Running Flow

Mihaly Csikszentmihalyi, PhD

Philip Latter

Christine Weinkauff Duranso

HUMAN KINETICS

Library of Congress Cataloging-in-Publication Data

Names: Csikszentmihalyi, Mihaly, author. | Latter, Philip, 1981- author. |
  Duranso, Christine Weinkauff, 1965- author.
Title: Running flow / Mihaly Csikszentmihalyi, PhD; Philip Latter, Christine
  Weinkauff Duranso.
Description: Champaign, IL : Human Kinetics, [2017] | Includes
  bibliographical references and index.
Identifiers: LCCN 2016049246 (print) | LCCN 2016057207 (ebook) | ISBN
  9781492535720 (print) | ISBN 9781492548928 (ebook)
Subjects: LCSH: Running--Psychological aspects. | Runners
  (Sports)--Psychology. | Happiness.
Classification: LCC GV1061.8.P75 C75 2017 (print) | LCC GV1061.8.P75 (ebook)
  | DDC 796.4201/9--dc23
LC record available at https://lccn.loc.gov/2016049246

ISBN: 978-1-4925-3572-0 (print)

This publication is written and published to provide accurate and authoritative information relevant to the subject matter presented. It is published and sold with the understanding that the author and publisher are not engaged in rendering legal, medical, or other professional services by reason of their authorship or publication of this work. If medical or other expert assistance is required, the services of a competent professional person should be sought.

The web addresses cited in this text were current as of October 2016, unless otherwise noted.

Acquisitions Editors: Tom Heine and Justin Klug; **Developmental Editor:** Tom Heine; **Managing Editor:** Tom Heine; **Copyeditor:** Joanna Hatzopoulos; **Indexer:** Nancy Ball; **Permissions Manager:** Martha Gullo; **Graphic Designer:** Denise Lowry; **Cover Designer:** Keith Blomberg; **Photograph (cover):** RyanJLane/ Getty Images; **Photo Asset Manager:** Laura Fitch; **Photo Production Manager:** Jason Allen; **Art Manager:** Kelly Hendren; **Illustrations:** © Human Kinetics; **Printer:** Versa Press

Human Kinetics books are available at special discounts for bulk purchase. Special editions or book excerpts can also be created to specification. For details, contact the Special Sales Manager at Human Kinetics.

Printed in the United States of America   10   9   8   7   6   5   4   3   2   1

The paper in this book is certified under a sustainable forestry program.

Human Kinetics
Website: www.HumanKinetics.com

United States: Human Kinetics, P.O. Box 5076, Champaign, IL 61825-5076
800-747-4457
e-mail: info@hkusa.com

Canada: Human Kinetics, 475 Devonshire Road Unit 100, Windsor, ON N8Y 2L5
800-465-7301 (in Canada only)
e-mail: info@hkcanada.com

Europe: Human Kinetics, 107 Bradford Road, Stanningley, Leeds LS28 6AT, United Kingdom
+44 (0) 113 255 5665
e-mail: hk@hkeurope.com

Australia: Human Kinetics, 57A Price Avenue, Lower Mitcham, South Australia 5062
08 8372 0999
e-mail: info@hkaustralia.com

New Zealand: Human Kinetics, P.O. Box 80, Mitcham Shopping Centre, South Australia 5062
0800 222 062
e-mail: info@hknewzealand.com

E6872

CONTENTS

PREFACE

Think about your most cherished running memory. Perhaps it was a race where you met a difficult challenge head on, where your mind and body were so completely tuned in that running your fastest time felt effortless. Maybe it happened while jogging through a beautiful landscape, a place so tranquil that your usually unruly mind couldn't help but shut off, allowing you to enjoy the simple pleasures of moving through the environment. You may have felt this same sense of engagement while conversing with your friends on a long run, a journey where 2 hours felt like 20 minutes.

Those moments are called flow moments, and they are usually among the most memorable and fulfilling in people's lives. **Flow** refers to an optimal experience during which the mind and body work harmoniously while honed in on a specific task. Flow is often associated with peak performance. When you are in a state of flow, you have no distractions, no deadlines, no querulous spouses to please, and no outside expectations to live up to. You simply have the present moment; in that moment, the pleasure comes from the act itself.

Flow may sound like a mysterious, ephemeral experience, but in truth it is a highly researched psychological phenomenon. Coauthor Mihaly Csikszentmihalyi (pronounced "ME-high CHEEK-sent-me-high" and hereafter referred to by the moniker "Dr. Mike") first identified flow in the 1970s. Over the past 40 years, hundreds of researchers have studied this phenomenon. Their work generally leads to this conclusion: People who regularly experience flow have happier, more fulfilling lives.

Anyone can experience flow by chance, but cultivating those experiences and benefiting from them requires knowledge and practice. Runners are fortunate because the sport offers numerous opportunities to experience flow. Racing allows competitive athletes to set goals, increase their skill level, and constantly challenge themselves to be better than they were the day before. Everyday runs offer plenty of challenges, too, making flow equally accessible to recreational and fitness runners. When you set goals and surmount challenges, such as running farther in the woods than before or staying in the moment while jogging along a busy bike path, you give yourself the best chance to experience flow.

The goal of *Running Flow* is to give you the knowledge necessary to experience flow on a regular basis. When you understand the variables that set the stage for flow, you can increase the likelihood of experiencing flow and living a happier, more fulfilling life. Flow experiences often coincide with personal bests and major achievements, making it a wonderful (and legal!) performance enhancer.

That said, no magic formula exists for creating flow. You cannot conjure it up by following a recipe or rigidly adhering to a series of steps. Although certain conditions must be present for flow to occur, their presence does not guarantee that flow will occur. Getting your body and mind in the proper place to achieve flow takes time and effort, which may explain why flow is not a fad. Its unpredictability makes it a hard sell to those seeking a magic bullet or step-by-step program.

Although you cannot conjure flow, you can nurture it. A significant amount of research over the past decade has helped us understand the antecedents that lead to flow, the flow experience itself, and its residual benefits. Functional MRI and CT scan technology, when combined with more basic questionnaires and personality assessment tools, have increased our understanding of who experiences flow most often, the brain's role in this process, and how it might improve quality of life.

All this talk can ring hollow if flow remains an abstract construct. For that reason part I of *Running Flow* focuses on the experience itself. Chapter 1 takes you deep into the flow experience of a relatable runner to illuminate what makes it unique and powerful. Chapter 2 builds on this concept by exploring the nine components of flow. Components of flow include your perceived skill level matching the challenge at hand (**challenge–skills balance**), having clear goals, and enjoying running for its own sake rather than for the promise of external rewards (**autotelic experience**). Chapter 3 examines what predisposes people to have flow moments and how these moments are affected by brain chemistry and personality traits. Part I concludes with chapter 4, which discusses why flow matters for people as athletes and as individuals.

Part II takes these ideas and applies them more specifically to runners. Chapter 5 is the longest in the book for good reason; it examines in full detail the factors necessary for flow to occur. Chapter 6 translates that knowledge to everyday, noncompetitive runs. These flow occurrences increase your enjoyment when training and make you more likely to experience flow moments in competitive situations. Chapter 7 is about competition, focusing on how flow helps you race faster even as your motivations turn ever more inward. Because experiencing flow is never guaranteed, the penultimate chapter deals with flow's limitations and how to cope with failure. The book concludes with chapter 9, which looks at how runners can take flow experiences and translate them to other aspects of their lives.

Although this book is grounded in scientific research, flow is such a personally powerful experience that we've reached out to a number of runners to learn from their peak experiences. These Olympians and everyday runners are profiled throughout, and they offer fresh perspectives on the topic. This book moves the concept of flow out of academia and into a realm where all runners of all levels can experience it. It provides practical tools, including a number of illustrations and tables to help you better visualize flow, as well as exercises (both mental and physical) that can help you find flow.

Dr. Mike's goal in researching flow for the past 40 years is as simple as it is noble—to help people lead happier, more enjoyable lives. Advancing this work into the realm of running, the goal of this book remains the same.

We wish you the best on your quest.

ACKNOWLEDGMENTS

Writing a book has a lot in common with running. There's the time commitment, the necessary work ethic, and the ability to push through when things aren't going smoothly. These obstacles can overwhelm even the most veteran writer, but every now and then the words explode on the screen and time seems to fly by. A feeling of confidence and empowerment sets in as the joy of writing blocks out all unwanted distractions. Writing, it seems, is an excellent conduit to flow experiences, just like running.

Those flow writing experiences never would have happened without the great foresight of editors Tom Heine and Justin Klug at Human Kinetics, who pieced together a world-famous psychologist, a professional writer, and a doctoral student who all shared a passion for flow and athletics. We'd also like to thank former *Running Times* editor in chief Jonathan Beverly for assigning a piece on flow that became the seed for this book and brought us all together. As much as we enjoyed the collaborative process, the patience of our spouses and children allowed us to plow through the research and find a way to make sense of this beautiful phenomenon. Words cannot express how much we appreciate your support.

Flow experiences can vary from person to person, but thanks to all the professional, amateur, and recreational runners who lent us their stories for the chapter introductions and athlete profiles, we believe any runner can now find flow in running. We especially thank the athletes who were busy preparing for the Rio Olympic Games for taking time out of their busy schedules to speak with us.

No amount of written research can replicate the gentle guiding hand of a genius in the field taking time to help us out. To Arne Dietrich, Cindra Kamphoff, and, yes, coauthor Mihaly Csikszentmihalyi, thank you for your wisdom and expertise. Your theories and research have made the world a happier, more positive place. We are all indebted to you for that.

PART I
Essence of Flow

CHAPTER 1

Experiencing Running Flow

On the most important day of her life, Shelby Hyatt woke up unable to breathe. The 16-year-old high school junior from Bryson City, North Carolina, swept her hands all around the nightstand trying to find her rescue inhaler, but in the pitch-blackness of an unfamiliar motel room her effort proved futile. Shelby sat up in her bed and tried to remain calm, but the stuffy, stale air churning from the wall heater did her no favors. She had to get out before it became any worse.

"My chest felt really tight," she says. "I could take breaths, but I couldn't take a deep breath. I didn't panic as much as you might imagine, because I didn't want to wake my teammates up. So I just tried to be calm and collected."

Outside seemed like a whole different world. A violent rainstorm pelted the motel's roof and left the parking lot in standing water. It was snowing back in the mountains surrounding her hometown, but here in the lower elevations of the Piedmont it was just blustery and miserable. Shelby huddled against the wall and inhaled the cold, fresh air. Bit by bit, her breathing steadied. It was 5:30 a.m.

For more than a year, Shelby dreamed and prepared for the events of this very day—the state cross country championships. The year before, as a first-year runner competing in the 1A (small school) division, she had placed 11th—one spot away from All-State honors. In the ensuing year, running became her passion; running defined her as a person. That confidence translated into other areas as well. Shelby earned a seat on the homecoming court and began dating a popular classmate. Buoyed by these positive events, she appeared right on track to achieving her All-State cross country dream.

Pneumonia changed all that. For 6 weeks in the middle of what was supposed to be her defining season, Shelby gasped her way through hard and easy runs alike. Some days were decent; some left her holding back tears. A naturally quiet person, Shelby said little about how the physical symptoms were affecting her mental health. Still, the effects were obvious as the rough days outnumbered the good ones. Her teammates and coaches tried to encourage her as she put out tremendous effort with little to show for it. Doctors tried various antibiotics, inhalers, and corticosteroids, but the results were minimal. As every major race turned out a little bit worse than the one before, training was proving to be an exercise in faith.

Sitting against the motel room door, her three Swain County High School teammates asleep inside, Shelby tried not to feel sorry for herself. They still had big goals for the day, even if physically she wasn't 100 percent capable. Knowing her team supported her eased her mind but increased her worry. *What if this happens again when I'm racing today?* she thought. *What if I can't do my best or help my team?*

Eventually her breathing calmed enough to go back inside the motel room. She lay awake for several hours. Outside, it continued to rain.

A few hours later at breakfast, she told her coaches about the breathing episode, but already she was starting to downplay the event. The rest of the day flew by in a haze of team bonding and race preparation. By the time she and her teammates toed the soggy starting line, Shelby felt calm and collected. Her face portrayed no anxiety. The warm-up run had gone well. Her legs felt snappy. Most important, her lungs could take in air. Whether the panicked breathing episode was a catharsis or the calm before the storm couldn't be known, so she stopped thinking about it.

"I felt really confident, like I knew that after everything that happened things weren't looking good for me, but I felt good," she says. "That helped with the pressure. I knew I wasn't expected to do so well in the race."

The starter barked out a 1-minute warning. Shelby stood on the line next to her teammates and surveyed the wide expanse of puddles and muddy grass in front of her. Deep breath in; deep breath out. The rain had ended, but she didn't notice. Her eyes showed a steely resolve and a narrowed focus. Nothing else mattered.

BANG!

In the ensuing chaos of the muddy start, Shelby stayed wide. The leaders pushed through the mud, battling the course as much as themselves. The northern wind howled at a steady 20 miles per hour (32 kph) as they ran headlong into it. Shelby tucked in with a couple of her teammates, confident that this was the best strategy. The first 7 minutes passed in a blur of mud and runners jostling for position. At the mile (1.6 km) she was in 40th place. Given her physical condition, it seemed wise to start at a moderate effort and continually increase the pace if possible. Her breathing remained steady and untroubled.

"After how good I felt the first mile, I decided, okay, I need to pick it up," she says. "This could go good or bad. I'm not sure. I just decided that I'd try to pick it up as much as possible and see what happens."

The next mile confirmed her suspicion. She felt better with each stride. With doubts about her breathing slipping into the background, Shelby aggressively worked her way through the field. She moved to 20th place, then 15th place, and finally crossed the 2-mile (3.2-km) mark just outside the top 10. Realizing her yearlong dream had merit, she redoubled her effort. Just ahead was her talented freshman teammate Emma. While Shelby's lungs fought through pneumonia, Emma quietly took the mantle as the team's number one runner. With clear goals in mind and no physical obstacles in the way, Shelby set out to reel her young teammate in.

The last mile of the race played out like a Hollywood script. Shelby moved into the top 10, then the top 8. With a half mile (800 m) remaining in the race, she caught Emma just as the course doglegged into an open meadow. The momentum catapulted Shelby past her teammate as her coach and spectators screamed support. Shelby was in sixth place and closing on fifth.

A flow experience helped Shelby Hyatt run the race of her life in the North Carolina state cross country meet.

Courtesy of Jeffrey E. Sides.

The girl with pneumonia—the one who had worked so hard but felt she had nothing to show for it—was now surging faster than she ever had in her life. She crested a small hill at a full-on clip, the muted late autumn sun silhouetting her against the dramatic backdrop. Charging harder and harder, Shelby passed one final opponent to move into fourth place with only 200 meters remaining. Down the final straightaway a small smile escaped her face as her focus widened and the magnitude of what was occurring settled in.

Counted out just that morning, Shelby Hyatt ran the race of her life and finished fourth at the state meet. In the process she not only achieved her All-State goal but also helped her team to a school-best third-place finish. The cherry on top was setting a personal record (PR) while running through mud puddles in a howling windstorm.

"It doesn't make sense to me, but it felt easier [than any other race]," she says. "My breathing, my body, my legs felt like they could go forever."

In the aftermath of the race, as exhausted athletes sought out their parents and coaches, Shelby got separated from her team. When she finally found her coach, they embraced in a warm hug filled with shock and surprise. As they separated, Shelby took a step back and smiled. "I think I flowed today," she said.

Phenomenon of Flow

Shelby was right. She experienced flow, a phenomenon people often call being **in the zone** or *locked in*. Few experiences in life are more memorable than flow moments; these moments make life worth living. A great benefit of flow is that this state of consciousness is available to all people who engage their passions and commit to achieving their goals.

Running is unique in that it offers opportunities to experience flow in various settings and with a high degree of frequency. Racing gives competitive athletes a structured, challenging environment to test their skills. Trail running presents technical challenges and thought-provoking scenery in an anxiety-reducing environment. Running on the beach can lull you into a meditative trance as the waves lap up on the shore. Even flat road running can be highly pleasurable if you lock in on the rhythm of a smooth stride and the wonderful sense of lightness it creates.

While this book primarily focuses on runners and their flow experiences, note that optimal experiences of this nature can occur any time you direct your full attention to a challenging task. Researchers have studied and validated the flow experiences of chess players, rock climbers, dancers, cyclists, gardeners, swimmers, writers, basketball players, and actors. Although the details vary by passion, flow's causes and feelings are universal.

In general, flow occurs when you believe you have the skills necessary to overcome a challenging situation. Your perception of time warps as your attention narrows to the task at hand. This attention is so sharply focused on the task that all extraneous thoughts and anxieties disappear. Clear goals drive your actions while all internal and external feedback verifies that the goal is achievable. Despite feeling invincible, you are aloof to what others think of you as your self-consciousness recedes into the background. All that matters is mastering the moment.

It is empowering, motivating, and above all else, enjoyable. Flow experiences are so enjoyable that people seek them out even at a great cost, when no promise of material return on their physical, emotional, or economic investment exists. That's because flow experiences are **autotelic**; the activity itself is the reward. A runner in a state of flow runs for the sake of running. That doesn't mean that flow experiences don't produce external rewards. Many of the world-class athletes you'll meet in the coming pages reported entering a flow state during races that produced Olympic medals and national championships. However, those same runners will be the first to tell you it's the experience, not the outcome, that resonates most strongly in their memories.

The overwhelming sense of pleasure that accompanies these experiences helps explain why engaging in challenging activities is still so prized, even as people live in a society where laptops and smartphones make leaving the couch unnecessary. As coauthor and esteemed psychologist Mihaly Csikszentmihalyi (hereafter referred to by his preferred nickname of "Dr.

Mike") pointed out in his 1990 bestseller *Flow*, enjoyment comes back to actively engaging our passions. "Contrary to what we usually believe," Dr. Mike wrote then, "moments like these, the best moments in our lives, are not the passive, receptive, relaxing times . . . . The best moments usually occur when a person's body or mind is stretched to its limits in a voluntary effort to accomplish something difficult and worthwhile" (p. 3). Hence the reason a morning 10-miler (16-km) usually brings a runner greater pleasure than having breakfast in bed.

As the flow experience resonates in the conscious mind, it increases the desire to pursue whatever task caused flow in the first place. This intrinsic motivation leads to increased desire to perfect your skills, leading to improved confidence in your abilities. As your skill level improves, you become better able to tackle bigger challenges, increasing the likelihood of flow. It is a highly positive cycle.

"Flow got me really excited about what was to come in running," Shelby says. "It changed my attitude. With the pneumonia I was feeling sorry for myself, and after that it was all over. A lot of times before I run, I go back to that memory and it helps."

Every runner deserves the chance to have an optimal experience like Shelby's. However, flow is a shifty phenomenon that doesn't respond directly to intentions. To increase your likelihood of experiencing it on a regular basis, it helps to understand how current understanding of flow has evolved to its present form.

History of Flow

The pursuit of happiness is nothing new. While it is impossible to know the exact motivations and desires of our ancestors before the agricultural revolution, it is safe to assume that humans have always craved pleasure in one form or another. Nurturing that pleasure into something more than a fleeting experience takes skill, and philosophers have pondered for centuries what it means to lead a truly happy, fulfilling life. For example, Aristotle believed happiness should be sought for its own sake and is credited with establishing the first science of happiness; Nietzsche, on the other hand, believed a so-called higher person would learn more from suffering and that seeking happiness for its own sake was "ridiculous and contemptible—that makes [mankind's] destruction *desirable*" (von Tevenar 2007).

In today's commercialized society, it is nearly impossible to separate the notion of happiness from the notion of money. At its most basic level, money is not interesting; it is little pieces of paper or bits of metal that through an unwritten cultural agreement have been assigned a given worth. What those pieces of paper and bits of metal can purchase (physical goods, power, peace of mind) makes people believe that money can buy happiness, even as they recite the cliché that it cannot.

In recent decades, Harvard professor Daniel Gilbert has headlined a great deal of research on this topic. His findings conclude that money matters only as long as people are struggling to meet their basic needs (Dunn, Gilbert, & Wilson 2011). After these needs are met, what affects happiness most are experiences, and in particular, the quality of those experiences. People whose experiences improve their sense of purpose and relationships with others report a greater sense of long-term happiness. Evidently, engagement is key.

Several continents away, Eastern religions such as Buddhism (the Zen sect in particular) have been tackling the problem of lasting happiness and engagement for several millennia. While they agree with Aristotle that happiness is worth pursuing in its own right, they differ in how to achieve it. Zen Buddhists focus extensively on staying in the present moment, which Western society often calls **mindfulness**. (However, note that mindfulness as it is understood today is the creation of American psychologist Jon Kabat-Zinn and has no religious affiliation). Consider some of Zen Buddhism's most famous sayings (Allan 2014):

- *Before enlightenment, chop wood, carry water. After enlightenment, chop wood, carry water.*
- *If you walk, just walk. If you sit, just sit; but whatever you do, don't wobble.*
- *When hungry, eat your rice; when tired, close your eyes. Fools may laugh at me, but wise men will know what I mean.*

Staying grounded in the present moment while maintaining a nonjudgmental view of life events is paramount in this philosophy. Practices such as meditation further enhance this effect by teaching the practitioner how to identify thought patterns and bring them under control until the mind is silent. Mental discipline is critical; in Buddhist philosophy true happiness comes from cultivating positive thought patterns and not relying on objects to bring joy (Gunaratana 2002).

In the 1950s in the United States, Abraham Maslow, the so-called father of humanistic psychology, attempted to synthesize many of these disparate ideas into a coherent psychological theory. Unlike most of his contemporaries, Maslow studied healthy people and was most interested in how they reached their full potential. He found that once people's basic needs were met—namely their physiological, safety, love, and self-esteem needs—they could focus on achieving their true potential. Maslow called this highest state **self-actualization** (Maslow 1954).

Self-actualized people are generally accepting of themselves and their life circumstances and are more concerned about societal problems than personal problems. They value privacy and autonomy but are open to the opinions of others. Above all, they appreciate life and the experiences it produces. Maslow believed that less than 1 percent of the population functioned at this level at any given time.

A related phenomenon to self-actualization is a **peak experience**. These moments are characterized by a sense of stimulation and euphoria combined with an intense feeling of connection with the world surrounding you. Peak experiences share many traits with flow, including a loss of self-consciousness, feelings of effortlessness, complete immersion in the present moment, and a distorted sense of time. Unrelated to flow, peak experiences also come with a burst of energy and are triggered by external events. After having a peak experience, people are more likely to view themselves and the world in a positive manner and actively try to experience such moments again. In addition to being powerful moments in their own right, Maslow believed that peak experiences were evidence of people's self-actualization (Maslow 1962).

If humanistic psychology had a downfall, it was a lack of empirical proof; theories often remained only theories. However, the ideas it generated were powerful and led to the modern-day field of positive psychology spearheaded by Dr. Mike. While a professor at the University of Chicago in the early 1970s, Dr. Mike began studying the behavior patterns of children at play. At the time it was accepted that children played to mimic the activities of adults, a form of modeling that would give them necessary skills in adulthood. Dr. Mike found that children also played for the inherent pleasure it provided, even when nothing was to be gained (Csikszentmihalyi 2003).

The idea of flow evolved philosophically from this discovery as Dr. Mike searched for a common thread among adults who also actively pursued passions that fully consumed them. At first he focused on highly successful people, such as talented teenagers, professional musicians, Nobel Prize–winning scientists, and elite athletes, although psychologists who followed his work also investigated the experiences of everyday people. After years of observations, interviews, and experiments, Dr. Mike determined that people experienced flow when they felt capable of meeting a specific challenge (Csikszentmihalyi 1975; 1988). He has continued this work at Claremont Graduate University in Southern California, where he founded the Quality of Life Research Center.

Since the 1970s, researchers have done hundreds of studies with thousands of subjects in order to better understand flow. Self-reports of individual experiences have contributed to a better understanding of the similarities as well as the variability in flow experiences. Some rather ambitious studies have even looked at the neural correlates of flow, using functional magnetic resonance imaging (fMRI) to track areas of the brain that seem active or inactive during specific flow-inducing activities. The loss of time, self-consciousness, and awareness of others that many report feeling during flow seems to be related to changes in brain activity, namely deactivation in the medial prefrontal cortex and the amygdala. Many people report feeling heightened positive emotions and blunted negative emotions during flow, which is also attributed to decreased neural activity in the amygdala. These findings are based on research with video game players and research subjects participating in technical mathematical problems with increasing levels of challenge that encourage the induction of flow (Dietrich 2004; 2011).

If you are a runner, you can appreciate the outcomes of the deactivation in the prefrontal cortex, because this experience is what allows you to get lost in a run. In flow you feel more intense positive emotions and fewer negative emotions (such as frustration) and are able to forget about the stressors that lurk in your day-to-day life. While you can be completely absorbed in the experience, you can simultaneously be completely unaware of the people around you. Research also suggests that experiencing flow allows the brain to unconsciously solve problems. If you have ever experienced writer's block or some other sort of mental standoff, you may also have experienced the joy of breaking through that barrier after a great run. That, too, is the result of flow, where allowing a problem to incubate in the unconscious mind while distracted by other mental or physical processes gives way to new solutions.

Like all scientific discoveries, understanding of flow is an imperfect and evolving science. For example, the fMRI studies are interesting, but they are also limited in scope because they are specific to tasks that are not physically taxing. It would be interesting to understand what is happening in the brain while experiencing flow during a run (e.g., what areas are highly active or inactive) and whether that differs from the results found in the experiments with chess players or video gamers. That type of research is unlikely to come about anytime soon, because fMRI units require that you lie very still inside them, which is clearly impossible to do while running.

For now, brain activity during running flow remains a bit of a mystery, but with technological advances, people may someday be able to retrofit a device on a headband or a hat to measure brain-wave fluctuations while running. Much like the technology surrounding heart rate monitoring and GPS has changed people's running experiences, the not-so-distant future will provide improvements in the way people monitor and thus understand the brain's response to running and flow.

Aside from brain studies with flow, other researchers have looked at varied contexts for flow, such as flow in the classroom, flow in dance, and flow amongst team members (**group flow**). It turns out that any team sport with rhythmic activity can result in flow within the group (Jackson & Csikszentmihalyi 1999). If you have ever watched a basketball game or a soccer game where an entire team seems to be in sync, knowing when and where to place the ball without any verbal communication, then you have probably witnessed group flow.

Shelby's teammates would certainly agree with the group flow theory. As Shelby and Emma led the way up front, their progress was relayed to the rest of the team by coaches and fans. Sure enough, the top six runners all continued to move forward aggressively throughout the race, seemingly keying off the positive momentum that was occurring farther ahead. On a day where course conditions generally slowed runners by over a minute,

Runner's High and Flow

When it hits you, it's all good. It comes at the end of a long run or a tough tempo, maybe even an interval session. Your mind is flooded with feelings of euphoria. The pain of training starts to melt away. Your thoughts are suddenly a little clearer and more profound. On your newly pain-free legs you feel like you can run forever, as if this were exactly what you were designed to do. Even when you finally do make yourself stop, the good feelings linger, sometimes for hours. Is anything better than a **runner's high**?

Recent research has found the term to be apropos. The two main chemicals responsible for a runner's high are **endorphins** (morphine-like opioids produced by various parts of the central nervous system) and **endocannabinoids** (your body's version of THC, the chemical in marijuana that makes people high). Unlike their synthetic counterparts, these chemicals are linked with positive mental health outcomes and don't lead to physiological addiction or dependence (Fetters 2014).

As a natural painkiller, it makes sense that specialized sites in the body, including the **prefrontal cortex**, would release endorphins into the bloodstream to help manage the trauma of distance running. Endorphins bind to opiate receptor sites to help dampen feelings of pain. Like all opioids, endorphins also increase the sense of well-being and reduce the effects of stress on the body.

Numerous theories abound as to why the body produces endocannabinoids when you run. The most popular holds that it is an evolutionary byproduct of the hunter-gatherer days, when humans needed incentive to burn additional calories and risk injury in pursuit of food (Gleiser 2016). Other animals that travel long distances for their food, such as dogs, display similar chemical responses to distance running. This response only occurs from more strenuous forms of aerobic exercise. For instance, walking does not increase endocannabinoid production.

Not all runner's highs are the same. Your body releases these chemicals as dictated by the demands of that day's training and in response to numerous other physiological factors. Some runs will leave you feeling on top of the moon; some will still feel like a slog that you're happy to have finished.

Also note that a runner's high is not flow. While they no doubt have some brain chemistry in common, flow relies more heavily on psychosocial factors and is directly related to funneling your attention on one specific goal for extended periods of time. A runner's high is a chemical response with a less pronounced carryover effect that requires no engagement.

A runner's high still matters, though. Flow is an oftentimes elusive experience that can require months, if not years of training. A runner's high asks that you get out the door and put in a little effort, and for that you'll likely be rewarded. And if you chase those runner's highs long enough, you might get rewarded with the ultimate flow experience when it matters most.

three of those six Swain County runners set personal records and the team's average time was the fastest of the entire season.

These runners were more apt to experience flow because they had made a conscious decision to place the team before the self in the hopes of accomplishing something as a group. The matter of choice is important, and it highlights other research on flow and the role of personality. For instance, a person with an **autotelic personality** is much more likely to have flow experiences frequently and to enter the flow state more readily than a person who does not have an autotelic personality. Later chapters discuss the autotelic personality and flow outside of running in more detail.

Research on flow continues to build. Like any area of study, the more you know, the more you realize you don't know. As a runner, you can capitalize on the information currently available to find ways to enjoy your own flow experiences as often as possible, knowing the next wave of research may someday make peak experiences more accessible than ever before.

Flow and Effort

Everyone loves different things. Some people are interested in physical activities such as running, hiking, or gardening; others are interested in sedentary enterprises such as painting or listening to music; still others are interested in more intellectual endeavors such as reading or writing. Most people would say they enjoy a combination of these examples. Dr. Mike discovered that when people become passionate about their activities, leisure or otherwise, they are more likely to set goals, be actively engaged and absorbed in them, and find greater satisfaction in them and in life, than if they choose passive pursuits.

This conclusion highlights a somewhat counterintuitive idea for many people: While most people *think* they are happier when they are relaxing or at rest, they are more likely to *report* being happiest when they are immersed in an activity or fully engaged with a challenge of some kind. Each of the highly successful people Dr. Mike studied spoke of their flow experience when deeply involved in their skill or in their work, and this experience kept them returning to the activities. Many of them spoke of their greatest achievements being accomplished during moments of total absorption and concentration. During those times they were unaware of anything else around them, including the passage of time. A scientist spoke of getting lost in a formula just as a rock climber recounted being so focused on foot placement that time passed without notice. Musicians described feeling completely at one with their compositions as their fingers caressed the piano keys. Later studies detailed professional swimmers and runners recounting their bodies feeling stronger than ever, responding to the demands of a race as never before. These are examples of the essence of flow—a peak moment in time when the body and mind are fully engaged in a specific task and when nothing else seems to matter.

Why is this idea of satisfaction in engagement in the pursuit of challenge so unusual? We have been conditioned in our culture to see our work (job, career, profession) as something we are forced to do. Think about how many times you have said, "I have to go to work." Compare that to the number of times you have said, "I get to go to work," and you will see how counterintuitive it is to believe we are happiest when we are challenged with a project or deadline.

Most responsible adults have to seek employment in order to provide for themselves, but how they do that is their choosing. It is in the choosing, in finding the work that suits your strengths and satisfies a sense of meaning that you can find flow and thus find fulfillment in it. Even if you are stuck in a menial job, you can find fulfillment in it by investing your unique talents or strengths in what you do and by reframing the way you conceive of your role in the company.

That is not to say that work can't be a draining activity. After finishing a challenging day at the office, the idea of idly sitting by and staring at a screen for hours often sounds enticing. Alas, watching television provides little satisfaction (Csikszentmihalyi 1990). Even if you are lucky enough to find something good to watch, it isn't long before you become bored and wish for something more engaging. An exception might be watching a game show, mystery, or sporting event in which you can be an armchair participant. The key to this exception is the active role you play in the process.

Finding leisure activities that challenge your strengths and provide a sense of meaning is your choice. You can use your leisure time to do nothing, or you can choose to use it more wisely, doing something goal oriented that offers an opportunity for personal growth. Odds are that if you've picked up this book, running is that passion. Lucky for you, few sports offer more pathways to personal growth and flow than running.

On those days when you don't feel your best or perform well, the hope of experiencing flow again can continue to motivate you, along with the hope that things might improve if you simply persevere. That hope can translate into reality. As she released her anxiety and changed her ambitions, Shelby found a means to achieve flow. Her willingness to accept that she could only do her best freed her to set a new goal, to start out slowly and assess her breathing and pace at each mile. For Shelby, this change was exactly what her body and mind needed. The incremental success she experienced in the first mile and then the second gave her confidence to increase the challenge, and her body responded positively.

This is why Shelby's story matters: Standing on the awards stage with a tear running down each cheek, Shelby had conquered a difficult challenge, overcoming internal and external obstacles in the process. She left that state championship a different person. It may come as little surprise that 7 months later she and Emma would once again stand on a podium together as members of a 4 × 800-meter relay team, only this time they would duck their

Chris Solinsky

Former American record holder and first non-African under 27:00 in 10,000 meters

Flow moment: Stanford Invitational 10,000 meters, 2010

AP Photo/Steve Yeater

In the fairytale retelling of one of the greatest races ever on American soil, Chris Solinsky is hailed as the underdog conqueror of both stereotypes and once unachievable records. The tall and burly debutant hangs on to a blistering pace, makes a dramatic move, and in an epic race against the clock becomes the first non-African to break 27:00 in the 10,000-meter race, lunging at the line for a 26:59.60 clocking. However, that retelling misses some of the finer points of Solinsky's race experience.

Going into the Stanford Invitational 10,000-meter race in 2010, all eyes were on American (and soon-to-be Olympic silver medalist) Galen Rupp. A long-distance prodigy under the tutelage of legendary runner and coach Alberto Salazar, the race was set up as a showcase for Rupp to break the American record of 27:13. His sponsor had banners and signs made up for the occasion.

Enter Solinsky. A national-class 5,000-meter runner, Solinsky was known as much for his height and muscular build as for his head-down, bust-through-a-wall racing mentality. Combined with his inexperience (this was his 10,000-meter track debut), he had all the makings of a nonfactor. But Solinsky was fit, confident, and curious.

"There was talk of Galen Rupp going after the American record," Solinsky says. "This being my first ever 10K, I was obviously a bit unsure whether or not I was quite that fit. However, it helped that I had raced Rupp many times before and usually beat him (at shorter distances), so I told myself that if he could run that fast, I definitely could. Training went really well leading up, and I knew I was in the shape of my life."

Through the early laps of the race, Solinsky got into the lead group behind the pacers and, in his words, was able to just "fall asleep." He relaxed and ran on autopilot, letting tens of thousands of accumulated miles do their work and pull him along at a lightning fast pace. It appeared effortless to the fans at Stanford and those watching the broadcast online, but Solinsky began to struggle with a side stitch halfway through. The distraction and pain caused him to slip off the pace for just a moment. But as the side stitch abated, Solinsky found himself immersed in the race as never before. He entered a flow state.

"I was able to respond to every surge, cover every gap because I was focused on doing whatever it took to beat Rupp," Solinsky says. "The pace picked up to splits that I otherwise would have heard and maybe slowed down from intimidation, but in that state of flow I didn't even think about it."

A mile (1.6 km) from the finish, Solinsky knew he had the win. Although a group of four runners remained intact, including Rupp, Solinsky felt restless, as though his legs had more running left in them. Flying around the track in high compression socks, Solinsky finally made his move with just over two laps remaining. The celebratory signs touting Rupp's American record would have to wait. This night belonged to Solinsky.

When he heard the bell ring, the clock read 26:02. There was no question he would break the standing American record of 27:13, but now he was entering sacred waters. Could Solinsky kick hard enough over the last lap to not just shatter that record but become the first non-African runner to go under the vaunted 27-minute mark, a time that was far more difficult to achieve than barriers such as the 4-minute mile?

With a half lap remaining, the clock read 26:32. It took Solinsky a few seconds to do the math, to realize he was on the cusp of history. Over the next 27 seconds he willed his body forward; nothing else mattered as the stadium roared in anticipation. As he crossed the line, Solinsky celebrated in disbelief. For years he had just missed making national teams and wondered if he could reach that highest level; now, in his first attempt at a new distance, he had become the best American ever. The clock read "26:59.60." His last half mile (800 m) had been run in 1:56, an excellent time by itself, to say nothing of after 23 laps. He had done it by locking in on a goal and pushing all distractions aside.

"Further proof of being in flow was that as I took my spikes off and changed into my trainers, I discovered a blister on my foot the size of a softball," Solinsky says. "I didn't even realize it was there until then."

In many quarters Solinsky's name has started to fade. A hamstring injury in 2011 and subsequent surgery hobbled him for months. He never fully recovered and ended up retiring for good in 2016. He has stayed in the sport as head distance coach at the College of William and Mary in Williamsburg, Virginia. Yet that 10,000-meter race will live on as a shining example of the ultimate flow moment, one that helped a good runner realize his greatness, and helped redefine what was possible for American distance runners.

heads down to receive gold medals. The satisfaction and personal growth experienced in those moments is the reason runners approach the starting line every day.

Key Points

- *Flow* refers to an optimal experience where the mind and body work together while honed in on a task. Flow is often associated with peak performance.

- Psychologist Dr. Mihaly Csikszentmihalyi first studied this phenomenon, and in the mid-1970s he coined the term *flow*.

- Flow is more likely to occur when you are fully engaged and challenged in activity rather than when you are at rest.

- Flow is an autotelic experience, meaning that the experience itself is the reward.

- Brain activity changes during flow. Studies suggest deactivation in the prefrontal cortex and amygdala, resulting in loss of time perception and self-consciousness, blunted negative emotions, and heightened positive emotions.

- While very similar, runner's high and flow are distinct. Runner's high results in chemical changes in the brain and feelings of euphoria, while flow results in changes in activity in the brain and greater focused attention on the task at hand.

- People with an autotelic personality are more likely to experience flow and to experience it more frequently than others.

- Effort matters. Most people are more satisfied with life when they spend time engaging in activities that are not particularly sedentary or passive. Passivity for very long results in frustration and agitation.

CHAPTER 2
Nine Components of Flow

Experiencing flow is one thing; understanding it is another. Many athletes have experienced moments when everything clicks but written them off as chance occurrences. They dismissed the easy sense of control and empowerment as a fluke, holding on to the belief that if you're not trying your hardest, you're not really trying.

Of all the paradoxes associated with flow, perhaps the greatest is how the mind and body functioning near their full potential can seem so enjoyable. Theoretically, peak performance should equal peak exertion. This apparent contradiction is the result of a complex series of steps that unfurl at both a conscious and unconscious level. Although it offers no guarantee of occurrence, understanding the rare occasions when your psychology and physiology fall completely in synch offers you the best chance of experiencing flow when it is needed most.

Shelby can certainly vouch for understanding flow. As a custom, members of the Swain County cross country team gather for team dinners in the week preceding major competitions. At a team gathering before the regional meet, Shelby and her teammates listened to coauthor Phil Latter (at that time, their head coach) vividly describe a flow experience and outline its nine components. The high-energy lecture left Shelby cautiously optimistic, even after the regional meet proved to be, in her words, another "major letdown."

"After the pneumonia and all that, I knew it would help a whole lot to flow at State," Shelby says.

Her hope was to fully engage the act of running and experience flow in its most powerful state. Since its conception in the 1970s, researchers have identified nine separate dimensions that add up to a complete flow experience. These nine dimensions still function as the consummate characterization of flow. However, newer conceptualizations emphasize that flow unfolds in a sequential manner. The process begins with these three proximal conditions, called **antecedents**: clear goals, the challenge–skills balance, and unambiguous feedback. Without the three antecedents in place, the six characteristics of flow (numbers 4 through 9, called **process outcomes**) cannot occur.

Antecedents

1. Clear goals
2. Challenge–skills balance
3. Unambiguous feedback

Process Outcomes

4. Focused attention
5. Merging of action and awareness
6. Sense of control
7. Loss of self-consciousness
8. Distortion of time
9. Intrinsic motivation (autotelism)

The relationship between these variables becomes even clearer when viewed in a linear model (figure 2.1).

Like many psychological concepts, being ignorant of flow doesn't preclude it from happening, and knowing about it doesn't guarantee its timely arrival. That qualifier notwithstanding, the more knowledge you have of flow (both its underlying conditions and the unique qualities it confers), the more likely you are to enter your runs in the proper state of mind and body necessary to achieve it.

Antecedents to Flow

As stated earlier, the nine dimensions of flow do not haphazardly or randomly present themselves. In almost all instances, the three antecedents must be in place in order for the process outcomes to follow. Just as years of training,

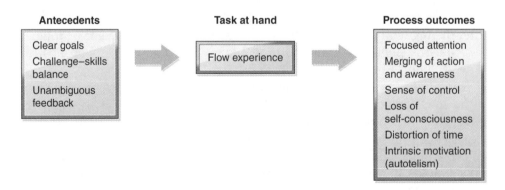

Figure 2.1 Current model of flow.

a good night's sleep, and proper hydration set the stage for a good race, you must have specific goals, an attainable challenge, and unambiguous feedback in place to experience flow.

Preparing yourself for flow actually begins well before the antecedents. You can't read this chapter and assume the mind will magically make up for a lack of physical preparation or overcome personal struggles that have left you emotionally wiped out. A sport such as running can take years to master. Understanding that mastery and where you want it to take you is paramount in the quest for flow experiences.

Clear Goals

Knowing what you want to accomplish is the first key to experiencing flow. Consider your runs. Sometimes you set out with no objective other than to enjoy yourself. You find value and pleasure in those runs for their own sake; hearing the rhythm of your breath, your heart, or your footsteps can be incredibly rewarding and peaceful. Other times you challenge yourself by setting concrete goals and pushing your body and mind to achieve them. These workouts and races test your limits.

The latter scenario is more likely to induce flow, even though the first run may be enjoyable in its own right. One important distinction between the relaxing run and the flow-inducing run is the type of goal. The first run exemplifies an abstract goal, one less tangible such as running for the sake of running. The flow-inducing run begins with a more concrete goal, such as running a predetermined distance at a specific pace. The quantitative nature of a concrete goal allows you to more easily measure performance. Knowing you're on the path to achieving your goal sets the stage for all the flow components that follow.

Think back to Shelby's flow experience. For months before her race, Shelby dreamed of placing in the top 10 at the state championships and running at a pace as close to 20 minutes for 5,000 meters as possible. These long-term goals drove her training objectives throughout the year, even as her health deteriorated. The panicked breathing episode the morning of the race left Shelby wondering whether those goals were still realistic.

"I honestly didn't believe that I could reach the top 10 that morning," she explains. "I felt confident that I would be okay while I was running, but I really didn't know what to expect from my body. I had trained since the end of track season for that moment, and I knew I had the fitness to reach my goal, but I just wasn't sure my lungs would keep up."

Despite those concerns, Shelby toed the line feeling well. She started with more conservative goals in mind, and as her body reacted well to the challenges at hand, she increased her expectations until they matched her season-long objectives. Those rising standards provided the necessary challenge to push Shelby into a flow state and led to an All-State performance.

Shelby's story provides examples of long-term, short-term, and moment-by-moment goals. Long-term goals provide needed directions on an epic journey. These directions can include a season-long training plan that successfully alternates hard and easy days, nutritional planning, supplementary exercises, and a tapering phase that helps you arrive on the starting line fit and fresh. Without a long-term vision directing your training, the odds of injury or staleness greatly increase. Setting long-term goals also helps you establish realistic expectations for progression over a series of months and years. If you run at a pace of 20 minutes per 5,000 meters, running that distance in 16 minutes by the end of the season is unrealistic. However, after 5 years of dedicated training, that goal may be attainable. Long-term goals provide the incentive necessary to keep training for an extended period of time.

Short-term goals are easier to bite off and dictate your daily training. Research in motivation (Dweck 1986; Emmons 1992) suggests that human beings are more likely to persevere toward larger, more abstract goals when smaller, incremental goals are present along the way. If the dream is to qualify for the Boston Marathon, then running a successful workout will increase your motivation to keep training hard enough to make it to the starting line in Hopkinton. With concrete goals in mind, a bad run or a bad week is much less likely to deter you in your long-term quest.

Having a moment-by-moment awareness of your goals makes them more pliable and can better fuel your motivation. These goals can be immediate (e.g., controlling your breathing up a steep hill) or a constant reinforcement of important short-term and long-term goals (e.g., running 3:10 in the marathon to qualify for Boston). As discussed later in this chapter, flow experiences narrow your focus almost entirely to the task at hand. By keeping your goals at the forefront of your thinking, you stand a better chance of achieving them. At the same time, being able to adjust your goals on the fly—if your skill level or the challenge at hand proves to be higher or lower than expected—better allows you to maximize your potential on that day.

No matter what type of goal you're setting, it should always relate to the activity. Setting a goal of experiencing flow sets you up for disappointment, and according to some research (Csikszentmihalyi 1990), it may actually hinder you from experiencing it. Shelby had hopes of experiencing flow while competing at the state meet, but her goals were specific to her race. Flow was the byproduct of a perfect storm, not the storm itself.

Challenge—Skills Balance

Finding an appropriate balance between your skills and the challenge at hand is arguably the most critical antecedent. Fortunately, the more experience you have in setting goals for yourself, the easier this becomes. Dr. Mike addressed this balance early in his research and created a visual model (figure 2.2) that demonstrates the varying outcomes associated with perceived skill and the challenge at hand.

To experience flow, you need to find a challenge that is within reach but still requires effort to achieve, as in the High Skills/High Challenge quadrant in figure 2.2. Achieving this balance is relative to your skill level. A high challenge for an Olympian might induce terror in a recreational athlete, while a recreational runner's goals might be too much for a neophyte.

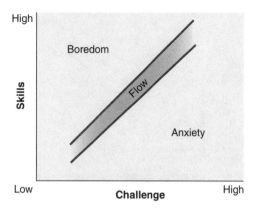

Figure 2.2 Challenge–skills balance outcomes.

Even at the individual level, people are far from static when it comes to their bodies and minds. A good challenge today may be too much or too little next week, depending on your mood, your physical health, and your fitness. Fluctuations in perceived skill level are normal, and they can even change mid run as you feel particularly good (or particularly bad). Being cognizant of your current skills and the available challenges out there is a never-ending dance between the two variables.

"Top 10 was definitely in my head starting the race," Shelby says, "but I just wasn't sure what would happen. As the race went on, and I was continuing to feel good, I kept getting different goals in my head, like 'Try to pass Ashlyn [a rival from a nearby school],' 'Go for top 10,' and 'Catch up to Emma.' As far as keeping to those goals, I didn't have to do much besides run my race, start off at an easy pace, and just pick off people as I went."

The **inverted-U theory of performance and anxiety** (Yerkes & Dodson 1908) posits that humans generally improve performance as the pressure to succeed heightens, but only to a certain point. Beyond that point the challenge becomes too high, anxiety sets in, and the performance suffers. Alternatively, when the pressure to succeed is too low, you are likely to become bored or even apathetic (figure 2.3). The **stimulus theory of human motivation** suggests that stimulation (challenge) is a necessary and innate need and that without adequate stimulation from our environment we become bored, agitated, and even disoriented. Therefore, you should consider the intensity of the challenge set for a run and how far reaching that challenge might be, given current skills. If you reach too high, anxiety overrides the moment; if you set the goal too low, boredom sets in and the desire to continue with the activity fades.

Not all runs should push you to your limit. There are valid reasons to set a goal for a run that is below or above your skill level. A difficult interval session in the middle of a high-mileage week will provide a strong training stimulus, but with heavy legs and a high degree or challenge it may not be conducive to experiencing flow. Conversely, a recovery run the day after that workout will likely fall into the relaxation zone in order to return the body

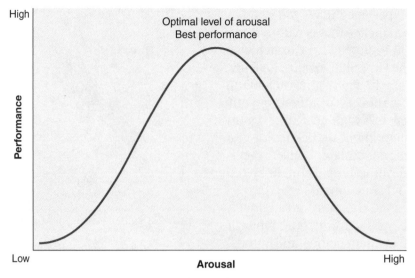

Figure 2.3   The inverted-U theory of performance and anxiety.

to equilibrium. Although perhaps not flow inducing, both of these runs are valuable from the perspective of a long-term goal.

Exceptions do exist to those rules. Recent research shows that flow can still occur when your skill exceeds the challenge because of the comfort level with the activity. Usually it would result in relaxation, but in this instance mastery can still invoke flow, although its intensity will be diminished. A similar effect occurs when the perceived importance of the activity is high. For example, an elite high school runner may experience flow at her conference cross country meet even if she runs unchallenged, because she believes she is leading her team to a major victory.

Aesthetics can also play a role. Going on a beautiful mountain hike may be a little less intense than a difficult flow-inducing run, but for some runners the beauty found in nature elicits a sense of satisfaction that invites flow. The more importance you place on an activity, and the more you value and prioritize it, the more likely it is to induce flow even if the challenge isn't high.

As you experience success in meeting your goals and facing challenges, you build **self-efficacy**, a belief that you have what it takes to accomplish the goals you set for yourself. As self-efficacy increases, you feel more comfortable risking failure by setting more challenging goals. Not only will you be more apt to have more flow moments, you will find greater personal satisfaction in your running altogether.

Unambiguous Feedback

Once you set a challenging goal, the next step is to consider the feedback you are receiving in real time. Much of Shelby's amazing run stemmed from identifying positive internal and external feedback and responding to it.

"During the race [the coaches] were flipping out cheering for me to keep it up because the way I was running was completely unexpected and unrealistic for that day," Shelby says. "There were also a lot of fans, coaches, and spectators from other schools that were also giving me positive words while I was running because no one expected me to be where I was. My body felt amazing, and everyone's words just kept pushing me forward."

More often than not the goal set at the onset of an activity requires adjustment along the way, and the experienced runner will learn to pay attention and adjust accordingly. Shelby did this when her body felt good and her breathing was steady; she picked up the pace and began to pass other runners with new goals in mind. Athletes steadily build a sense of kinesthetic awareness, knowing their own body more keenly over time. For a runner it comes down to better understanding the implications of certain muscle contractions, breathing patterns, heart rate, foot strike, stride length, and cadence. As you learn to listen to your body, you also begin to understand what is beneficial to good running and goal completion and what is not.

During some runs, the information you gather from your body tells you to adjust your pace, your distance, or both. In Shelby's case, she was feeling physically strong during her state meet, so she altered her goal and her performance accordingly. She increased the challenge, her body responded positively, she performed well, and she experienced flow. Sometimes the information your body gives you is less positive, and you need to heed that information in order to prevent injury. When your body sends that message, listen to it; adjust the goal to something less taxing to find a more appropriate challenge–skills balance.

Internal markers are not the only data you need to monitor for feedback on performance. Externally, you need to attend to your environment, your opponents, your teammates, your coaches, and even spectators if you are running competitively. Everything from monitoring distance traveled to knowing the ambient temperature can influence your strategy.

Feedback can also come from those running with you. Your position relative to your opponents may suggest that you are not pacing appropriately. If your goal is to cross the finish line ahead of a particular competitor or teammate, viewing them in the distance may tell you it is time to speed up. Your coach may tell you it is important to relax given upcoming challenges of which you are unaware. Spectators can also provide welcome positive feedback. A rise of encouragement from the crowd may suggest you are approaching a pivotal moment and need to pay attention for further feedback.

For runners who run alone and are not necessarily competitive with others, gathering internal data is more important. Aside from your surroundings indicating distance traveled, information can be gleaned from technology you might be using. A heart rate monitor, GPS device, or fitness watch can provide important details about performance that can aid your understanding of your progress. These modern marvels can tell you if your pace or heart rate is too high or low for your given goals. You may need to alter your pace or adjust your breathing after processing the information. If you make modifications, your body will respond positively, improving the chance that flow might take place.

GPS Watches
When Is Too Much Data Too Much?

If you want to hear something unique to current culture and time, stand at any mile or kilometer mark of any major race. As the runners approach, you will be treated to a unique musical treat: thousands upon thousands of chirps, beeps, and vibrations as a sea of humanity passes an arbitrary distance marker (give or take a few feet).

This symphony is the product of GPS watches, those magical devices that track your every step and convert a complex series of math equations between a watch and a distant satellite into real-time, highly digestible nuggets of information. Many runners have become wholly reliant on these watches to assess their pace and distance, and for good reason. With an accuracy rate of 99 percent in most locales and software that transfers that data to computers and smartphones, GPS watches have made the once arduous task of measuring courses and filling out running logs all but obsolete.

With its ability to render instantaneous feedback, on the surface a GPS watch seems like a valuable tool in experiencing flow. In certain situations, it is certainly true. If you have an opportunity to run a personal best on a flat, fast course where the weather is good, rapid feedback is ideal. Measurable data allow you to contrast perceived effort against time and distance and adapt your pace accordingly. This same principle holds true when you're running a workout with specific time goals or on a day when you feel especially fast and want to know exactly how quickly you were traveling.

In other instances, GPS data can be counterproductive to flow running. Imagine you are on a serene wooded trail in the mountains. The scenery is calming and restorative; you feel happy just to be immersed in the quiet natural world. Suddenly your watch chimes in with this message: Mile 1 [1.6 km]: 13:45. Usually you run 9-minute miles on your easy day. But 13:45? It must be a mistake, you think. Did the foliage affect the watch's accuracy? Are you out of shape? Tired? This can't be right.

Odds are the watch is right, or at least right enough, which is fine. Wooded trails are slower than paved roads, and mountainous ones are even more so. To be a slave to pace is to lose the ability to enjoy these jaunts in the natural environment or anywhere else your pace might be affected. Which of these runs is more beneficial: a run at a pace of exactly 7:30 per mile (1.6 km), or a run at an 8:45-mile pace done in the company of friends?

All that said, most runners like their GPS watches and the tracking they provide. They have no plans to ditch them anytime soon. So how can you still enjoy a run while you're being monitored?

- *Disable the auto lap function.* Almost every GPS
offers the option of automatically taking splits at each mi
distance of your choosing). While this can be very info
on days when you feel great, other times you may want
The watch will still record your total time and distanc
longer distract you from the moment.

- *Switch the display.* If pace fixation is a problem o
pace disappear. Most watches offer the ability to scroll
of information. Pick a non-threatening one to have dis
rate or cadence. If your watch doesn't offer those, cor
of day. Sure you could do the math and make some ca
at least you've given yourself a chance to think abou
instantaneous pace.

- *Change your perception.* Perhaps the best way to get over pace fixa-tion is through a trait that is generally frowned upon—apathy. Not caring what the watch tells you on easy days, exploring days, or running-with-friends days offers you the freedom to listen to internal cues from your body and trust your instincts when running. As great as GPS watches are, they can never fully replace your ability to interpret your own biometrics (heart rate, perceived ex-ertion, and breathing). If your body tells you to slow down and enjoy the view, heed its advice.

Listening and tending to the internal and external feedback you receive takes practice. It is an active process in which you must engage in order to make flow more realizable. The more you focus your attention on messages from your body and your surroundings, the more capable you will become at interpreting that information and using it to adjust your performance.

When taken together the three antecedents emphasize how important it is to have a realistic understanding of your own skills and potential. Flow is predicated on being able to rise up to a challenge. Unrealistic or vague goals, an overwhelming or underwhelming challenge, and inconsistent feedback all run counter to that prerequisite.

Characteristics of Flow (Process Outcomes)

When the antecedents for flow are in place, the opportunity for the human mind and body to approach their fullest potential emerges. As the mind concentrates on the task at hand and the body readies itself for the difficult challenges that await, other disquieting thoughts and concerns disappear. As the challenge increases, the mind steadies itself by locking in on a moment-by-moment awareness. In some instances, this concentration can lead to the mind-altering state of flow.

Flow should not be confused with other forms of mind alteration. Flow is not a form of escapism, nor does it come with the host of side-effects that accompany psychedelic and hallucinogenic drugs that people might use to feel similar effects. Flow is about engagement, control, and highly focused attention. Alcohol, drugs, and other forms of consciousness bending all lead to the opposite effect.

That doesn't make the flow experience any less enjoyable than its chemically-induced counterparts. The six characteristics of flow (process outcomes) are all highly pleasurable in their own right. In fact, this sense of pleasure differentiates flow from other forms of peak experience. Not only are you running your fastest in a near effortless state, you are loving every footfall and heartbeat along the way. Staying locked into that moment is critical for staying in a flow state. For that reason, this section begins by examining the role of focused attention.

Focused Attention

It's not easy to stay focused in the modern world. How many times do you sit down to relax with a few minutes of television only to get sucked into a binge session fueled by 300-plus stations and on-demand content? How often do you start a conversation with a family member only to be interrupted by a text message or notification from your phone? People think of being home when they're at work and think of work when at home, and somehow they never seem to embrace the present moment. This lack of full presence is common in a culture that further embraces instant gratification and omnipresent technology.

Even when people want to fully engage a task, their brains are limited in how much they can process at a time. The central nervous system constantly filters information; without those filters you'd be paralyzed by an unending assault of sensory data. Fortunately, the brain has become quite adept at prioritizing information. This is why you might barely acknowledge all the pedestrians walking safely on the sidewalk as you drive by in a car, but you would immediately slam on the brakes when a child wanders out into the street.

When you actively engage thoughts and occurrences in your conscious mind, you are paying attention. Attention is what enables you to swerve around that child in the road, step over a root in the middle of a trail, or respond to a competitor's surge at the end of a race. Paying attention is an active process that can be improved over time through techniques such as mindfulness, yoga, and meditation (see Mindfulness, Meditation, and the Power of Attention).

Attention is at its fullest in a flow experience. For once your mind doesn't wander in a million directions but instead becomes completely engulfed by the task at hand. When you experience it in a race situation, you are fully aware of the internal feedback your body is providing and the external feedback coming back from competitors and spectators, your position in the race, and the clock. Superfluous thoughts about work, family, relationships, or what's for dinner disappear as the race takes precedence.

Mindfulness, Meditation, and the Power of Attention

It may seem that sustaining focus is beyond your control. Today's world is one of immediacy, where every text message necessitates an immediate response and being unplugged for just a few minutes leaves you sprinting back to your phone or computer to see what you might have missed. For some, running is the only time they escape this modern bombardment of information. For others who might run with a phone, they might not even escape it then.

Learning to sustain focus is worth the effort. While flow increases your ability to sustain attention on a single task and the relevant feedback, it is also true that if you are able to engage and maintain attention for longer periods of time on your own, you are more able to experience flow. It is a chicken-and-egg scenario; both sides offer the opportunity for a great experience.

One of the most popular ways to increase your attention and channel your focus is meditation, particularly mindfulness meditation. Meditation practices have their roots in traditional Asian cultures, although they have been well adapted to the Western mode of thought.

People have practiced meditation for centuries. Meditation involves quieting the mind through controlled breathing, a comfortable position, focused attention on a single word or the sensation of breathing, and a nonjudgmental stance toward passing thoughts. According to the U.S. National Institutes of Health (2016), meditation has been clinically proven to reduce pain, high blood pressure, and symptoms from certain psychiatric disorders. It may also positively alter the brain, increasing the number of outer folds (helpful when processing information), and helping the amygdala better process emotions.

Mindfulness meditation is an American-based version that begins with short bouts of directed attention (usually 10 minutes at a time) centered on the sensation of breathing and gradually increases in scope. During these quiet times, the goal is to focus solely on the present, making note of any thoughts, feelings, or emotions that pass in a nonjudgmental way. The same holds true for the environment around you. In this way, "mindfulness is the nonjudgmental observation of the ongoing stream of internal and external stimuli as they arise" (Baer 2003). As you progress in your mindfulness practice, it can become a grounding philosophy and a way of life. Just as in a flow experience, when you adopt a nonjudgmental stance in the present moment, you leave no room for fear or rumination. This boundary is good, because mindfulness reduces symptoms of pain, anxiety, depression, disordered eating, and depressive episodes (Baer 2003).

(continued)

Mindfulness, Meditation, and the Power of Attention *(continued)*

The best-known practice in this field is the mindfulness-based stress reduction (MBSR) program. Developed by mindfulness founder Jon Kabat-Zinn, MBSR is an 8- to 10-week course designed for large groups who meet weekly. During these sessions, participants do exercises such as body scans, where they lie prone on the ground and direct attention to different areas of the body sequentially. Yoga poses and traditional meditation are also used to help these practitioners experience the mind and body in a new way. In all these practices, participants are asked to direct their attention toward a movement or breathing pattern. When thoughts, memories, and daydreams cross their minds, practitioners are asked to note them briefly and then return their attention to the present moment and task (Baer 2003).

In running, meditation's propensity for increasing your attention span is of greatest importance. Meditation is considered to be a long-term practice; advanced practitioners feel they achieve their best control after many years. However, recent research by Tang et al. (2007) found that after 5 days of practice (at 20 minutes per session), participants scored much higher on attentional tests, making even short-term adoption worth a try. Joining a mediation or mindfulness group is probably the best way to learn the practice, although books and online videos also offer a wealth of information.

Not only is your attention fully on the race, but it remains on the race for the remainder of the flow experience. This narrowing of focus keeps out negative self-talk (e.g., "I can't wait for this to be over") and doubts (e.g., "My legs feel so heavy, I'm not sure I'll be able to hold this pace much longer"). It also frees up more mental energy for you to respond to what occurs during the race.

The unusual fact about attention during flow is its effortlessness. As Arne Dietrich and Oliver Stoll write in *Effortless Attention: A New Perspective in the Cognitive Science of Attention and Action* (2009),

> *Theories of attention and action . . . assume that higher task demands require more effort, both objectively, in terms of caloric consumption by the brain, and subjectively, in terms of perceived mental effort. In flow, however, the opposite appears to be the case. Here the perceived mental effort decreases, sometimes to the point of utter effortlessness, yet such seemingly automatic action is associated with superior performance (p. 160).*

One reason this effortlessness occurs is repetition (Dietrich & Stoll 2010). The more you practice a skill such as running, the less mental energy it takes to replicate it. Think of a young child learning to write. Every line and squiggle requires full care and attention to complete. In the time it takes a 4-year-old to write "ABC," you likely could have written the previous paragraph. After a certain point of mastery, your brain can automate the activity and allow it to be controlled by less specialized parts of the central nervous system.

At that point it is governed by the **implicit memory** instead of the **explicit memory** (described in more detail in chapter 3).

This mastery worked in Shelby's favor at the state meet. Without having to think about each stride and breath, her attention locked in completely on working her way through the race. "I just remember thinking about how in the world I felt so good," she says. "I kept getting closer to people in front of me, and my thought would be to catch up to them and move on to the next. After the first mile I had Emma in my head and I wanted to catch up to her. I never really had a specific time in my head because of the weather conditions (everyone was a little off), but when it came down to the second mile I realized I could easily break 21 minutes [her 5K personal record at the time was 20:49]." With her attention freed to higher-order concerns, Shelby pushed through the mud to record a PR of 20:41.

Effortless attention can be equally powerful in noncompetitive flow environments. On a mountainous trail run, your attention will be directed toward the footing on the trail or the beautiful scenery. On a flat road you may find yourself completely locked in on the rhythm of your stride and breathing pattern. The stakes may be lower in these recreational settings, but that doesn't diminish the intensity and narrowness of your focus during flow. That is because one competitor always remains, namely, you. Competition against the self can be just as potent for inducing flow as competing against others.

Merging of Action and Awareness

When your attention is fully absorbed in the task at hand during a flow experience, you feel completely at one with your actions. When this curious phenomenon occurs, everything feels automatic, because no separation exists between your thoughts and actions. Contrast this phenomenon with how often people describe actions as done by a separate body. "My legs had nothing today," they say after a hard run, as if those appendages were somehow alien to the person and process.

While a basketball player in flow might talk about making a move on pure instinct, or a softball player might describe her bat or mitt as an extension of herself, for runners the merging of action and awareness most often translates into a sense of lightness and ease. No longer do you think about picking up the pace and then execute it. Instead it occurs simultaneously. It is as if the very spark of a thought wills it into action.

"I have never run so effortlessly in my life," Shelby says. "Yes, I would think about picking people off and getting in the top 10, but my body just kind of did it without me having to make myself."

Flow earned its name, in part, because so many early research subjects described their experiences using that term. Things just *flowed* along effortlessly, as Shelby described. Writers, painters, and rock climbers used the same words as runners when describing the phenomenon.

Amy Hastings

Two-time Olympian, 2:27:03 marathon PR
Flow moment: 2016 U.S. Olympic marathon trials

Adam Davy/PA Photos

Some days, the universe seems to throw it all at you. Sweltering temperatures with no shade and no heat acclimatization because it's mid-February? Check. A repetitive, uninspiring urban course through the middle of a concrete jungle? Ditto. Dirt covering the road from recent construction? You bet. Oh, and how about in these conditions running 26.2 miles with a trip to the Rio Olympics on the line? Absolutely.

The media, fans, and plenty of competitors locked in on these miserable variables and declared the race would be a "suffer fest." Amy Hastings was not of the same mind. The Kansas native and former All-American at Arizona State University had already endured the cruelest fate professional running offers, finishing fourth at the Olympic trials marathon in 2012 in a race where only the top three qualified for the London Games. At the prime marathoning age of 32, Hastings wasn't going to enter this race on a downer vibe.

"Ahead of time, you heard so many negative things," Hastings says. "The number of turns on the course, the heat, the dirt on the road. It gave me a little more confidence. After we checked out the course, I realized if I can be okay with these things, it's going to be an advantage. I made the decision I wouldn't let the little things bother me."

Instead Hastings and her Bowerman Track Club teammate Shalane Flanagan ran comfortably in the pack early on, then around the halfway point they found themselves up front. Over the next hour they would become the face of these Olympic trials as they led the field in front of a national television audience. The teammates shared fluids and small conversation, much to the amusement of the commentators. Their fluidity and comfort in the horrendous conditions spoke to Hastings' commitment to achieve greatness on that day. She was in flow, and she knew it.

"It's a very specific feeling and I kind of know it now," she says. "I've gotten better at getting myself into the right frame of mind where it'll affect my physical self. It's something I can absolutely recognize when it happens, and it does happen fairly regularly."

A kinesiology major who had learned about sport psychology over the years, Hastings frequently evaluates her physical and mental state to make sure they are optimized for the right day. For Hastings this means zeroing in on her goals and ridding herself of anxiety. She does so by finding a quiet place before a major race and focusing on her breathing. "I remind myself that races are supposed to be exciting," she says, "and that helps a lot."

For 23 miles (37 km), the only excitement in the trials seemed to be whether Hastings and Flanagan would win by 2 minutes or 3 minutes. Hastings felt the pace was manageable, as though she wasn't even racing yet, and even then she and Flanagan were gaining 5 to 10 seconds on the field every mile. Eventually the heat caught up with Flanagan. That same national television audience now watched Hastings encourage Flanagan, and when words could no longer do the trick, they saw her selflessly slow down to stay beside her teammate. Not far behind, 2012 Olympian Desi Davila gained with each step. With the gap under 30 seconds and only a few miles remaining, Hastings wished Flanagan luck, then surged away from her competitors to win the trials in impressive fashion. Davila finished second, with Flanagan collapsing across the finish line into Hastings' arms for third.

It was a fitting end to a perfect day, one where the ability to block out the negative and focus solely on the goal at hand allowed her to perform her best when it mattered most. "I had been thinking about that race for years, thinking about everything leading up to it," she says. "When it came down to it, I was incredibly confident and in a very happy state and excited state. Physically I felt like I was ready to do it. It was one of those days where I felt whatever happened, whatever was thrown at me, I could handle it because of where my frame of mind was."

This idea of an effortless flow is partly an illusion. While it may appear that no energy is being expended, it's certainly true that as a runner you need to maintain both mental concentration and physical engagement in the sport in order to achieve your goals and stay in a state of flow. This requires a good bit of energy. However, because the mind and body thoroughly lock into the task at hand, the usual thoughts that might creep in and make you aware of this energy usage ("Am I going too fast? Should I back off and save some energy for later? Did I make my move too soon?") are blotted out. With these thoughts rendered irrelevant, you become one with the act of running.

What causes this phenomenon is partly up for debate. As Dietrich and Stoll (2009) point out, mastery of a skill leads to it being performed by the implicit memory. When the implicit memory is in charge, the less you think about a task the better you perform it, thus it appears effortless. At the same time, many of flow's characteristics appear related to the progressive down-regulation of the prefrontal cortex region in the brain. Put simply, making the human body move is an incredibly difficult task for the brain to take on, even with the implicit memory in charge. Various regions of your brain may begin to lower their demands in order to free up energy for the task at hand. The brain may induce this energy diversion through a change in attention (such as mentally preparing for a big race) or by the rhythmic motion of running.

In both instances, the result is an altered state of consciousness, one that leaves you precious little room to second-guess yourself.

Sense of Control

Before we delve into the sixth component of flow, take a look at what you have accumulated so far on your journey toward flow. You have a clear goal in mind. You have a belief that your skill level is competent to meet the challenge at hand. Every bit of feedback is confirming that belief. Your attention is like a laser beam, totally locked in on accomplishing a task but at seemingly no mental cost to you. Finally, your mind and body are working together in such a manner that you can't tell where your thoughts begin and your actions end.

Is it any surprise, then, that these combined factors would lead to an incredible sense of control? Usually even the most optimistic person would admit that one can control surprisingly few things. Think about running. You cannot control the weather, the actions of your competitors, the flow of traffic that impedes your rhythm, the virus that comes home from school with your child, or the last-minute job request that keeps you off the trails and in the office an extra 2 hours. Throw in death, relationships, and taxes, and it's a wonder people function as well as they do.

These limits disappear in flow as your focus narrows down to what you can control, namely, yourself and your actions. All feedback is pointing in a positive direction, so you experience a sense of empowerment, as though you are fully in charge of your destiny.

"I'm not really sure how to explain the control I had over my body besides the fact that I felt good, like I could just get faster and faster, like nothing could have stopped me," Shelby says. "I didn't have any pain in my lungs and my legs just continued to feel fresh the whole race. I was able to run my exact race, just working my way up."

Remember that Shelby still held in her mind a realistic view of her current potential. Thanks to genetics and training, several runners in the field were simply a different caliber. But among those runners who Shelby felt equal to in terms of raw ability, a belief grew that she could triumph. As Dr. Sue Jackson writes in *Flow in Sports: The Keys to Optimal Experiences and Performances* (1999), this belief is what matters most.

"More than actually being in control," Jackson says, "it is knowing that if you try hard, you *can* be in control: you trust your skills and you know that the task is doable. The outcome of this knowledge is a sense of power, confidence, and calm" (p. 26).

As Shelby powered over the final hill on the course and moved into fourth place, she never doubted her actions. She had complete and utter belief that it would prove to be successful. That doesn't mean you can't exaggerate this sense of control. In fact, believing you have too much control leads to arrogance and bravado, traits that will snap you out of flow immediately. It pays to be confident yet humble.

Jackson also cautions that you can lose this sense of control if the challenge suddenly increases or you find your skill level wasn't as high as predicted. This rude awakening will pull you out of flow just as quickly as arrogance. In those instances, the key to getting back into a good rhythm is to adjust your goals and expectations to more realistic outcomes on the fly. These cautionary tales serve as great reminders that the sense of control is all about you (your effort and potential), not what's happening around you (your competitors and unexpected environmental factors).

Loss of Self-Consciousness

It may seem paradoxical to lose your sense of self-consciousness at the exact moment you feel most in control of your actions and destiny, but it can happen in flow. With your attention firmly centered on the task at hand, no additional mental energy remains to entertain self-doubt or worry about others' perceptions of your performance. The ego is quieted in a most wonderful way.

All too often people are their own harshest critics. Perfectionism, defined by Dietrich and Stroll (2010) as "the disposition to regard anything short of perfection as unacceptable," can be a great benefit when it comes to learning and developing a skill such as running. The quest to master the minutest details of the sport may result in rapid improvement as no stone is left unturned in a quest for achieving one's potential.

Unfortunately, perfectionism comes with a heavy price. The need to always be proficient leaves perfectionists too self-critical of their actions and behaviors. It is difficult to lose self-consciousness or quiet the ego if you are struggling with overly critical thoughts, are excessively distracted by the fear of failure (another side-effect of perfectionism), or if your goal is focused on outperforming others instead of outperforming yourself. Both **positive-striving perfectionism** and **self-critical perfectionism** are covered in more detail in chapter 3.

Much of people's identity is also wrapped in how they believe others perceive them. Charles Horton Cooley (1902) dubbed this the "looking-glass self" more than a century ago. More recent social psychology has focused on the roles different social groups play and what cues and opinions people take from them. In both instances, it is made clear that people's sense of self is greatly tied into the views (real and imagined) of those around them.

This type of self-consciousness can be detrimental to performance because it impedes instinctual responses. If you spend time worrying about what others will think of your actions and their outcomes, then a disconnection occurs between your actions and awareness. However, if you have complete belief in yourself and your abilities, then your mind is free to focus on more pressing needs.

"Everything in me was focused on the race," Shelby says. "Not one time did I think about anyone's opinions or anyone who was watching me. All I thought about was running and getting faster because I felt good."

Much like action and awareness merging, a sense of oneness and unity with the environment around you can form from a loss of self-consciousness. As you run along a wooded trail, you feel part of the trees and rocks and earth. As you navigate your way through a crowded urban marathon, you feel a strong connection to the competitors and spectators around you, feeding off their energy but not aware of yourself as anything more than a piece of a larger, wondrous whole. This kinship with the world around you can only occur when the ego is subsumed by complete immersion in the task at hand.

A loss of self-consciousness does not equate a loss of the self. When you're engaged in a flow activity such as running, the need to focus for longer periods of time while performing a task means you can't zone out and forget who you are. Doing so would be detrimental to your performance and would snap you out of a flow state immediately.

For Shelby, losing her self-consciousness was no guarantee. Her health issues had made her and those closest to her hyperaware of all the bad outcomes that could happen in the race. Despite her "body feeling really well and relaxed," she recognized that others believed she might not be up to the challenge.

"After the asthma attack I had that morning, I was worried and I knew the coaches were too," Shelby says. "All morning I just heard from my coaches and teammates that everything would be fine, and I would be able to run my race. We set my standards lower, like top 25 I think, and that's how I knew [the coaches] were concerned. The night before and the day of the race I had so much anxiety I actually had to keep texting my mom to calm me down. My family, friends, and my church family had been sending text messages of encouragement and prayers my way all morning, and without that I probably would have had a mental breakdown the morning of the race. Everything my coaches, teammates, and family had told me that day was encouraging and positive, but I knew my coaches were still concerned by the way we talked and lowered my goals."

Fortunately for Shelby, those concerns evaporated on the starting line as her focus narrowed to the point of exclusion. With all feedback pointing in a positive direction, Shelby blocked out any previous concerns and instead directed all her energy into the race, increasing her goals as her body proved willing. By doing so, she was able to tap into the fitness that had been buried under the pneumonia for 6 weeks and begin a charge that would take her all the way to the podium.

Distortion of Time

Think of some of the most pleasurable and engaging moments of your life. It could be your wedding day, the time you wrote an entire short story in one sitting, or the best hike of your life up a scenic mountain. Very likely, those disparate examples had this one thing in common: They all seemed to play out at a different speed than normal.

Now think about some of your best runs. They could be effortless races where you set a big PR, long runs spent in the company of good friends, or solo sojourns that found you totally lost in thought. Once again, a common theme is likely to be a distortion of time.

Escaping the tyranny of time is no easy task. Many people wear a watch, and those who don't find their phones and computers reminding them of the time of day at every glance. Awareness of time can be positive, such as when an interval split shows you're having a great workout, but all too often people become infatuated with time when they want to be doing something more pleasurable. Instead of embracing the present moment for what it offers, they become lost in a countdown waiting to be released from the less-than-desirable activity.

This obsession with time doesn't happen only at work. Most runners steal more than a few glances at their watch during a run. During a truly difficult day, you may find yourself flipping your wrists up every few minutes in the hopes that your self-induced hell is nearly over. With no engagement in the present, the mind drifts between the past ("What did I do to feel so badly today?") and the future ("I can't wait to get back to the house").

In a flow state, the opposite occurs. As you find yourself immersed in a pleasurable task, your sense of time is distorted. A 30-minute race feels as though it's over in a blink of the eye. A 2-hour-long run with friends leaves you shocked at how many miles you covered; after all, didn't the run just start a few minutes ago? Even with your conscious mind fully aware of all the roads and trails you're navigating, you still have a sense a wonderment that it passed by so quickly.

"The race seemed to fly by," Shelby says, "and it's not so much that the memories were more vivid, but they were good, and I want to remember them."

In other instances, time may seem to slow down. During a particularly good workout, you may find yourself noticing every stride as you feel totally in control of your body. In a race, it may seem as though you're watching a slow-motion replay as you match your competitors' moves. On a scenic trail, every second feels more intense and memorable than usual.

Once again the causes for this distortion may be a mix of neurology and psychology. The prefrontal cortex regulates our sense of time, and with its downregulation comes a diminished ability to perceive how much time has passed. Similarly, the intense focus of a flow experience prevents you from thinking about your watch every few minutes and lets you fully engage the activity. Negative thoughts that are prone toward stealing your attention (such as "How much longer do I have to do this?") are not possible in a flow state.

Intrinsic Motivation (Autotelism)

When you love something, you do it more. When you do something more, you get better at it. When you get better at it, you increase the challenge.

When you increase the challenge, you are more likely to experience flow. When you experience flow, you love it more. When you love it more, you do it more. And so on.

This beautiful cycle of flow begins and ends at the same place—a love of the activity you're doing for its own sake. Flow isn't possible for a runner who only competes for trophies and prizes. Those runners may find pleasure in the outcomes that running far or fast provide, or they may get a rush from a runner's high; but without an intrinsic love of running, flow is not available.

Flow certainly can increase your love for an activity. Not only does the effortless state make running seem more pleasurable, but the level of success that accompanies flow experiences makes it more intrinsically and extrinsically rewarding. Consider Shelby's relationship to running:

> One reason I like running so much is honestly because I'm pretty good at it. I have a good team, and we can compete well. My mom has always told me I played sports when I was little just so I could get more trophies than my older brothers. So I have always liked winning, but in [reflecting on] that race, I think about how good I felt, and I still can't manage to figure it out. Everything was against me, and I ran the best race of my life and felt amazing the whole time. Looking back, I first think about how good I felt and how I would love to have that same experience again.

Developing this internal love of the sport is doubly important as you increase your skill level. Professional athletes often report that as they experience incremental successes and gain more external support for their accomplishments, the pressure of meeting others' expectations can thwart their intrinsic motivation, thus impeding flow. Motivational research with children shows similar findings. When you flood the environment with external rewards, it dampens the development or awareness of intrinsic rewards and quashes intrinsic motivation.

Fortunately for Shelby, her love of running grew as she had more success, which in turn made her train harder to have even more success. Adding flow into the mix raised the bar even higher. Not only did it increase her intrinsic love of running, it also provided an important memory, one that keeps the fire burning a little bit brighter each day.

"Remembering those moments is what helps you get through the harder times of running," Shelby says. "You can have a week where you feel like absolute crap, but thinking about times like that [flow race], it's like, 'Why can't that happen it again?' It motivates you."

More Than an All-or-Nothing Proposition

Experiencing flow is a very personal thing. Each person will experience the components of flow at different intensities and in different orders. Sometimes flow experiences will encompass all nine of the components listed; other times, it may be fewer. According to several studies that looked at athletes' experiences in flow (Jackson 1996; Sugiyama & Inomata 2005) the majority reported experiencing five or six of the nine components of flow during a single flow experience.

The direct relationship between all nine components is still being studied, but newer research (Stavrou, Jackson, Zervas, and Kerteroliotis, 2007) has found the three antecedents, sense of control, focused attention, and an autotelic experience are often reported together. Other characteristics, such as time transformation, occur less frequently. The absence of one or more components does not dilute the flow experience; by its very definition, it is still highly pleasurable.

So far this book has painted a beautiful picture of flow, but is it an egalitarian one? Do some people experience flow more readily than others? If so, what personality traits and characteristics give those people a leg up? To answer that question, read on to chapter 3, which describes and explains flow personality.

Key Points

- Flow has nine components: three are antecedents and six are outcomes. The antecedents include clear goals, challenge-skill balance, and unambiguous feedback. The outcomes are focused attention, merging of action and awareness, sense of control, loss of self-consciousness, distortion of time, and intrinsic motivation.
- Clear goals are concrete goals. Be specific.
- If your goal is to experience flow, it is not likely to happen. Set a running goal, not a flow goal.
- Setting an appropriate challenge–skill balance can vary based on mood, fitness level, sleep, and other variables such as personality and how much you value the activity.
- The inverted-U theory of performance and anxiety states that humans like challenge, but too much challenge results in anxiety. Anxiety inhibits flow, so be careful not to set the bar too high if you want to experience flow.
- Practicing meditation is a great way to improve focused attention.
- Flow begins and ends with intrinsic motivation, a pure love for the activity.
- Each person experiences flow a little differently, with varied intensities and reports of all or only some of the outcomes being present. It is always enjoyable, regardless of the intensity or the outcomes experienced.

CHAPTER 3
Flow Personality

Kaitlin Goodman has a simple mantra: *Run joyfully*. On the night of April 3, 2015, Goodman tested that intonation at the prestigious Stanford Invitational. Competing over 10,000 meters (6.2 mi; 25 laps) on the track, Goodman lined up against a world-class field of 35 that included U.S. record holder Shalane Flanagan, Ethiopian star Geleta Burka, and Canadian marathon record holder Lanni Marchant.

None of those ladies were particularly concerned about Goodman. Nominally a professional runner since graduating from UC Davis in 2010, Goodman had never qualified for a U.S. Olympic trial or won much on the roads. Her personal best of 33:01 was almost 3 minutes slower than Flanagan's best of 30:22. Still, she loved the sport, so she continued to eke out a threadbare career while following her husband's medical training across the country from California, to Ohio, to Rhode Island.

From the moment the gun fired, Goodman felt smooth. She ran in a large chase pack of professionals and elite collegians, well behind Olympians Flanagan, Burka, and Marchant. As the laps clicked by, Goodman's confidence increased. She monitored the pace and her breathing; all systems were go. She felt a lightness, a sense of ease. Hearing her father yelling encouragement and fast splits brought her comfort every lap. Her attention never wavered. She was locked in; she flowed.

With five laps to go, Goodman knew the time had come. She picked up the pace a hair. It was just a few seconds faster per lap, but it splintered the chase pack immediately. Goodman and one other runner (future Australian Olympian Dominique Scott from the University of Arkansas) found themselves in the hinterlands between the safety of the chase pack and the third-place Marchant, who still held a half-lap lead. Several thousand fans in the stands cheered. These track aficionados recognized Goodman's effort and the move she was making. It would take a minor miracle to catch Marchant, who regularly trained in Kenya, but Goodman pushed on.

Every lap felt better. Scott ran right by Goodman's side, relieving the mental burden of going it alone. When the bell sounded, indicating one lap to go, Goodman pounced. All the years, all the miles that led to this single moment, came charging out with 400 meters remaining. Goodman spotted Marchant 10 seconds ahead and pushed harder. Her form never wavered. Smooth and efficient, she gained and gained. On the final straightaway, with the crowd screaming and on its feet, Goodman found one last gear. She smoothly passed Marchant and kept her focus locked in until crossing the line. Then she looked at the clock; it read *32:09*. Goodman was going to the Olympic trials.

"The last 100 meters of that race is something I will remember to the end," Goodman says. "It was just so . . ." She pauses to find the right word. "It was a lot of validation of years and years of hard work, and work that wasn't always translating into the results I wanted. So it was very validating. It was just so fun."

As with all flow experiences, Goodman experienced a strong sense of pleasure as her focus narrowed. Her effort was intense but enjoyable, her goal of making the Olympic trials and placing highly in the competition guided her actions, and the encouragement of her family and spectators told her she was strong enough to achieve her goals.

But what about her mantra, *Run joyfully?* Did that simple coda give Goodman an advantage in finding flow? What about her level of expertise, her dedication, or even her temperament? For the last 20 years, researchers of flow have spent much of their time asking those questions, seeking to figure out what determines the frequency and intensity of flow experiences.

One area that has received increasing attention is personality. While personality is fairly stable, people can modify personality traits marginally, given some effort (Hudson & Fraley 2015). This fact is important to keep in mind when you look at traits that may hinder the frequency and quality of flow experiences later in this chapter; it is virtually impossible to not see yourself described, but it is not hopeless to have some of these traits. You can use the knowledge gained in this chapter to make some adjustments in perspective and attitude so that you can increase the likelihood of frequent and intense flow.

When examining flow, currently researchers describe several approaches to personality, including the **autotelic personality**, penned by Dr. Mike. The autotelic personality is a broad framework for understanding the behavioral tendencies, attitudes, and dispositions of a person who experiences flow frequently and fluidly. Before examining the autotelic personality, this chapter outlines research that has used other personality measures to identify traits that correlate with self-reports of frequent flow experiences. When combined with the autotelic personality, these reports help to build a composite of the flow personality.

Individual Traits

The five-factor model of personality (McCrae & Costa 1990) measures personality on five major dimensions. These dimensions are commonly ordered by the acronym OCEAN and described as follows:

Openness to new experiences

Conscientiousness

Extraversion

Agreeableness

Neuroticism

This model formed from a methodology known as factor analysis and attempts to reduce the many variables of a person's personality down to five traits that appear time and time again.

Fredrik Ullén, a flow researcher in Sweden, studied personality in flow-prone people with several colleagues using the five-factor model of personality. After several rounds of data analysis, they found that flow-prone people score high on conscientiousness and low on neuroticism. Openness to new experiences, extraversion, and agreeableness didn't play a significant factor (Ullén et al. 2011). Conscientiousness is characterized as a behavioral tendency toward self-discipline, reliability, ambition, organization, and initiative; neuroticism is characterized by emotional instability, anxiety, and passivity (McCrae & Costa 1990; Goldberg 1990). With that in mind, the following sections examine these two relevant factors of the five-factor model of personality.

Conscientiousness

People who measure high on the personality trait of conscientiousness are self-disciplined, appreciate achieving goals, and develop plans to achieve those goals (McCrae & Costa 1990). Conscientious runners periodize their training to include base building, long runs, tempo runs, hill work, ancillary training, and planned rest periods, because these elements help prepare them to meet their long-term running goals. These runners persevere through difficult runs, races, or weeks because such speedbumps are to be expected and are often necessary in order to achieve long-term goals.

Runners who are highly conscientious are less likely to engage in spontaneous behaviors that might negatively affect their training. They're also less likely to act impulsively while training. For instance, a runner with this trait would be unlikely to race a teammate during a workout or run a risky trail only days before a major competition. Their sense of order and purpose keeps those potentially dangerous thoughts at bay.

It is not surprising that these traits work in a runner's favor when seeking out flow. After all, conscientious runners set goals (the first antecedent from chapter 2), are acutely aware of their level of preparation, allowing them to set the appropriate challenge–skills balance (the second antecedent), and constantly monitor feedback to ensure they're on the right path (the final antecedent). The extra time spent preparing, when combined with the wherewithal to accept their present mental and physical condition, can do wonders when it comes to inducing positive psychological states while running.

Neuroticism

As much as conscientiousness encourages flow, the qualities of neuroticism are equally discouraging (Ullén et al. 2011). People who measure high on neuroticism are prone to anxiety, struggle with internal and external distractions, and are easily frustrated (McCrae & Costa 1990; Goldberg 1990). When you are overwhelmed by anxiety and distractions, it is difficult to focus on monitoring progress toward your running goals. This focus is critical, because processing feedback about your progress is one of the major antecedents.

Neurotic runners worry excessively over external factors, such as their safety, the actions or reactions of other people around them, and their outward appearance. Everyone has at some time felt concern over these same factors; being concerned for your safety while you are running on a remote trail or dark street is reasonable. You also may have gone out of your way to impress a fellow runner, competitor, or friend in the stands. These factors become categorized as neurotic only when they are excessive and keep you from focusing on the more relevant elements in your environment.

Internal factors pose equally large problems for people with neurotic tendencies. A good run is often typified by the joy of losing yourself in your thoughts or in no thought at all. This state is a pleasurable running outcome. For a neurotic runner, silencing the mind is nearly impossible, and the thoughts that resonate are mostly negative. Imagining how others will dissect your performance, your form, or even your outfit creates an uninviting mental space for flow and keeps the neurotic runner from enjoying the act of running itself.

These negative internal dialogues leave neurotic runners ruminating over past failures. They in turn become pessimistic predictions about future failures (McCrae & Costa 1990). All of this mind noise makes flow difficult, because less cognitive energy is available for you to focus on your goal and your progress. The tendency to give up and stop running can be very tempting. For runners who struggle with high anxiety levels, finding ways to quiet internal noise, quell the distractions around them, gather focus, and replace pessimistic predictions with optimistic expectations can open the door to flow and much more satisfying running experiences. Part II of this book examines ways to quiet the mind and shift it toward more optimistic thought patterns.

Perfectionism and Motivational Tendencies

One trait many dedicated runners share is the desire to perfect their craft. Where the desire stems from and how it is applied can make all the difference in whether this trait produces or inhibits flow.

Arne Dietrich, a prolific cognitive neuroscience researcher at the American University of Beirut in Lebanon, believes that people who practice positive-striving perfectionism are more likely to experience flow than those who practice self-critical perfectionism (Dietrich & Stoll 2010). **Positive-striving perfectionism** is a behavioral and mental tendency to set high standards for yourself, to set specific benchmarks to measure progress toward or achievement of those standards, and to exhibit the drive necessary to persevere. When push comes to shove, these people show that they have the tenacity and grit to keep striving.

On the other hand, **self-critical perfectionism** mirrors neuroticism in many respects. Self-critical perfectionists set high standards but are critical of themselves when expectations do not match the performance, tend to be highly anxious about potential mistakes, and are rather pessimistic about the potential to meet the high standards they set in the first place. This approach not only impedes performance but also dilutes the potential for flow to unfold.

Both types of perfectionist set high standards and expectations for themselves, which can be stressful. The critical difference is in how each one copes with the stress and how they reason their failures. The positive-striving perfectionist tends to feel energized and motivated by the stress of a challenge, feeling capable of managing the task. This perfectionist perceives failure as part of the growth process or learning curve. Failure is not a personal flaw but a natural part of life. A positive-striving perfectionist is also an **approach-motivated person** who enjoys challenges, seeing risk and failure as opportunities to improve. An additional benefit of being an approach-motivated person is that you tend to see memories through a positive lens, even those that felt neutral or negative when they occurred (Strachman & Gable 2006).

If you practice approach motivation, not only do you enjoy the challenge of a good run (or any challenge in life), you also appreciate the challenge of a tough run. In doing so, you're able to frame the memory of a bad run or bad performance in a positive light. This reframing doesn't entail manipulating the memory of the run into something less than truthful. Instead you simply dilute the negative aspects and find something positive to learn from the experience (Strachman & Gable 2006). You might call this an ability to find the silver lining around any of life's clouds. It is no surprise that these behavioral tendencies are highly correlated with life satisfaction (Elliot et al. 2006).

Self-critical perfectionists interpret these same situations very differently. They set high standards and difficult goals for themselves, but they are anxious and highly critical of their own performance toward their goals. This preoccupation with the critical analysis of their performance may be a learned behavior, but it may also be a result of biology encouraging continued activation in the prefrontal cortex (and possibly the amygdala), where higher order reasoning resides (Dietrich & Stoll 2010). As mentioned in the previous chapter, Dietrich's flow research suggests that when you are in flow, your prefrontal cortex deactivates (Dietrich & Sparling 2004) or rests. The energized prefrontal cortex in the self-critical perfectionist would prohibit the onset of flow.

Just as the positive-striving perfectionist is practicing approach-motivated behaviors, seeking out challenge and appreciating the failures as opportunities to learn and grow, the self-critical perfectionist is likely to practice avoidant-motivated behaviors. The person who tends to be **avoidance motivated** often aspires to avoid failure, not achieve success. This is a subtle but important distinction. Think about toeing the starting line for a race. What thoughts engulf your mind? Are you thinking about achieving a particular pace, place, or PR? Or are you thinking about not losing, not falling, not finishing last? The former will propel you forward toward your goal with progress that is clearly measurable. The latter provokes anxiety from the beginning of the run to the very end, keeping flow away.

You could fall at any time, and your competitors could pass you at any stage of the race. Because the risk of failure exists through the entirety of the race, you can't measure progress or achieve your goals until its completion, when you realize you didn't fall and didn't finish last. Not only is that a flow crusher, it also steals joy from the race. Little pleasure exists in acknowledging you finished a run still on both feet.

Self-Esteem

Another area of personality that affects frequency and quality of flow is self-esteem. Self-esteem is a combination of attitudes and beliefs about your own competency and the resulting emotions from those attitudes and beliefs (Smith & Mackie 2007). When you have **high self-esteem**, you feel worthy and capable. You are proud of yourself and your achievements. This attitude allows you to set goals that are appropriately aligned with your skills, which in turn encourages flow.

Inflated self-esteem stems from a misjudgment of skill. In this instance you believe you have greater abilities than you do. This misjudgment impedes flow, because you work excessively hard at trying to meet a challenge you're not prepared to tackle. Just as the challenge–skills balance outcomes (see figure 2.2) indicate, if your abilities are not up to the task at hand you are likely to experience anxiety, if not extreme fatigue and frustration.

Low self-esteem resides on the opposite side of the spectrum. People with low or no self-esteem believe they are not worthy, not capable, and should be ashamed of themselves. This belief results in a misjudgment of skill that is lower than their actual potential. Low self-esteem impedes flow, because people who have it are likely to feel apathetic and bored—if they engage in the challenging task at all.

Neither inflated nor low self-esteem calls for an honest assessment of skills. Honestly assessing your skills not only increases the likelihood of flow, it also makes your runs more satisfying in the end. Therefore, in terms of flow, high self-esteem provides an advantage.

Mastery Orientation Versus Performance Orientation

According to Jackson and Roberts (1992), taking a mastery approach toward your running will encourage flow, while practicing a performance orientation will make flow less likely. Their study also found that high levels of perceived ability predicted flow as well. A person with a **mastery orientation** is focused on the process and the experience, while a performance-oriented person is more concerned with the outcome. **Performance orientation** is more common in a person with low self-esteem and high anxiety; this person also frequently practices social comparison (e.g., *How am I doing compared to everyone else?*). These conditions make experiencing flow much less likely.

Experiencing flow in running isn't the only reason to consider working on a mastery approach. Research in academic settings suggests that students who prefer performance orientation may perform well on tests, but those that focus on the experience of learning test equally well, retain information longer, and seem to enjoy the learning process more (Dweck 1986). Generalizing on this concept, if you run for the joy of running and embrace the elements of the experience like a mastery-oriented runner, you are not only more likely to experience improvement in your runs and to run in flow, you are more likely to enjoy the experience regardless of the outcome.

Effortless Attention

Experiencing flow requires the ability to focus attention and process information gathered from your surroundings. It includes time spent running and distance traveled. Researchers originally assumed a correlation between flow proneness and intelligence, given that intelligence requires the ability to practice effortful, or **focused attention** (Ullén et al. 2011). To their surprise, the data did not support this assertion. Instead it may be the ability to practice effort*less,* not effortful, attention that plays a role.

Focused attention is related to intelligence, while effortless attention is not. **Effortless attention** is the result of significant practice and repetition and is visible in the reflexive responses of an expert in any field, including sport. After practicing an activity for a long period of time, whether it is driving or running, portions of the experience become hardwired into your memory, specifically your **implicit memory**.

How Long Can You Flow?
A Profile of the Prolific Ellie Greenwood

In running, races such as 5,000 meters, 10,000 meters, and even marathons offer a good window of time to immerse yourself in the act of running and blur everything else out. However, what if your idea of a fun time is 100 miles (160 km)? Can you find flow over the long haul and maintain that focus without losing your mind?

Courtesy of Jan Heuninck.

Not much research exists on this topic, so we decided to ask the top female ultramarathoner in the world for her opinion. Born in Great Britain and based in Canada, Ellie Greenwood has taken the ultramarathon scene by storm since her first race in 2008. She is a two-time world champion in the 100 kilometers and holds the course record at the venerated Western State 100-miler and the JFK 50-miler. Following is an edited version of our conversation.

***Running Flow*: Before we dive in, is flow something you experience regularly?**

Ellie Greenwood: Yes and no. If training is going well for a period of weeks or months then often running itself, even at higher efforts and intensities, can seem relatively easy and effortless, in which case I would say I experience flow quite regularly. In these moments I switch off, and although I am aware of my surroundings, I find myself so absorbed in the moment that I can pass landmarks and junctions on a trail without really being aware of it. However, there are other periods in my training when I am maybe peaking for a race or am pushing my training to a limit where my running by and large seems like much more hard work. My legs ache, I struggle to achieve what seems like a suitable pace, and as such I do not achieve flow. Running seems like it is a conscious effort rather than a natural movement.

***RF*: Trail races by and large take place in beautiful environments, which have been shown to increase the likelihood of flow. Do you think training and racing on trails help you get into this state?**

EG: Yes, I would agree with this. Primarily, I would wonder if this is due to the fact that if I am running in an urban environment then it is impossible to switch off from the interruptions of my surrounding and "lose" myself in my run. Traffic lights, road crossings, other pedestrians, and cyclists are all things that I need to be aware of, and so I cannot drift off into just running. I can, however, experience flow when running on a treadmill or on a closed racecourse, where traffic and outside interference is minimal. The treadmill strips running down very bare—no distractions, no interruptions, and no need to think about route choice. It is very simple running, and so is a situation where I can achieve flow.

But certainly running on trails or mountain terrain, I achieve flow more frequently when running. I feel relaxed and refreshed in a natural environment away from the stresses of noise and people of everyday life. In addition, on the trail one is often focusing in on the task in hand, for example how to place one's next footsteps, looking out for roots and rocks, et cetera. That absorbs my focus rather than thinking about, say, work or other day-to-day stresses when road running.

RF: Feedback is a critical part of flow, too. Without mile markers on the course, and with the hills and terrain making GPS data not very relevant, how do you judge your effort?

EG: I think it can be easier to assess how I am feeling on the trails due to the fact that it is more about perceived effort than actual pace. When road running, we often become overly reliant on external factors like a watch and thinking we should be hitting a certain pace without really thinking about how we feel. But because trail running involves varying terrain and hills, one cannot look at a number on a watch to see how one is doing. Instead one has to focus on how one feels and run more "with the flow," which can lead to a more natural effort suited to one's current fitness level.

RF: Tell us about the sheer amount of time you're out there during a race or long training run. Where does your mind go during a 10-hour race?

EG: I never consciously think about where my mind is going or try to steer it, unless I find myself in a tough spot and sinking into a negative mindset, which can occur in long races. In that case I do consciously try to think of positive things to pull me out of a lull. When I am completing a long race on the trail my mind can wander between a state of flow or thinking about things that are nothing to do with the race (like daydreaming, future races, and friends), to thinking about race tactics and race logistics, like which aid station is coming up or who is ahead of me. I think about what to eat and what gear to change. I often find in long races that I look forward to aid stations as landmarks of progress, but when I actually get to an aid station I want to get out as quickly as possible because I find the noise and number of people is too overwhelming and too much in contrast with my solitary time on the trail in my own little world. I generally don't talk to fellow racers much during a race but can enjoy running in silence or exchanging the occasional word. It can be nice to get into a rhythm behind another racer's footsteps and really mentally zone out.

RF: Does time often seem to speed up for you in those instances?

EG: Definitely, I lose concept of time when in flow. For this reason, in long races I don't like to have the time of day on my watch as it pulls me back to reality. "Oh,

(continued)

How Long Can You Flow? *(continued)*

it's lunch time!" It makes me realize how long I have been running for or how much longer I have to go. When in flow everything feels easy and effortless. It's easy to daydream and soon time passes without really noticing. Faster efforts can definitely feel easier. Sometimes I think it is more of a case of a hard effort feels just as hard, but I can embrace it and know I can maintain it. It pushes me to work even harder.

RF: **What's your best flow moment?**

EG: My win and course record at Western States 100-miler in 2012. When asked afterwards by an interviewer if I had had any tough spots, I really felt that I hadn't. It was a race of 16 hours and 47 minutes, and I just ran all day. In some ways one could describe it almost as boring or uneventful as I never wavered physically or mentally all through the race. I simply ran, worked my way from one aid station to the next without fuss or drama, I refueled when I needed, I enjoyed seeing friends at aid stations, and I enjoyed running hard. Although it was not effortless, it seemed very manageable.

Recall driving for the first time, and you likely remember how difficult it was to process all of the variables that required your attention. Oncoming traffic, stop signs, and even the simple act of keeping the car in your lane all required focused attention. Since you were still learning the tasks, this information was processed by your **explicit memory**. Over time, and with lots of practice, driving became nearly reflexive (implicit). This process, much like any activity that you undertake, still requires energy, but the exertion seems more effortless than before (except when you encounter something that throws you off and makes you rely on your explicit memory, such as when navigating an unfamiliar city or working your way through heavy traffic). Many aspects of running can become implicit (effortless) over time and with practice, which frees up the mind to focus on goals, feedback, and the challenge–skills balance necessary for flow.

Understanding the specific traits that enhance or detract from experiencing flow is helpful. However, personality traits don't make up the whole picture. Dr. Mike offers a more positive, broad, and complex understanding of the life of a flow-prone person. Dubbed the *autotelic personality*, you will notice similarities to some of the research on personality and flow that were just discussed.

Flow significantly enriches running, and provides a satisfaction that can permeate other areas of your life. The autotelic personality (discussed next) is a blueprint for the overall disposition, attitude, and behavioral tendencies of the flow-prone person. To date, it offers the greatest chance to experience flow regularly.

Autotelic Personality

The word *autotelic* originated in the Greek language and means "self-directed" or "self-rewarding." An **autotelic personality** embodies those traits. Self-reward doesn't reflect a selfish nature but a desire to engage with activities that are rewarding in their own right. This idea is also called *intrinsic motivation*; the pleasure found in the activity is itself the reward.

Autotelic Personality Traits

Curiosity

Engagement

Achievement/goal oriented

Intrinsic motivation

Enjoyment of mastering new skills

Appreciation of challenges

Enjoyment of life experiences more than pursuit of power, material things, or accolades

As an autotelic personality, you are curious about the world and your surroundings, so you engage them. You enjoy a sense of achievement and accomplishment and are goal oriented. The satisfaction of achievement is not in the external acknowledgements or gains but in the personal pride found in your successes and in the process itself. You enjoy selecting activities that allow for skill development because you enjoy the process of setting goals and working toward them. Adjusting your goals and performance based on the feedback you receive isn't injurious; it's simply a reflection of where you are at present and what heights you can still reach.

This approach isn't limited to passions such as running. With an autotelic personality, you approach daily chores and long-term dreams with the same vigor and excitement. Because you find such satisfaction in personal activities and achievements, you see little need for the pursuit of power, material items, or accolades. Experiencing life and engaging in meaningful activities is the source of your fulfillment (Csikszentmihalyi 1997). The joy of life comes from the act of living.

As an autotelic personality, you have the ability to experience a satisfying balance between the pleasure of finding challenge and the discipline of building skills (Csikszentmihalyi et al. 1993). People with this trait believe they have a high degree of control over the events in their lives. They can therefore achieve their goals with the right amount of dedication. People with an **external locus of control** believe they have little influence over their circumstances, and they ascribe most outcomes to the hands of others, fate, or destiny. Goal setting is harder for those with an external locus of control, because investing all that time may prove to be worthless given the bevy of outside influences that could derail them from achieving their goal.

If you are a runner with an autotelic personality, you run for the joy of running, not to boast about it to others or to gain popularity. The pleasure comes from moving through space, feeling the snap in your stride, and the power in your heart. You enjoy setting goals for today's run, and you immerse yourself in the experience, putting aside the demands of the day. Because you are a curious person, you like to see how far you can push yourself in the run, how well you can encourage your body to respond to the requests you present, how you can measure improvements over time, and what you might ask of yourself the next time you run. Your internal locus of control allows you to feel optimistic about your ability to improve and to set ever more challenging goals for yourself into the future. Although a great satisfaction exists in beating a rival, it isn't your main motivation.

Flow Personality

Even though the five-factor model and autotelic personality are not directly related, many commonalities exist. This overlap produces the core of the **flow personality**. People who possess these traits or work hard to develop them are flow prone; they are more likely to experience flow on a regular basis and find enjoyment from the act of running and whatever other passions in which they partake.

People with flow personality are goal oriented but not goal focused. They find intrinsic value in the process of learning or developing a new skill and become mastery oriented. They enjoy the process because they have a realistic perception of their abilities and set goals that are attainable; it shows in their high levels of self-esteem. Their internal locus of control gives them a sense of control over their environment, skill set, and future. Because they feel in control, they have goals to strive for and feel optimistic about their potential for goal achievement and life more broadly.

Flow-prone people are conscientious (figure 3.1), which means they like achieving. They know they may need to persist through difficulties and challenges; failure is a real possibility that is accepted as part of the process of improving. Because they measure low on neuroticism, the risk of failure and its possible implications doesn't lead to anxiety. Instead these people plug into their activities, their goals, and their life as a whole.

Don't be surprised if you've seen yourself reflected in personality traits that are both conducive and counterproductive toward experiencing flow. Every person has a mixture of strengths and weaknesses, many of which can be addressed through subtle shifts in approach and thought patterns (as you will see in part II). Many researchers in the field of psychology have found support for the malleability of personality and character traits, such as those discussed so far. For instance, one major concept in neuroscience and developmental psychology is neuroplasticity, the fact that the neural networks (brain wiring) that regulate and initiate thought processes and behavior are constantly changing as a result of experiences. This concept is often referred to as "neurons that fire together, wire together." Rick Hanson, a senior fellow at the Greater Good Science Center of UC Berkeley, studies,

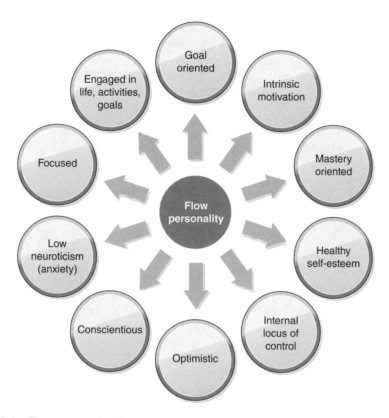

Figure 3.1   Flow personality diagram.

speaks, and writes about neuroplasticity and notes that when you focus on the good things in your life (or runs), you can rewire those neurons to fire together for more positive thoughts and behaviors (Hanson 2013). Even if you feel as though stress dominates your life right now, it's quite possible to *run joyfully* like Kaitlin Goodman in the near future.

Speaking of Goodman, you might wonder how her personality profile matches up with the previously mentioned models. After taking a 41-item personality test (www.personalitytest.org.uk) published by University of Westminster (UK) professor Tom Buchanan, Goodman rated "relatively high" in measures of openness, conscientiousness, extraversion, and agreeableness. She rated "relatively low" in neuroticism.

Goodman's positive, goal-striving personality gives her a leg up when it comes to experiencing flow. She believes running offers a chance for positive experiences that can ultimately transcend the sport.

"*Run joyfully* is for me," she says, "but whether that's *walk joyfully, swim joyfully,* or anything else, it's just getting out and being active. That's kind of my mantra, not just in competing but in my life and relationships and my work in health and wellness promoting healthy lifestyles. You don't have to be running, just do something joyfully.

"The other part [of my outlook] comes from a place of gratitude," Goodman continues. "I actually stole it from my dad who's a cross country coach in Davis, California. He always counseled his athletes to run joyfully and to remind themselves that they're the luckiest kids to be alive and able to do this. You're not wanting for anything. You have a roof over your head, you're not in a war-torn country, fighting chaos in your country. Just appreciate the opportunity that you have to be out there. And that for me with still racing [professionally] and being able to pursue this dream, I should absolutely not be complaining about running when it's cold. I should be grateful for having the opportunity."

Goodman's ability to experience flow when it mattered most earned her a ticket to the U.S. Olympic trials. This experience keeps her happy, humble, and training hard. However, most runners don't have realistic Olympic aspirations and cannot train full-time to meet such a lofty goal. The average runner may ask, "Why does flow even matter?" It's a valid question, and chapter 4 explores it in detail.

Key Points

- Dr. Mike coined the term *autotelic personality,* which describes the thoughts, attitudes, and behavioral tendencies of the person who experiences flow frequently.
- OCEAN is an acronym for a model of personality. Two of the factors, (high) conscientiousness and (low) neuroticism, are associated with flow.
- Positive-striving perfectionism is related to flow, while self-critical perfectionism makes experiencing flow very difficult.
- The term *flow personality* is a composite of traits and tendencies related to flow frequency. The flow personality include goal oriented (not goal focused), intrinsically motivated, high self-esteem (not low or inflated), optimistic, internal locus of control, mastery orientation, approach motivation, high conscientiousness, low neuroticism, and a tendency to "plug in."

CHAPTER 4
Why Flow Matters

On the starting line of the Warrior Dash World Championships, the runners shook their arms and danced in place. Some jumped up and down. They stood in a lush valley, the type that radiated a resplendent green. In each direction that green carried up steep hills and knolls. The foothills of southern Tennessee didn't climb to the dramatic heights of the Great Smoky Mountains to their east, but they rose and fell all the same. The competitors knew they would soon do the same.

Up front the elites eyed one another. Several Olympians toed the line, as did a handful of others for whom running was their primary occupation. National championship races attracted these types of fields. Pacing strategy wouldn't matter on this type of course. The runners waited for the starter's command.

The first clue that this was a different sort of race occurred once the gun went off. Instead of sprinting down a road to the cheers of onlookers, flames shot out the top of a timing platform adorned with a large Viking helmet. The runners didn't flinch but instead locked in on climbing the first grassy hill.

The hills were relentless and steep. Every runner interviewed after the race would comment on their ferocity. But the hills were also the easiest part of the course, for awaiting each of the 300 competitors were obstacles with names such as *Goliath, Deadman's Drop,* and *Diesel Dome.* There were wooden platforms to climb, cargo net tunnels to navigate, and mud pits that threatened to swallow the entire lower body. Some of the more accomplished obstacle racers complained that the course was too easy.

Into such a race went Max King. The defending world champion, King had long ago brought an air of respectability to the rapidly growing sport of obstacle racing (whose other main brands, besides Warrior Dash, include Tough Mudder and Spartan Racing). His résumé included a 2:14 marathon at the 2012 U.S. Olympic trials and an 8:30.54 personal best in the 3,000-meter (1.86-mi.) steeplechase, a track race that entails jumping 35 barriers, including 7 over a 12-foot/3.7-meter long water pit. That combination of strength and speed helped King earn two berths on the U.S. national team at the world cross country championships. Never one to rest on his laurels, King followed those accomplishments by blitzing to world titles and course

Kevin Winzeler Photography

Always seeking new running challenges, Max King has an autotelic personality.

records at distances up to 100 kilometers (62 mi.) and winning a score of world titles on the trails and roads at shorter distances.

However, halfway into the world championship, King still had company. Josh McAdams, a 2008 Olympian in the steeplechase (with a faster personal best than King), and Brett Hales, a 2016 U.S. Olympic marathon trials qualifier and trail race champion, continued to push the pace. They knew the bona fides of the man lurking behind them.

King didn't mind the tactics. In fact, he relished them. Competition is what makes King tick. Eventually he would pull away from McAdams and Hales for the win and the $30,000 grand prize. A week later he'd return to the trails to race a half marathon in his native Pacific Northwest. King just keeps going and going. His reasoning is simple. "I made the conscious decision that as long as I was enjoying what I was doing I would keep doing it," he says.

Thirty thousand dollars aside, it makes sense to consider why King is not content to stick to one race surface, much less one distance. Clearly he has the talent and the drive. Why not specialize and push the envelope in one area?

"For me [the variety] keeps me motivated to train hard," he says. "Doing one thing over and over isn't as much fun as varying things to keep it interesting. That's the basis for it, but I also just like competition and to see how I can do at a new challenge. I do races that I know are my strong suits, like half-marathon trail races or flat 50-milers, but I also do races that I know will be a huge challenge for me, like a big elevation mountain race. I love every aspect of running, so I'm willing to put myself out there to try something new."

Given King's quest for greater challenges and his curiosity about available experiences, it's safe to say he matches the description of the autotelic personality given in chapter 3. In fact, King is somewhat of a flow junkie. He trains 80 to 130 miles (128-209 km) per week in order to maintain the fitness necessary to tackle as many challenges as he can find. That regimen includes times when the challenge far exceeds his skill. The quest to bring his skills up to par with the challenge is what keeps him pushing through.

"I know that flow goes out the window as I get into something that I'm not skilled at, such as mountain racing, but I continue to go back to it for the challenge and to see if I've gotten better at it," he says. "Maybe it's to see if I can achieve that flow state . . . in something new."

King's response begs a bigger question: Why does flow matter? Clearly flow is a highly desirable state that produces a harmonious interaction between mind and body and is often associated with peak experiences. More than that, flow can also elevate your mood, increase your motivation to train, alter your brain in positive ways, and improve your skill. Pursuing flow is anything but frivolous.

Flow and Happiness Revisited

Chapter 1 touched on the concept of flow and happiness. Although they are distinct phenomena, the two are undoubtedly related. Thousands of interviews conducted with people immediately after their flow experiences confirm that participating in flow-inducing activities is pleasurable and leads to a profound sense of happiness after the fact.

The key word is *after*. Few people experience true emotion while immersed in flow. In fact, many experience no emotions at all. With all your attention directed at the task at hand, emotions such as happiness, sadness, and anxiety—all of which require a sense of self-awareness and extra energy to process—can't form (you'll see why later in this chapter). To experience happiness would actually be distracting and would alter your state of attention. If one feels an emotion during flow, most often it's something along the lines of curiosity (Engeser and Schiepe-Tiska 2012).

That is not to say that flow isn't pleasurable. By its very definition, it provides pleasure and satisfaction. However, **event-specific enjoyment** (e.g., enjoying the act of running) is not the same as **global happiness** (feeling happy as a state of being). Not surprisingly, given the importance of the challenge–skills balance, the degree of pleasure experienced during an activity is strongly related to perceived skill level. For instance, one study asked participants to immerse themselves in the computer game *Tetris* and then measured their flow scores (Keller and Bless 2008). Gamers playing an adaptive version that mirrored their skill level reported higher degrees of pleasure and more flow experiences than those who played the most basic or advanced level repeatedly. From this information one can infer that runners

Testing for Flow

Flow is an experience that engages all your senses and fills your mind with pleasant memories on which to reflect. However, testing for flow isn't simple. Walking up to someone and asking them if they're in flow isn't likely to elicit much of a response. Even worse, if they were in flow, asking the very question is likely to snap them out of it.

Dr. Mike pioneered research on testing for flow, and he created the experience sampling method (ESM). Research participants would be given a pager that went off at random intervals over a period of 1 week. When the pager sounded, the participants were to open up a journal with identical pages and fill out a sheet recording their thoughts, feelings, and observations at that precise moment. These data could then be collected and analyzed to see which tasks throughout the day and week produced flow.

Drs. Sue Jackson and Herbert Marsh developed a standardized version of this process (Jackson & Marsh 1996). Developed in 1996, their Flow State Scale offered 36 questions to participants. It could be used retroactively when remembering previous flow experience. Each of the questions corresponded to one of the nine flow variables identified.

More recently researchers have turned to the Flow Short Scale (Rheinberg, Vollmeyer, & Engeser 2003). With 13 questions and three sliding scales, this test is at this point the shortest and simplest device used to measure flow. Unlike the Flow State Scale, the Flow Short Scale groups responses by the antecedents and the outcome variables. Because it is concise, it allows respondents to quickly lay out their immediate recollections.

As much information as paper tests have produced, it can only produce correlations, not definitive causations. Fortunately, technology has advanced to the point where the next wave of flow testing will rely heavily on brain scanning devices such as functional magnetic resonance imaging (fMRI). Functional MRIs measure blood flow to the brain. Study volunteers can be hooked up to an fMRI scanner while immersing themselves in stationary tasks such as video game playing, allowing researchers to monitor changes in brain activity. These results can then be overlaid with the participants' recollections, creating a fuller picture of the interplay between brain physiology and psychology in the creation of a flow state.

who understand their skill level and find appropriate challenges are more likely than others to experience flow. Keep in mind that what challenged you a week, month, or year ago may now be too much or too little of a challenge.

Keller and Bless (2008) did find one interesting moderating factor when evaluating their scores. Only gamers who had a higher internal locus of control and high action orientation reported flow under these circumstances. Those who felt they had little control over the game (external locus of control) or who preferred to patiently study possible outcomes (state orientation) did not have the same experience, even when playing the *Tetris* levels best suited to their talents. According to eminent German psychologists Anne Landhäußer and Johannes Keller (2012, p. 72) "[t]his can be interpreted as evidence for the assumption that individuals differ in their readiness to experience flow." In other words, those with autotelic personality traits are more likely to experience flow under a variety of settings, even when they are less familiar with the task at hand. That's a tremendous advantage, because research (Csikszentmihalyi & LeFevre 1989) has shown that being in flow accounts for more of the quality of experience than whether people started a task feeling happy or sad, creative or dull, or engaged in a task with which they were familiar.

This idea explains in part why runners like King constantly seek out new challenges. A 3,000-meter steeplechase and 100-kilometer trail race have almost nothing in common, yet King attacks both with equal vigor. "I think for me once I've achieved flow in a particular discipline, it no longer has the same reward the next time," he says. "Then I'm looking for a new challenge where I can learn a new skill. Once that flow state is achieved (in the new discipline) then it's a bigger sense of accomplishment."

Finding new challenges isn't a prerequisite to experiencing flow, but experiencing flow frequently may very well be a prerequisite to leading a happy life. More than just the sum total of pleasurable experiences, experiencing flow allows you to constantly test your limits and achieve goals. As Moneta (2004) and Dr. Mike (Csikszentmihalyi 1982) have found, frequent flow experiences lead to personal growth and development. However, it doesn't work in both directions. While flow leads to residual happiness, being happy when taking on a challenge does not increase your likelihood of experiencing flow (Landhäußer & Keller 2012). The depth of the experience (i.e., how many flow components were experienced and to what degree) matters far less than frequency when determining how much flow experiences will affect your general sense of happiness.

"I've been lucky to have running take over my life," says King, "so much of the time I'm working on being in the flow of training. I definitely think that there's a connection between how much flow you can achieve in your free time to how happy you are during the rest of your day. And you can work on achieving that flow in whatever you do; it doesn't have to be exercise related. I often find when I'm writing that I can get into a flow state and the words pour out on the screen. It makes the job easier and more fun."

Motivation and Persistence

Imagine for a moment you're Shelby Hyatt, Kaitlin Goodman, Max King, or any of the other athletes profiled in these pages. You've just run the race of your life. Not only did the run go well, it was pleasurable. You lost your sense of self in the activity because you were so focused; time seemed to fly by in an effortless manner. Throughout the run you felt confident, and everything you encountered indicated that you were on the right path. When you finished, you were hit by wave after wave of pure happiness. You had a true flow experience. As the excitement wears off, you're struck by this simple thought: *I want to do that again.*

At an intuitive level it makes sense that flow produces motivation. When a task is pleasurable and rewarding, you want to do it again, even when the activity is challenging. In fact, whether you experience it at home or at play, that very challenge is what opens up the opportunity for flow in the first place.

A three-part study of marathoners (Schuler & Brunner 2009) found that runners who experienced flow during their first marathon race were more highly motivated to continue training. That increased motivation led to increased training, which led to better performances in the study. On the surface it seems like a simple equation: experiencing flow → increased motivation → increased training → faster performances.

Another level of complexity resides below this intuitive observation. Flow experiences don't just produce a basic want to experience that high again; they actually increase the ability to push through rough patches in a given discipline. Deeply ingrained in the brain, these flow memories may explain why people continue to come back and tackle large challenges even when many obstacles may be in the way of achieving success (Baumann 2011).

German researcher Nicola Baumann (Baumann & Sheffer 2011) dubs this phenomenon **achievement flow** to emphasize that it occurs while working on a challenging task (although the flow experience itself is the same as would be found in any other endeavor). When confronted with a challenge, the brain responds by analyzing numerous outcomes. In order to achieve flow, you must first believe that the task is achievable. You can only do so if you believe you have the skills necessary to meet the challenge. When you have had prior success or extensive training, your implicit memory takes over and simplifies the process. This is especially true when the activity has a high degree of personal meaning. With your actions now automatic in a challenging situation and your attention fully devoted to the challenge, you are more likely to experience flow. In this way past flow experiences induce confidence that you will successfully manage the challenge.

Persistence in a task such as running develops when you find pleasure in it and are able to successfully meet the challenges you encounter. It's a critical trait for a runner to develop, because years of consistent training are what lead to the greatest external successes (such as faster times or longer distances covered).

The coming pages and chapters address how flow can increase your skill at running (and vice versa) in the immediate and long-term future. Flow also plays a role in pushing you through challenging times. In any given week, you're likely to experience some periods where running feels light and effortless, and other periods where you feel lethargic and weighed down. These rises and falls in physical and emotional readiness are a natural outcome of training variability and should not be mistaken for a rapid rise or decline in fitness (Pfitzinger & Latter 2015). If you finish your longest long run of the year on a Sunday, you're liable to feel tired on Monday, Tuesday, or Wednesday.

Periods of lethargy and low motivation can stretch out for a number of physiological or psychological reasons. Heavy periods of training, stress at work, lack of sleep, anemia, dietary deficiencies, and other compounding factors can make training more difficult than usual. Past flow experiences can buoy you during these periods, while an internal locus of control and achievement motivation can help you seek out solutions to lingering problems.

Running success is also not a purely linear process. Inevitably running performances will stagnate sometimes. When on these plateaus, having a deep-seated belief in your abilities and an autotelic love of running can help you persevere.

"Finding a sustainable approach that keeps me from burning out has a lot to do with how much time I'm in that flow state and enjoying what I'm doing," says King. "That's kept it fun for me."

Performance Enhancement

If you're a fan of clean sport (performing without using performance-enhancing drugs), 2015 wasn't the greatest calendar year. In January, three-time Boston Marathon champion Rita Jeptoo received a 2-year ban from competition after both her urine samples tested positive for the oxygen-boosting compound EPO. In November, fellow Kenyan and two-time World Cross Country Champion Emily Chebet earned a 4-year ban for taking a drug-masking agent. In between, the largest drug scandal since the Berlin Wall came down revealed a state-sponsored, systematic doping program and corrupt labs in Russia, where more than 50,000 urine samples were destroyed. This sting led to the arrest of former International Association of Athletics Federations (IAAF, track and field's international governing body) president Lamine Diack. He was accused of taking bribes to cover up positive drug tests before major athletic competitions, such as the Olympics and IAAF World Championships.

After doping scandals already rocked sports such as cycling and baseball (and still get swept under the rug in sports such as American football), it may seem that the only way to achieve your maximum potential is by ingesting foreign substances that alter your body's blood chemistry and muscular strength. Whether prescribed as such or used off label, these drugs have the power to let you train harder and recover faster.

As proponents of clean sport have shown, drugs are not the only way to achieve success. In the same way that savants reveal the true potential of the brain's enormous capacity to learn, flow experiences often reveal latent potential hidden inside the body. The causes of these experiences occur both in the conscious mind and deep within the central nervous system.

Since the 1990s, numerous professional athletes and teams have employed sport psychologists in an effort to more readily achieve peak performances. One common approach involves reframing obstacles into challenges that offer room for growth. When combined with goal setting and a mastery orientation, the aim is for athletes to more readily achieve peak performances by entering a flow state.

Consider the approach the United States Tennis Association (2016) has taken towards sharpening the so-called "mental game:"

> One benefit of sport psychology training is that it enhances performance on the court. Winning is one of the main objectives in tennis, but winning requires consistent performance at a high level. Mental proficiency helps ensure this consistency, guarding against fluctuations in performance. As the game becomes more sophisticated, coaches who fail to properly utilize psychological tools place their players, and themselves, at a disadvantage in performance and satisfaction. A full investment in sport psychology may spell the difference between high achievement and mediocrity for players.

This sentiment is echoed by the IAAF in their *IAAF Medical Manual*. As authors Betty Wenz and Keith Henschen (2012) write,

> It has long been acknowledged that psychological skills are critical for athletes at the elite level. Athletes with the requisite "mental toughness" are more likely to be successful. In the past, it was assumed that these skills were genetically based, or acquired early in life. Now, it is commonly accepted that athletes and coaches are capable of learning a broad range of psychological skills that can play a critical role in learning and in performance (p. 63).

Many of the attributes of a flow experience overlap nicely with those found in peak performances. Runners experiencing flow engage with the task of running, filtering out unwanted information. They focus on the task at hand and their present goals, relying on feedback to determine how well they're meeting the challenge. With negative thoughts unable to enter the conscious mind, these runners lose their sense of self-consciousness and are able to focus on running faster, smarter, and more efficiently.

Jackson and Roberts (1992) studied the relationship between flow and peak performance and found that most athletes performed their best when they focused on the process instead of the outcome. Athletes focusing mainly on the end results were less likely to experience flow and more likely to perform below par. Several other researchers have reported similar findings (Garfield & Bennett 1984; Loehr 1984; Ravizza 1973, 1984). All assert that the relationship between peak performance and flow is due to an athlete's ability to focus and become completely absorbed in the task.

As action and awareness merge, implicit processing kicks into high gear for those in flow. This state brings pleasure and confidence; after all, the mind and body are fully synchronized in a way that makes one feel powerful. Researchers have long understood that athletic performance is at its best when directed by implicit processes (Masters 2000; Masters, et al. 1993; Maxwell, et al. 2000). Relying on the complex but cumbersome processing abilities of the explicit memory would slow things down to a crawl.

The Yips!

Imagine a professional golfer having the round of his life. He comes to the 18th green with a chance to win for the first time in his life. But with the ball on the green and close to the pin he panics. Instead of lining up and putting as if he has practiced the last 10 years, he stares at the ball and the line in front of him, going over and over every calculation possible. In the end his stroke is jerky, and he misses the putt and his chance at victory.

The implicit memory is a wonderful thing. It lets your body make lightning-fast decisions and react to situations instinctively. Whether you're running a 5K, driving a car, typing a report, or even reading a book, the implicit memory keeps things humming along. In doing so, it frees up mental processing power for other tasks or objectives.

Nervousness, anxiety, or overanalysis can lead you to use the explicit memory instead of the implicit memory at times. It's not pretty, but it does have one of the best names out there—the yips.

The golfer in the previous example had the yips. Given the amount of time available for introspection and the need for perfect mechanics, it's no wonder that golfers came up with the term *yips*. The yips can take all sorts of forms. More than a decade ago New York Yankees All-Star second baseman Chuck Knoblauch suddenly lost the ability to throw a baseball from second base to first base, right around the time St. Louis Cardinal's pitching phenom Rick Ankiel lost the ability to find the catcher's mitt behind home plate.

"Lost the ability" is of course an exaggeration. Both Knoblauch and Ankiel could still physically perform the act of throwing a ball to a target. They were well-paid professional athletes at the peak of their powers. But once a series of miscues forced them to continually examine their mechanics, their explicit memory took over. (If you want to see how the explicit memory works for motor skills, try throwing a baseball or writing your name with your nondominant hand.)

To their credit both players revived their careers, albeit in nontraditional ways. Knoblauch transitioned to left field and Ankiel, always a good hitting pitcher, moved to center field when their yips persisted. Even though the distance was four times farther, neither athlete had trouble throwing accurately from the outfield. The change of scenery and the resulting drop in pressure and expectation allowed both athletes to return to implicit processing.

Runners are fortunate in that they are unlikely to forget how to run. However, critical central nervous system functions are made much easier and faster by the implicit memory. Imagine if you had to tell every muscle in your legs to contract with every step. More realistically, imagine if you had to process and adjust your pace with every stride. It would be an analytical nightmare and more than the explicit memory could handle.

Nervous runners may occasionally feel this scenario creeping up before a big race. Many people call it "paralysis by analysis." Fortunately, the act of running tends to calm the mind down and allow implicit processing to return. If you feel overly anxious before a race, try to keep your composure and rest assured that the implicit memory will soon help you keep on keeping on.

With the implicit memory in charge, the body reacts without hesitation to running-related thoughts. *Hold 6-minute mile pace, cover that move, take shorter strides on the uphill, breathe.* These thoughts are acted on automatically at a level that the conscious mind cannot describe. At the same time it feels fluid, because the body and mind are entirely on the same page. This powerful feeling produces a keen sense of control. In these instances one can manage strategy and pace without effort. As Dr. Mike (Csikszentmihalyi 1990) once said about transitioning into flow, "Alienation gives way to involvement, enjoyment replaces boredom, helplessness turns into a feeling of control, and psychic energy works to reinforce the sense of self, instead of being lost in the service of external goals."

Bill Rodgers

Four-time winner of the Boston and New York City Marathons
Flow moment: 1975 World Cross Country Championships

Before he was known as "Boston Billy," an affable but mythical runner who won four titles each at the Boston and New York City marathons and who inspired an entire generation to get out and run, Bill Rodgers was just a runner. In college he was overshadowed by his roommate, future 1968 Boston Marathon champion Amby Burfoot. At times his talent showed, such as when he ran an 8:58 2-mile race. Most of the time, though, Rodgers was content to get by on talent and enjoy the party life of the late 1960s. When the Vietnam War escalated, Rodgers registered as a conscientious objector and took to transporting dead bodies at a Boston hospital

Frank O'Brien/The Boston Globe via Getty Images

to stay out of combat. He didn't jog a step.

However, running was in Rodgers' blood. Soon he kicked his poor habits and started to train (after being fired from his hospital job for trying to organize a union). The initial results were less than inspiring. He failed to finish his marathon debut at Boston in 1973 and only ran 2:28 in his first complete race. Undeterred, he started putting in serious mileage, averaging 120 miles (193 km) per week for months on end. Even after a disappointing 2:35 marathon in New York in 1974, Rodgers kept clawing away at his dream. The work paid off as Rodgers placed third at the U.S.

cross country selection race and earned a trip to Rabat, Morocco, for the 1975 World Cross Country Championships.

Back in the 1970s, the world cross country championships was one of the most competitive races in the world, bringing together the best runners at all distances from the mile up to the marathon together in one race. John Walker (the world's fastest miler) would be there. So, too, would reigning Olympic marathon champion Frank Shorter. At the time Rodgers was still a relative unknown, but he had great faith in his training. He found this faith a key to experiencing flow.

"I always aimed to run a way that allowed me to run with flow, that is to run within myself," he says. "Maybe that means I knew I could handle the pace and was therefore relaxed, which further helps with racing. This was achievable if I raced smart, used my head, and/or conditions were conducive—cooler, low humidity days [for instance]."

In Rabat, Rodgers ran beside Shorter through the early miles, then pressed on when Shorter dropped back with a side stitch. Soon he found himself beside Ian Stewart of Scotland (who had won the European indoor track title for the 3,000 meters 7 days prior) and Spain's Martin Haro. Haro and Rodgers would aggressively push the pace around the racehorse track in Rabat, trying to break away from the field. Entering the last lap, the lead group was down to those three. Rodgers wasn't checking names, though.

"My World Cross Country Championship was where I felt flow the most keenly," he says. "I wasn't thinking of any specific runner I was facing; I simply raced. Time, of course, didn't matter since it was cross country."

With the goal of winning becoming more realistic by the second, Rodgers continued to grind away with Haro up front and eventually took the lead within sight of the finish. In the final straight, Stewart surged by them both to win the 12-kilometer (7.4-mi.) race. Rodgers finished third to earn the bronze. Since then, only four Americans have ever placed that highly at World Cross Country Championships.

That race in Rabat would prove to be a watershed moment for Rodgers. Two months later he won his first of four Boston Marathon titles in an American Record time of 2:09:56, enchanting the home crowds. Rodgers saw those crowds often; he loved to race. In 1978, perhaps his finest year, he won 27 of 30 races he entered. It also made flow harder to achieve at times.

"Perhaps because I tended to race too much, I often failed to reach this perfect combination of mind–body effort and relaxation," he says.

Today Rodgers owns the Bill Rodgers Running Company in Boston, gives lectures, and does promotional work all around the country. Even in his 60s, Rodgers still enjoys the thrill of competition. And he hasn't given up on finding himself in the zone.

"As I've aged, I've found this flow effort less reachable, maybe because I travel so much, which leads me to feel tired at many races," he says. "Yet when I aim for certain races, I can still find fleeting periods when I am racing and running smoothly."

The Brain in Flow

As is evident from the discussions of implicit and explicit memories, many aspects of flow occur well beyond your consciousness. Thanks to new technology such as positron emission tomography (PET) scans and functional magnetic resonance imagining (fMRI), scientists are now peering into people's brains like never before. Their findings are showing that flow is anything but a mind trick. They are also showing that flow experiences are not the process of people's minds expanding, but rather stripping down to the most basic elements needed in order to keep on moving.

Arne Dietrich (introduced in chapters 2 and 3) has been at the forefront of studying how the brain responds to heavy demands. He dubbed his findings the **transient hypofrontality theory (THT)**. At its core, his findings show that as demands grow greater, the brain slowly **downregulates** (shuts down) nonessential functions. In this case, that means the prefrontal cortex, the part of the brain responsible for higher-level thought (including perceptions of the self), is the first to go.

"Hypofrontality means that the very pinnacle of human evolution, the prefrontal cortex, must be downregulated, which [means] you lose these higher cognitive functions which makes us so special," Dietrich said in a *TEDx Talk* lecture from Beirut (TED 2011). "Whenever the brain is under assault, whenever it changes its *modus operandi*, it needs to hunker down and focus on the basics. It's kind of like a sinking ship. As soon as the ship starts sinking, it needs to throw overboard ballast. Just as in an altered state of consciousness, the deeper and deeper you go, the more ballast you need to throw off."

Dietrich's most recent research (Dietrich & Audiffren 2011) leads him to believe that the brain begins to deactivate nonessential sections after about 30 minutes of running. This subtraction shuts down blood flow to parts of the brain that are not necessary for running (such as the prefrontal cortex) and increases blood flow to other areas of the brain and body that require more energy while running (such as the motor cortex, which coordinates movement). In moments of extreme need, such as a competitive race, it seems reasonable to conclude this would happen much sooner.

While the brain may be trying to conserve calories and reallocate energy behind the scenes, the effects of THT are significant in your moment-by-moment awareness when fully engaged in running. With more energy suddenly available, the motor cortex is able to coordinate a smooth gait, proper posture, and effective heart rate and respiration rate. In other words, you are able to run more efficiently at faster speeds.

The shunted areas of the brain play just as big a role in your ability to perform your best. With the prefrontal cortex downregulated, you lose the ability to worry excessively about your present experiences (Takizawa 2014) or to focus too intently on the details that are best left to the reflexive nature of your implicit memory (Dietrich & Audiffren 2011). This downreg-ulation also reduces depressive symptoms and other forms of stress. Good performance, as well as flow, requires silencing this internal soundtrack. When focusing on your goal rather than on the details of past failures or the present potential for failure, you stand a better chance of succeeding. If you allow distracting thoughts to drive your present run, the explicit (conscious, rational) part of your memory may override the implicit part of your memory and impair your ability to perform at your best (Masters 2000; Masters, Polman, & Hammond 1993; Maxwell, Masters, & Eves 2000). Implicit memory is the result of hours of practice that have imprinted good form and strategy in your brain so that you no longer need to expend energy thinking about them; they essentially become automatic (Dietrich 2004). Loosening the grip of anxiety and rumination frees you to breathe, to move, and to feel a sense of calm optimism.

"The mystical oneness, the merging, [it] occurs between you and [the world around you] simply because you no longer have the computational capacity to compute the difference between you and the other," Dietrich said in the 2011 *TEDx Talk*. "The calm and the serenity that comes from being in the here and now is simply because you can no longer do the fancy mental footwork to extract yourself from the here and now because that takes a lot of brain power."

These processes may also explain why people so often describe flow expe-riences as effortless even when they involve a great metabolic (energy) cost and high levels of mental concentration. Athletes running their fastest times in flow often report lower levels of perceived exertion and pain (Jackson and Csikszentmihalyi 1999). This performance-enhancing effect won't allow an athlete to circumvent a lack of fitness, but it may change how athletes interpret physiological stress (deManzano, et al. 2010). Put simply, if you're in flow and doing what you love, fatigue and pain stop being interpreted as negatively.

In *The Tao of Pooh*, author Benjamin Hoff (1982) overlays the principles of Taoism onto the characters from the children's book *Winnie-the-Pooh*. During one section Pooh, who is considered an ideal Taoist, gently scolds Owl for learning knowledge for knowledge's sake instead of spreading it around for the betterment of others. Owl, it appears, is more concerned about appearing intelligent than actually gaining anything approximating wisdom from all the reading he has done.

Now that you have a base of knowledge of flow, you can move toward finding it. The chapters in part II discuss applied methods for making it part of your runs and your life. Talking about implicit memories and hypofron-tality does little good if it doesn't somehow offer up the chance for a better run or, better yet, a life better lived.

Key Points _____

- Flow experiences are pleasurable; however, most people don't report feeling happy *during* flow.

- Flow experiences seem to provide an opportunity for personal growth and development, which contributes to global happiness (feeling happy as a state of being).

- Testing for flow is rather challenging, so most research relies on self-reported reflections on flow experiences.

- Dr. Arne Dietrich developed the transient hypofrontality theory (THT), which explains changes in the brain that result in greater focus, less distraction, and muted emotion. Downregulation of the prefrontal cortex and the amygdala are the changes implicated in this theory.

- THT explains why flow contributes to peak performance in the moment. It helps filter out unnecessary information so that you can focus on the important elements around you, while it also allows your implicit memory to manage the well-practiced portions of your performance.

- Flow contributes to improved performance over time because of persistence and resilience. Your desire to experience flow again serves as a motivator for continued practice or vigilance in the activity, even when it is difficult or uncomfortable.

PART II
Finding Flow

CHAPTER 5
Antecedents to Flow

Against the roar of 80,000 people, Leo Manzano circled London's Olympic Stadium track among 11 of the fittest, fastest men on the planet. They eyed each other carefully, no one wanting to miss the move that would alter the race and, by extension, the course of their lives. The Olympic 1,500-meter final would take less than 4 minutes to complete, but during that short period of time these athletes would call on years of aerobic training and hundreds (if not thousands) of punishing interval workouts to give them the needed edge. Only two laps remained. The move would come soon.

Like hundreds of millions of runners across the globe, Manzano loved the sport and how it made him feel. His talent, when combined with a decade of rigorous, well-planned training, had brought him to the precipice of greatness. Now, with just over a lap left in the race, he saw Algeria's Taoufik Makhloufi surge to the front. The 12 men, who for almost 3 minutes had been bunched in a pack, immediately spread out in pursuit. Makhloufi led through the bell, the sound a Pavlovian reminder to pick up the pace with only one lap remaining.

Most of the runners immediately covered Makhloufi's move, Manzano didn't. It was not because he didn't want to; Manzano had trained for more than a decade to shine in a moment like this. His legs and lungs just didn't respond. A wave of disappointment surged through Manzano as he thought of his poor upbringing in Mexico, his father illegally crossing into Texas to find work, and the better life it promised. He thought of the tens of thousands of miles, the hard workouts, and the 4-hour "easy" days filled with lifting and drills. His family sacrificed for him. He sacrificed for his body. Now his dream was literally running away from him. It hurt like hell.

"My legs felt so done," Manzano says. "I'm thinking, I don't know if I can do this. I'm thinking this is hard, this is tough. I'm thinking this in front of 80,000 people. Then all of a sudden, something in my mind went, 'No. I'm giving up. I can't give up. All the sacrifices with your family . . . down the drain?' In my mind, it was kind of like I woke up. And when I woke up, I had this burst of energy."

Manzano thinks for a moment before adding with a smile, "Maybe it wasn't a burst of energy. Maybe it's that everyone else was getting tired."

Makhloufi wasn't done. As he hit the backstretch of the track for the last time, he sprinted. He would cover the next 100 meters (109 yd.) in an unheard-of 12.0 seconds. Seven runners would follow in his wake, beginning their all-out kick almost 200 meters (218 yd.) earlier than they planned.

Meanwhile, Manzano was recovering. The Zen-like concentration of the first three laps had broken for sure, but so had the self-pity. As Manzano's legs recovered and he reengaged the race, a thought crossed his mind: *They're running too fast. They're going to come back.*

So began one of the most heroic 40 seconds in United States Olympic history. Manzano, in ninth place, began to weave his way through faltering limbs and dreams. His thinking was right. The pace was too hot. With 200 meters remaining, he passed Nick Willis, the defending silver medalist. For a moment that overwhelmed Manzano. *Should I be passing such a great runner?* But then he realized the feedback was good; his goals had validity.

"At that point I knew I needed to go," he says. "Every time I passed someone, I gained more and more momentum. As I'm gaining that momentum, I'm passing more guys, which in turn gives me more momentum to keep moving forward."

Manzano had moved up to sixth place as he hit the final straightaway. His mind cleared. His body felt strong and responsive. Only 12 seconds remained in his race, and he needed to pass at least three people to earn an Olympic medal.

"I remember thinking, 'Here it is,'" Manzano says. "I laid it down on the line. Almost in a praying mode, 'Man, just give me the strength to do this.' And sure enough, I went right by those guys. I didn't even just come up to them, I went right by them. And then I crossed the finish line, and that's when I knew I had an Olympic medal."

Almost immediately cameras raced around Manzano, eager to see the reaction of the man who had ended the United States' 44-year medal drought in the 1,500 meters. Later he would stand next to Makhloufi as the Olympic silver medal was draped around his neck, but first he looked up at 80,000 faces in the stands and millions of viewers back home and shook his head in disbelief. Everything had come together when it mattered most.

"There were so many emotions," he says. "So many mixed emotions. You know, I'd gone through all these hardships, always being the underdog, of course. At the same time, all this joy and all this excitement [hit me]. It was phenomenal."

Today the Olympic medal is tucked away in Manzano's home in Austin, Texas. The silver brought a higher level of fame and numerous opportunities Manzano's way, but it's the memory of the flow experience that keeps him running.

Few runners will ever stand on an Olympic starting line, much less earn a medal, but every runner can aspire to master running at a personal level. As you enter part II of *Running Flow*, the text moves away from theory and more toward practical application. Setting the stage for flow requires controlling the

Chuck Myers/MCT via Getty Images

A flow experience carried Leo Manzano to a silver medal in the London Olympics.

controllable, namely these antecedents to flow: clear goals and objectives, a proper balance of challenge and skill, and unambiguous feedback pointing you toward success. These antecedents don't guarantee flow's arrival, but they put your mind and body in a position to experience it. They are also prerequisites for peak performance, making them relevant to any endeavor.

Clear Goals and Objectives

Leo Manzano didn't earn an Olympic silver medal by accident. It came as the byproduct of a decade's worth of hard work and commitment on the trails and tracks of Texas. That work ethic was fueled by a belief in his goals, which included making it to the Olympics (first achieved in 2008) and medaling (2012). By holding himself accountable to those goals, Manzano found an endless source of motivation to help him push through hard workouts and difficult patches of training.

Not everyone can win the genetic lottery like Olympic athletes, but everyone has the ability to set goals and work toward achieving them. Creating goals that are motivating and realistic can be a challenge. Often people are told to shoot for the stars while keeping one foot on the ground (or any other number of mixed metaphors). Figuring out the balance between a challenging and unrealistic goal can be a challenge itself.

For those reasons, using the SMART method of goal setting offers an ideal way to map out a goal and see it through to its completion. George T. Doran coined the mnemonic acronym SMART in 1981 to help business leaders and others in management roles achieve their business objectives. Over the last 35 years the acronym and its usage have gone through many permutations. This book uses its most common current form. The SMART method states that all goals must be all of the following:

Specific

Measurable

Attainable

Relevant

Time bound

This framework offers the advantage of letting you see a goal through multiple angles. By setting specific goals that can be measured, are realistically attainable and relevant to your life, and have deadlines to keep you on track, you are far more likely to highly achieve in your endeavors. The higher the challenge, the greater the reward (Locke & Latham 2006).

Specific

All goals result from a deficiency or need of some sort (Locke & Latham 2006). In order to create motivation and focus, these needs have to be clearly identified. Vague goals are hard to pinpoint and harder to measure. Specific goals address your deficiencies or desires and then precisely outline what you're hoping to achieve. That precision allows you to monitor progress toward your goal.

For instance, consider the goal of running a Boston Marathon qualifier. For many runners making it to the starting line in Hopkinton is a tremendous accomplishment; it is their own personal Olympics. Minimum qualification standards are very clear. A 37-year-old man wishing to run Boston knows he has to run at least 3:10:00 (7:15/mile pace) to be eligible, just as a 53-year-old woman knows she has to break 4:00:00 (9:09/mile pace). Therefore, setting a goal to qualify for the Boston Marathon is very specific.

Contrast that specificity with the goals people often make, especially around the beginning of a new year. The following lists the 10 most popular New Year's resolutions of 2015. With the exception of quitting smoking, these goals are too vague, none of them narrowing tightly enough to develop a game plan. Open-ended goals such as *lose weight* offer no quantification. Is losing 5 pounds enough? How about 10? What about 20? Another common open-ended goal is *getting in shape. Fitness* is a fluid term, so how do you know when you are in shape? Not surprisingly, a 2015 University of Scranton survey found that only 8 percent of Americans successfully achieve their New Year's goals (Statistic Brain, 2015).

Top New Year's Resolutions, 2015

1. Lose weight
2. Get organized
3. Spend less, save more
4. Enjoy life to the fullest
5. Stay fit and healthy
6. Learn something exciting
7. Quit smoking
8. Help others in their dreams
9. Fall in love
10. Spend more time with family

Source: University of Scranton, 2015

Vague goals can be helpful early in the brainstorming phase when all options are on the table. Often they point to underlying desires. You want to run faster. You want to run more. You want to be a more well-rounded athlete, lose weight, or find training partners. This dissatisfaction with the status quo fuels your desire to make a change. The key is to take the next step; use that general idea to work toward a specific goal. A 3:15 marathoner may want to run faster, but by setting a goal of running 3:10 she has given herself a specific objective. A 190-pound (86-kg) runner may want to lose weight, but by saying he wants to reach 175 pounds (79 kg) on the scale he now can determine what constitutes a success.

Where a goal comes from is less important than you might think. Success rates are nearly identical whether a goal is assigned to you, whether you come up with it jointly with another, or whether you set it yourself (Locke & Latham 2006). That information is reassuring for those who coach and those who are coached.

Measurable

Setting a specific goal is the first step toward achieving it. Finding a goal that can easily be measured and monitored is the second and arguably just as important.

The sport of distance running offers no shortage of black-and-white metrics. Time and distance (and their byproduct, pace) give runners concrete ways to measure progress. If your training runs last year were at a mile (1.6 km) pace of 8:00 on your favorite training loop and now they're at a pace of 7:50, you've made progress if the level of effort feels the same. If your goal is to someday average a pace of 7:45 on those runs, you now have clear proof that you're heading in the right direction.

The previous example highlights another benefit of having a measurable goal, namely, seeing incremental progress. Consider the example of quitting smoking. Some people who are addicted to nicotine quit abruptly; this minority doesn't require incremental encouragement. However, most smokers go through a long cessation period, during which they cut back on the amount of nicotine they ingest over a period of weeks and months. Seeing that two packs of cigarettes a day has been reduced to one offers a strong incentive to keep pushing ahead with a difficult task.

Runners find similar incremental gains helpful. Consider this hypothetical example of a runner trying to qualify for the Boston Marathon: Sam the Marathoner enters the year with a personal best of 3:22. He knows he needs to run 3:10 to meet the minimum eligibility standard for Boston. In his first race of the year Sam the Marathoner runs 3:16. Sam the Marathoner can interpret this one of two ways. Either he (1) failed to achieve his goal or (2) made progress toward his goal. Considering the race knocked 6 minutes off his personal best, indicating improved fitness, it seems that he made incremental progress and is much closer to reaching his goal.

This same principle holds true for short-term and intermediate goals (discussed later in this chapter). If your goal is to run 10 miles (16 km) in 80 minutes, then it makes sense to run on a measured path or use a GPS watch so that you can get feedback on your pace throughout the run. If your goal is to lose 10 pounds (4.5 kg) by the end of next month, it makes sense to step on a scale once a week to see how well you're progressing.

For all their apparent definitiveness, numbers always need to be interpreted through a lens of life and environmental factors. Some races are windy. Some runs come after all-night study sessions. Some holidays you're going to eat more than you planned. It happens. Instead of berating yourself for a poor run or tipping the scales more than usual, take a wider view and figure out what changes need to be incorporated.

Attainable

Norman Vincent Peale supposedly said, "Shoot for the moon. Even if you miss, you'll land among the stars" (We say "supposedly" because, like so many other common phrases in the English language, this one is attributed to multiple great minds.) Poor astronomy aside, this oft-used quote is used to motivate people to push beyond their limits and see what is possible. There's nothing wrong with dreaming big. Few aspects of modern life would exist without people who had high aspirations, but setting a goal that is beyond your genetic or lifestyle limits can lead to failure and disappointment.

At the same time, challenging goals make striving hard worthwhile. Studies have found that achieving difficult goals positively affects mood and sense of well-being, whereas achieving easy goals does not (Wiese & Freund 2005).

Runners face this dilemma between what's possible and what's realistic at all times in their lives. Competitive college runners often find their running aspirations at odds with paying off student loans upon graduation. Middle-aged runners may want to lose weight or strength train more, but their time and energy are limited by family and career demands. In addition, whether they want to accept it or not, all runners will eventually slow in an absolute sense as their bodies age.

Understanding your limitations is good, but it doesn't have to put a low ceiling on your ambitions. The point is to make goals attainable, not easy. A goal of running 20 miles (32 km) a week isn't useful to someone already running 50 miles (80 km) a week. On the other end of the spectrum, it can be daunting to declare you want to run an ultramarathon (anything over 26.2 miles) if you've never even run 10 miles before.

Ideally, your goals would expand in difficulty and scope as you progressed in the sport. For instance, Manzano once aspired to high school state titles in the 1,600 meters. Next he wanted to win an NCAA title in the 1,500 meters (he achieved that twice). When he graduated and signed a professional shoe contract, his goals grew to encompass winning national championships and representing the United States in international competitions such as the Olympics and World Championships. After making the 2008 Olympic team, Manzano kept raising his sights over 4 years until at last he was chasing an Olympic medal. Even with all of that under his belt, Manzano still works just as hard at other goals such as running a sub-3:50 mile and making future Olympic teams. The thrill is in the chase.

Figuring out what constitutes a realistic goal takes time and practice. As you put in years of training, gains are harder won. A novice marathoner might take off 30 minutes between his first and second race, while a seasoned marathoner might rejoice if she is able to drop as little as 30 seconds from her personal best. Your age, training history, availability of time and resources, and desire will all play a role in figuring out an ideal goal.

Not all goals need to be physically challenging. In fact, many of the toughest goals revolve around establishing better habits. Adding two strength training sessions per week might not be too taxing on the body, but altering your weekly routine to fit them in poses a challenge. The same goes for stretching, cross-training, eating better, or any other habit that indirectly benefits your training. The automaticity that comes from establishing good habits can be worth the initial effort, because it frees up your mind from consciously deciding whether you want to engage in a beneficial task or not.

Relevant

Any goal that is going to produce flow is by nature challenging to some degree. Turning on a television doesn't produce flow; climbing a mountain does. With those challenges come a host of struggles. When those struggles crop up, you need to care a lot about what you're trying to accomplish.

Otherwise, odds are the struggle will be greater than your desire, and you'll end up moving on to less challenging pursuits.

This resiliency stems from caring about what it is you're pursuing. You could easily change the word "relevant" in the SMART equation to "passion," "desire," or "interest" (though that would make a much less catchy acronym). If you care about the task at hand and the goal you're trying to achieve, then odds are you'll push through the mental and physical roadblocks that inevitably pop up.

Keep in mind that your emotional capacity and ability to focus varies from day to day. Sometimes it's easy to go for a run; sometimes the very act of putting running shoes on seems impossible. Even world-class athletes like Manzano struggle with this uncertainty. In January 2013, when coauthor Phil Latter met him for a feature in *Running Times,* Manzano lacked a sponsor and wasn't competing during the indoor season. The emotional high of medaling at the biggest race of his life had been replaced by the day-to-day realities of being a first-time father struggling to figure out his future. It would have been easy to rest on his laurels, take some more time off, and try to profit off his name by giving lectures. Instead, Manzano remembered his dreams of running faster, representing his country, and taking care of his family through the sport. In doing so, he kept one foot moving in front of the other and went on to run his fastest times in the ensuing years.

Even when running isn't your livelihood, you can still feel passionate about it. Whether as a competitor or fitness athlete, running can be a core part of your identity, and as such you take great pride in doing it well. While you don't want to cast aside major personal responsibilities just to run a few seconds faster, there's no shame in pursuing excellence in the sport to the best of your ability.

Time Bound

Deadlines are everywhere in life—work, school, taxes, you name it. Deadlines are rarely pleasant, but they're highly effective at creating a sense of urgency. This tug to get something done keeps you moving forward toward your goals, even when obstructions appear.

This phenomenon is nothing new. Consider this excerpt from the great 18th-century British writer Samuel Johnson (1840):

> *The distance is commonly very great between actual performances and speculative possibility. It is natural to suppose that as much as has been done to-day may be done to-morrow; but on the morrow some difficulty emerges, or some external impediment obstructs . . . and every long work is lengthened by a thousand causes that can, and ten thousand that cannot, be recounted. . . . He that runs against Time has an antagonist not subject to casualties (231).*

Time may not be subject to casualty, but it can motivate you to achieve your goals before it's too late. Specific goals tend to produce timeliness organically. Manzano knew that if he wanted to win gold in London, August 7, 2012, was the day to do that. If you're a high school athlete trying to qualify for a state championship, you know you have a certain number of weeks to get in your training before the qualifying meet.

This same urgency can help in matters ancillary to performance. Consider a goal of losing 10 pounds (4.5 kg). If you give yourself 3 months to achieve this goal, then you can measure progress toward the goal by weighing yourself every week. If you put no end date on the calendar, you can easily delude yourself into thinking you'll start trying to lose weight later down the road, perhaps when it's more convenient.

Open-ended goals offer less accountability. Phrases such as "I'm working on it" or "I'll get there eventually" seem plausible when no end date holds you accountable for your actions. In reality, without an end date, you are likely to feel apathetic and cease working toward the goal, particularly when a rough patch emerges. With no motivation to finish, it's easy to give in.

Goals don't simply expire at their end date. They can be evaluated for progress and reformed for future seasons and years. After running his 3:16 marathon, Sam the Marathoner comes back that fall and runs 3:14. Once again he has made progress, but it's still not a 3:10 Boston qualifier. At this point, it behooves Sam to take a critical look at his training, judge it against what he believes is his potential, and start working toward a new goal for the following year. It may be that 3:10 is unrealistic. It may be that Sam the Marathoner got stuck working 60 hours a week all summer and wasn't able to train much. Either scenario would cause Sam the Marathoner to build new goals for the coming year based on that feedback, plus his expectations for the future.

Goal Planning Range

Everyone has dreams. People who achieve dreams often do so because they've mapped out a path to success. Strategic planning entails having a mix of short-term, intermediate, and long-term goals. By plotting out a series of goals, you give yourself specific checkpoints along the way to measure success toward an ultimate goal. Figure 5.1 illustrates this hierarchy.

Long-Term Goals

Near the top of the goal-setting pyramid are long-term goals. These goals tend to be the most difficult and require the greatest amount of work to achieve. At the same time, successfully reaching a long-term goal tends to bring with it a sense of lasting satisfaction and an increase in self-efficacy. Increases in self-efficacy (most easily understood as a belief in one's abilities in a given task) help people choose more challenging goals and increase their resiliency (Locke & Latham 2006). In turn, this increase in challenge and resiliency leads to ever-greater levels of success.

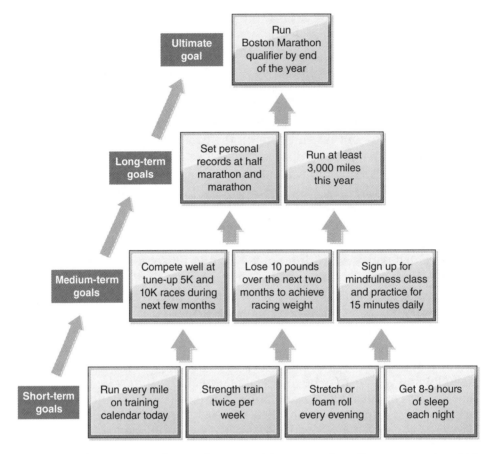

Figure 5.1 Short-term goals contribute to achievement of medium-term goals, which eventually lead to the accomplishment of long-term goals.

Most runners would consider yearly or seasonal goals to fall into this category. Like Manzano, some runners may map out their plan even further into the future to ensure that long-term gains aren't sacrificed for short-term successes. In this way long-term goals can act as a type of check and balance against the temptations of more immediate goals that may not align with big-picture thinking. For example, doing speed work on the track in January may create rapid increases in your racing ability in February and March, but if your goal race is in June you may be sabotaging your season by heeding only short-term thinking. Often people are most successful when they let long-term goals drive their actions in the immediate and not-too-distant future.

Sam the Marathoner's long-term goal remains to run 3:10 and qualify for the Boston Marathon. Simply saying he wants to run that fast isn't enough. Sam has to plan his training and modify his lifestyle accordingly. To do so he needs to take action in the present and near future while letting his long-term goals steer his actions. Framing those actions as goals in their own right gives Sam a better chance of achieving his ultimate goal.

Medium-Term Goals

If everyone had the ability to visualize long-term success and properly enact a plan to achieve it, the world would be a much simpler place. Alas, humans have a wide capacity for folly. Long-term goals can feel too distant and overwhelming. For many runners, looking at a 20-week marathon training plan, to say nothing of a 2-year plan, is too much to ingest. Instead, you can rely on intermediate goals to give you something to shoot for in the near future yet still keep you on your long-term path.

Medium-term goals can range out from 2 days to 2 months. Usually they will fall in the next few weeks. They aren't ultimate goals, but rather opportunities to measure success and see progress. In order to achieve his long-term goal, Sam the Marathoner maps out a season of training. Included are several tune-up races. These races are of lesser importance, but Sam the Marathoner knows those races will provide needed feedback and a sense of accomplishment in their own right. Sure enough when Sam runs 1:30 in a tune-up half marathon, he realizes he is well on his way to achieving his 3:10 marathon goal.

These goals don't have to merely relate to racing. If you have a goal of losing 15 pounds (6.8 kg) in 3 months, then setting an intermediate goal of losing 5 pounds (2.2 kg) in the first month offers a good way to measure success. If your goal is to run 200 miles (321 km) this month, then setting a weekly goal of 50 miles (80 km) is a good way to ensure compliance with the larger goal.

Short-Term Goals

In flow, one of the biggest unifying factors is being totally immersed in the present. Short-term goals relate to the now—the doing of things. These smaller, short-term things make long-term goals possible. A short-term goal for Sam the Marathoner may be getting his run in at the prescribed pace, making a nutritious meal, or getting an extra hour of sleep.

Frequently achieving short-term goals increases positive effects and self-efficacy. These small victories add up. The sense of confidence in your abilities and the resiliency to overcome obstacles makes it far more likely you'll ultimately achieve your long-term goals.

Developing Physical Skills

If goals serve as signposts directing you where to go, then developing skills and finding suitable challenges is the adventure itself. In order to be successful, all good adventures require preparation. This preparation can be daunting to some, but the wisest runners end up finding great pleasure in the journey itself.

To truly enjoy the journey you need to be well prepared. Preparation takes the form of skill development (both mental and physical). An athlete like Leo

Manzano, who aspires to win an Olympic medal, dedicates his life around the pursuit of running. On an average day, up to 4 hours are dedicated to training-specific activities, including warming up, running, body-weight exercises, strength training, hurdle mobility exercises, stretching, and plyometrics. Even when he's off the clock, Manzano still keeps his running performance a priority by eating well (he loves kale), getting lots of sleep, and resting in between training sessions.

Little doubt exists that Manzano would be an excellent runner on half or even a third of that training; that's how great his talent is. However, Manzano isn't aiming to be a good or even national-class runner; his goal is to be the best in the entire world. To reach that pinnacle requires a focus on skill development that pushes most other priorities to the side.

Unless you have otherworldly talent (or lots of time on your hands), you shouldn't reasonably prioritize running to that extent. Instead you're better served by scaling your goals and skill development to the level of time and availability you have. Table 5.1 shows the level of commitment and skills needed to successfully compete at a given level assuming you have the requisite background and innate ability. A runner aspiring to compete at the national or regional level in the marathon can expect to devote a lot of time to running-related activities. A recreational runner looking to set a PR will need less to achieve that goal. Before committing to a goal, make sure you have the time necessary to properly prepare.

Table 5.1 Skill and Time Required to Achieve Goals in Running

Pursuit	Skills needed	Time commitment
National-class marathoner (sub-2:25 male)	Endurance (high), stamina (high), efficiency (high), injury resistance (high), muscular strength (moderate), flexibility (sufficient)	15-20 hours per week 2 hours per day on average, longer during long runs and workouts Plus strength training, stretching, plyometrics, cross training
Regional 10K runner (37:00 female)	Endurance (high), stamina (moderately high), speed (moderately high), muscular strength (moderate), flexibility (moderate), injury resistance (moderately high)	10-15 hours per week 45-90 minutes on typical day, longer during long runs and extensive workouts Plus stretching and bodyweight exercises
Recreational marathoner	Endurance (moderately high), efficiency (moderately high), stamina (moderately high), injury resistance (moderate)	8-12 hours per week 45-60 minutes on typical day, longer during long runs, likely 1 or 2 days off per week Plus light stretching and cross training
Beginner 5K runner	Endurance (sufficient), injury resistance (sufficient)	2-4 hours per week 20-45 minutes per day, multiple days off from running per week

If your goals and level of physical commitment are aligned, then it's time to start building the needed skills. Although it is beyond the scope of this book to describe training plans in detail, this book touches on some of the best ways to develop the skills outlined in table 5.1. If you are interested in taking your running to the next level, there's no shortage of good books out there. Some favorites include *Daniels' Running Formula* by Jack Daniels, Ph.D.; *Faster Road Racing* by Pete Pfitzinger and Philip Latter; and *Better Training for Distance Runners* by Peter Coe.

Endurance

Endurance is the body's ability to repeat an action, such as running, for a long period of time. Often called aerobic capacity in scientific circles, increasing your endurance allows you to run progressively farther with less fatigue. Every distance running event from the mile up is primarily fueled by the aerobic engine, making it the top priority of everyone from elite ultramarathon runners to local 5K runners.

Jared Ward

Member of the 2016 U.S. Olympic team

Flow moment: 2016 U.S. Olympic marathon trials

When the move came, it came suddenly and dramatically. At mile 16 (25.7 km) of the 2016 U.S. Olympic trials men's marathon, Tyler Pennel of ZAP Fitness decided it was time to try and secure his ticket to the Rio Olympics. On a sweltering hot day, Pennel dropped the pace below 5:00 per mile (1.6 km). Immediately, the large pack of runners splintered, with eventual champion Galen Rupp and former Boston Marathon champion Meb Keflezighi joining

AP Photo/Kelvin Kuo

Pennel at the front. As the pace stayed red hot and the gap back to the chasers widened, many onlookers wondered if the Olympic team had been decided.

Jared Ward tried not to worry as the three leaders ran away with potential tickets to Rio in hand. Until then, he'd conserved not just physical energy but mental

(continued)

Jared Ward *(continued)*

energy as well. The early miles were for sorting things out, taking in the scenery, and getting a handle on fluids and gels. "I approach marathon races from the start with a fairly broad focus," he says. "Early in the race I'm reading the funny *My grandma can run faster than you* and *Only 26 miles to go* signs. I focus on my fueling and my pace, but I'm not very focused on the competition."

Ward's career until then had followed an untraditional path. A graduate of Brigham Young University, Ward delayed his college career for 2 years by going on a traditional Mormon missionary trip. Even as he went on to be a multi-time All-America runner, he did so by training only 6 days a week (to the tune of 120 miles/193 kilometers per week, no less). Today he spends that Sabbath with his family, keeping his priorities balanced.

Pennel's move at mile 16 (25.7 km) threw things out of balance and brought Ward's quest into sharp relief. Ward honed in on the trio ahead and attempted to run at the fastest sustainable pace he could imagine holding for the next 10 miles (16 km). This was the part of the race that always brought flow into the picture. "Flow experiences are what I live for in athletics," Ward says. "I find that honing in on the competition gets me closer to flow. I start to feel competitive; I begin thinking about how I can maximize my potential."

Realizing his potential came from a place of patience. Ward stuck to his game plan, and by mile 20 Pennel was wilting from the heat and pace. Ward passed him by mile 22 (35.4 km). Now he was in the driver's seat, holding on to the third and final Olympic spot if none of the other chasers caught him. It was time to buckle down and fully immerse in the task. He did it by removing thoughts of fear and other mental interferences and taking control of the race with every mental and physical tool left at his disposal.

"I felt that by not burning through all my adrenaline early in the race, I was able to save the mental focus to bring me home over the final stretch," Ward says. "I would say I flowed through the next few miles. The ingrained goal of making the Olympic team fueled me, alongside thoughts of loved ones who had sacrificed so much to put me in a position to live my dream."

Those positive thoughts were necessary at the end, for as his body's glycogen (blood sugar) stores depleted, so, too, did his ability to maintain focus and stay in flow. Over the last mile, Ward seriously wondered at times whether his body would collapse from the exertion. But his goals and willpower were enough to get the Utah resident across the line for the third and final Olympic spot, even as his body told him to stop. As he crumpled to the ground with an American flag in his hand, the biggest dream of his life realized, he fully understood the power of the body and mind working together.

"Getting to flow is what I race for," says Ward, who followed this race up by placing an unexpected 6th at the Rio Olympic Marathon. "The feeling of competition that supersedes pain and any other type of interference is incredible. Mastering how to get my body there is the art."

Endurance is best developed through moderately intense runs, usually performed between 60 to 75 percent of your maximum heart rate. Runs as short as 30 minutes and as long as 3 hours help develop this system by increasing the number of capillaries in your muscles, the stroke volume of your heart, the strength of your muscles, and the number of red blood cells in your bloodstream (to say nothing of more complex developments, including gene expression). Generally, if your effort level allows you to hold a conversation while running, you're in an aerobic zone that is building endurance.

The vast majority of your mileage each week will fall into the endurance zone. How much mileage you'll put in depends on the event you're training for and your skill level. Table 5.2 shows typical in-season mileage numbers for beginning runners and more advanced runner. The number farthest to the right reflects what a professional athlete puts in.

Table 5.2 Mileage Requirements by Event in Miles per Week (km/Week)

Event	Beginner range	Elite range
5,000 m	20-30 (32-48)	50-100 (80-160)
10,000 m	25-35 (40-56)	55-120 (88-193)
Half marathon	30-40 (48-64)	65-130 (104-209)
Marathon	35-50 (56-80)	80-140 (128-225)

Stamina

When your body has sufficient endurance, it can hold a faster pace for longer periods of time. This ability is your stamina, and it plays a major role in how fast you can run and race.

Endurance training will naturally increase stamina over time. You can directly increase stamina by performing more challenging runs at a higher heart rate (75-85% of maximum). These runs include lactate threshold runs, also known as tempo runs. Tempos are generally 20 to 30 minutes long and are performed at a pace roughly equivalent to what you could race for an hour (generally 10K pace for slower runners, and 15K to half marathon pace for faster runners). These runs can be broken into segments, known as cruise intervals, run intermittently in the form of a fartlek workout, or you can make them more challenging by alternating moderately hard and hard segments in a continuous, high-effort workout.

Faster workouts performed at 3,000-meter or 5,000-meter race pace also help increase your ability to withstand fatigue and run fast for an increasingly long period of time. These classic interval sessions (such as 800-meter or mile repeats) increase your $\dot{V}O_2max$ (the maximum amount of oxygen your muscles can use while exercising). This factor is a top predictor of performance at any running distance, particularly 5,000 and 10,000 meters.

Efficiency

As runners become better trained, efficiency is one area that often still needs improvement. Also known as running economy, efficiency is a measure of how much oxygen you require in order to run at a certain pace. Biomechanical flaws such as excessive arm movement and overstriding limit your efficiency; the same is true if you are muscularly weak.

Increasing efficiency is the product of some debate among coaches and exercise scientists, but most believe it is a combination of two systems. On one hand, explosive exercises such as weight training and sprint training teach muscle neurons to contract more forcefully in a shorter period of time. Because each stride is more explosive, it takes less energy to move at a given pace. Jumping exercises (plyometrics) are particularly effective for explosiveness. On the other end of the spectrum, running thousands of miles over a period of years teaches the body to better recruit the right combination of muscle fibers. With less energy wasted on unneeded muscles, you conserve more energy (Jung 2003).

Speed

Although it is not the number one determinant of success in distance running, speed still matters. Or, as the old sports adage goes, *speed kills*. Every run you do is at a percentage (fractionalization) or your all-out capabilities. If you can run 200 meters in 30 seconds (4:00/mile pace), then running an easy run at 8:00 per mile is roughly 50 percent of your all-out capabilities. A person who can only run 40 seconds for 200 meters (5:20/mile pace) may find that same 8:00 pace much more difficult unless the person has compensated for it in some way, such as having high endurance and stamina.

In many ways, speed represents your genetic limitations; no matter how hard you train, we're unlikely to catch 9-time Olympic champion Usain Bolt in a 100-meter dash. However, you can develop greater speed through short strides, 200- and 400-meter repetitions, strength training, and plyometrics (Paavolainen et al. 1999; Daniels 2004; Pfitzinger & Latter 2015).

Muscular Strength

One training element many runners abhor (or skip altogether) is strength training. Many runners do not feel confident walking into a gym surrounded by weightlifters. However, strength training is beneficial. It increases resistance to injury, makes you more efficient and explosive, and helps you fight through fatigue in the latter part of a race.

You might think lifting for a runner would center on a high number of repetitions at a light weight, such as lifting a barbell at the gym 50 times. It turns out that runners benefit most from lifting a moderately high weight 4 to 8 times in 2 or 3 sets. For instance, if your maximum bench press was 100 pounds (45 kg), you would get more benefit from lifting 80 pounds (36 kg) in sets of 4 repetitions than you would by lifting 50 pounds (23 kg), 50 times. This benefit may be because running already maximizes the endurance systems, making light lifting redundant. Instead, big gains come from developing more power and explosiveness, which in turn translates into increased efficiency (Jung 2003).

Flexibility

An oft-misunderstood element of running, flexibility is your body's ability to move through a normal range of motion unimpeded. Runners in the 1970s and 1980s did entire static stretching routines before running a step. After research in the 1990s questioned whether stretching might inhibit muscle power, many runners stopped stretching at all.

Recent science has shown that short bouts of static stretching don't impede power and even more effective is dynamic stretching. These exercises take muscles through a full range of motion before beginning, improving blood flow and flexibility in a functional manner. These stretches include leg swings, trunk rotations, and various skipping exercises and form drills. Longer static stretching exercises, such as hamstring grabs, are recommended for after a run. If you feel an urge to stretch out your Achilles before a run with a long hold, don't worry; you won't be slower for it.

Injury Resistance

The biggest predictor for success in running is generally thought to be consistency. Getting in a run every day it's called for may sound trivial, but it's the only way to truly develop the endurance and stamina necessary to thrive. Those systems don't develop unless you're able to stay healthy, making injury resistance a key variable.

No magic formula exists for preventing injuries; if it did, many physical therapists would be out of a job. However, you can take small steps to minimize the risk of sitting out a long time with an injury. Chief among these steps is the relatively new idea called *prehab*. Unlike rehab, which occurs after an injury has sidelined you, *pre*hab involves treating a minor flare-up aggressively. Treatment includes icing the affected area, using compression, reducing training volume, and taking anti-inflammatories if needed. Flexibility and strength training can also help you avoid being sidelined by increasing functional strength and range of motion.

It can be difficult to fit in every one of these training elements on a consistent basis, so it's important to prioritize based on your personal goals and the demands of the distance. Even if you only run for fitness, make sure you have a good grasp on what you want to achieve and how much time and energy you have to commit to that goal before embarking on your journey. The better prepared you are physically, the higher the likelihood that you will be ready to experience flow when the time is right.

Developing Mental Skills

In addition to becoming a better runner physically, you can engage in techniques and exercises to become stronger mentally. They take these two primary forms for runners seeking flow: visualization and mindfulness.

Visualization

At the 2014 Sochi Olympics, the U.S. Olympic team brought nine sport psychologists to Russia. One of their primary goals was to help athletes with visualization. This practice consists of creating mental images that correspond to the event you're participating in and visualizing positive outcomes. The practice began in the 1960s, but it has become increasingly common among professional athletes in the last decade (Clarey 2014). At its highest level, visualization can be similar to guided hypnosis.

Visualization techniques have become more advanced in recent years. Athletes today often write out scripts of their events, then practice visualizing them from start to finish. Athletes in highly technical events, such as gymnastics and ski jumping, imagine each step of their routines from the warm-up area to the final landing. Seasoned athletes use all five senses to create vivid, lifelike images that help them feel as though they are actively participating even when they are sitting on the couch.

Creating mental pictures of your success does more than lift the spirits. Scientists have found that visualizing yourself moving a muscle and actually moving a muscle created similar brain pattern activity. In fact, studies have shown significant strength gains for athletes who only visualized activity. Visualization also affects motor control, attention, perception and planning, and it increases your likelihood of experiencing flow (LeVan 2009).

Competitive runners can benefit from imagining the scents, smells, and apprehension of the starting line, getting out fluidly at the start, finding a comfortable rhythm, tackling hills or wind with great power, and finishing smoothly. They can visualize keeping up with their competitors, establishing a quick cadence and smooth takeoff with each stride, and even pushing through the strain at the end of the race. By rehearsing all possible scenarios and seeing triumph in each one, you give yourself a better chance to experience success when it matters most. Like regular running training, most sport psychologists recommend daily practice (at least 10 minutes) to truly master visualization.

Mindfulness

The word has been tossed around so much in recent years it may seem like a fad, but mindfulness training offers a plethora of benefits to a runner. As mentioned in chapter 1, mindfulness is, in its simplest form, a state of mind that keeps you locked into the present moment. Thoughts are allowed to come and go as they please, but past regrets and future worries are filtered out as you focus on the present moment and whatever it holds. Taking it all in with a nonjudgmental stance is the key to making mindfulness meaningful. It also differentiates it from other forms of cognitive mind control, such as thought suppression, by encouraging acceptance of the mind's state (Aherne, Moran, & Lonsdale 2011).

Mindfulness benefits you by keeping you locked into the task at hand. That means when you're running you're focused on each individual stride, not the big hill looming a mile down the path or the chemistry homework waiting on your desk. By giving actions your full attention, you turn off certain automatic processes and bad habits that might otherwise disengage you from the moment (Brown & Ryan 2003). Other benefits include stress reduction, better working memory, better focus, less emotional reactivity, and more cognitive flexibility. More recent research has started exploring mindfulness's effects on health, including better immune system function, decreased psychological stress, and overall improvements in well-being (Davis & Hayes 2011).

Continuing to practice mindfulness over time appears to have a positive, cumulative effect. Rachel Thompson and her colleagues (2011) found that long-distance runners who practiced mindfulness for more than a year improved their mile times compared with runners who stopped practicing. Thompson et al. theorize this occurred because mindful runners withheld judgment of pain sensations, allowing them to better push through physical discomfort.

Early research in the field is also showing mindfulness training as an effective way to increase the number of flow experiences. Researchers in Ireland asked a small group of elite, college-aged athletes to fill out a questionnaire related to their experiences in their sport (Aherne, Moran, & Lonsdale 2011). The experimental group was then given four mindfulness exercises to perform twice a week over a 6-week period: breath awareness, breath and body sensations, standing yoga, and a body scan (where participants focused on different parts of their bodies over a short period of time); the control group received no further instruction. The first three exercises took 10 minutes each; the body scan was closer to 30 minutes.

At the end of the experiment, participants once again filled out the questionnaire related to their sport. Athletes who had undergone mindfulness training reported having clearer goals, better feedback, and a stronger sense of control. In short, they experienced flow more readily by undertaking a relatively short course of mindfulness training (Aherne, Moran, & Lonsdale 2011).

You can better experience mindfulness in in your own life in several ways. Mindfulness-based stress reduction (MBSR) courses are becoming increasingly common. They offer the benefits of a trained practitioner walking you through the finer points of the practice. You can also do it on your own in a less structured manner by paying close attention to others' words in a conversation without passing judgment—or focusing exclusively on your breathing and the environment around you while running. Keeping negative, irrelevant thoughts out of your conscious mind will allow you to better experience the world around you and have the focus necessary to stay engaged in the task at hand when running toward a flow experience.

Finding Suitable Challenges

When your skills reach a certain level, it's time to assess your gains. Whether in the form of competition against others or yourself, challenges allow you to see how much progress you've made. All goals that you set are challenging to some degree. This degree of difficulty is a major player in whether a challenge enhances or inhibits the likelihood of flow.

Since Dr. Mike first conceptualized the challenge–skills balance in 1975, athletes have attempted to find the optimal balance that would push them into a flow experience. Although some researchers and sport psychologists have framed this optimal arousal zone as just beyond your current skill level, at a practical level it makes more sense to think of it right on the edge of your highest capabilities. Figure 5.2 shows a newer conceptualization of flow that takes these factors into account.

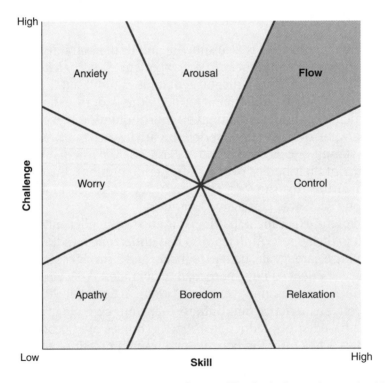

Figure 5.2 Flow is most likely to occur when a difficult challenge is matched by highly developed skills.

Recent research suggests that achieving flow in a highly challenging environment stems from two factors: how desirable the activity is and your personal predilection for challenge (Keller & Landhäußer 2012). These two psychological traits underscore the interaction between mental and physical processes. A highly trained runner racing a marathon may mentally give up when the challenge becomes great if he were doing the event because a friend dared him to (or any other external reason). Similarly, a less physically prepared runner may be able to push through and run a great time if that same marathon holds a great deal of importance to her or if she likes testing her physical limits. In fact, this sense of importance allows less challenging activities to turn into flow experiences. An elite runner who is the top athlete in her area may experience flow even if she's in the "control" or "relaxation" sections of the diagram in figure 5.2 if the race she's competing in (say a conference or regional championship) is especially meaningful.

The greatest magnitude of flow exists when your skill set is pushed to its absolute limit in a very meaningful event. It's no surprise that Manzano would report experiencing flow while chasing an Olympic medal. By its very definition, an Olympic medal is a rare, exceedingly hard thing to come by. Manzano was willing to fight through fatigue and doubt in order to win his sport's most exclusive prize. In doing so, he surmounted the greatest challenge of his life.

Balancing Challenges, Goals, and Skills

Just as in goal setting, finding a challenge that is specific and measurable gives you a better chance of success. For runners, this balance usually takes the form of the metrics they frequently use: time, distance, pace, elevation gain, and heart rate. Trying to run a 10K in 40 minutes or covering 8 miles (12.8 km) on a mountainous trail run with 1,000 feet (304.8 m) of vertical gain is specific and measurable. Other challenges might include running a certain total distance in a week or performing a workout at a given intensity (measured by pace or heart rate).

If your goals extend beyond the act of running itself, framing challenges in the same way can improve your likelihood for success. A goal of losing 15 pounds (6.8 kg) in the next 3 months is both a goal and a challenge. If it were easy, you wouldn't have the weight to lose in the first place. By accepting the goal's challenge and periodically measuring your progress toward it, you'll know where and when to make adjustments.

It can be distressing to see some of your peers more readily tackle challenges. These highly active people seem to function on a different level, turning any activity into a challenge worth pursuing. It turns out that people's ability to get moving toward a task and stay motivated has a genetic component. In *The Sports Gene* (2013), author David Epstein sheds lights on European studies with fraternal and identical twins that have shown that the frequency and amount you exercise is 50 to 75 percent determined by heredity. Researchers believe this tendency comes from the way the brain's dopamine system rewards you. Some people have a higher reward mechanism from doing continual aerobic activity, whereas others get less pleasure. This incentive may be enough of a tipping point to keep some people running a lot and others not running at all.

For those that do enjoy moving toward a physically demanding goal, it's important to remember that all challenges exist on a spectrum. An easy run around the block is much different in degree than running a 100-mile (160.9-km) race. Being able to determine the appropriate intensity for a given challenge is a byproduct of personal experience. Most well-developed training plans call for a variety of runs at various intensities over a period of weeks. Each will present its own challenges, big and small. Continually seeking greater challenges can actually be deleterious to your training if it impairs your ability to recover and run fast on designated days.

As you put in frequent, consistent miles, you develop a keener sense of your body's strengths and limitations while also learning how to better manage the discomfort that challenges produce. You may enter some challenging days overly fatigued and have to adapt the workout. Other times you may feel fresh and decide to run faster than planned. Being adaptive and observant will allow you to challenge yourself appropriately on any given day.

To be successful, challenges need to be consistent with your goals and skills. It may sound obvious, but it's amazing how many long-term goals go unfulfilled because of training errors or a poor estimation of skill. Say Sam the Marathoner has been putting in some great training. His goal of running 3:10 is looking more and more realistic. A week before the race he runs with a friend who has run 2:30 for the marathon. Although the pace is much faster than usual for their 10 miles (16 km), Sam the Marathoner keeps up. His scheduled workout the next day is harder than planned because of residual fatigue. His friend calls the following day, and Sam the Marathoner once again agrees to run. This time, though, he can only keep up for half the mileage. He's tired the next day and logs only half his mileage. Come marathon morning, Sam the Marathoner is still fatigued and ends up running 3:20 on a perfect weather day. He immediately regrets challenging himself too much on days that didn't call for it.

He may have come up short, but Sam the Marathoner did have the requisite skills to achieve his goal of 3:10. Other times, though, people set goals that cannot be physically achieved or that are well below their standards. A 100-meter sprinter deciding to do a 10K on a whim is in for a world of hurt and frustration, just as a 10K runner racing a 100-meter sprinter is likely to lose and possibly pull a hamstring. Your muscle fiber types are genetically determined, and although specialized training can alter their functions to a degree, a true sprinter will always be a true sprinter just as a true distance runner will always be a true distance runner.

By that same token, no amount of physical training can overcome genetic limitations. If you've averaged a 6:00 mile (1.6 km) pace for mile repeats at 5K pace the last 2 months, mental willpower won't push you to a 5:00 mile pace at the local 5K. Better to shoot for a 5:55 mile pace, knowing that the adrenaline of race day and the tenacity of chasing something you love might earn you a few extra seconds.

This assertion backs up another interesting point regarding the skills you possess when attempting a challenge, that it's all about perception. If you're physically capable of running a mile pace of 5:55 but believe prior workouts were a fluke, then you probably won't run miles under 6 minutes. If you think you're exhausted or are overly anxious, the effect is the same. A certain amount of nervousness is good; it primes the sympathetic nervous system for the exertion that is about to come. However, being overly nervous pushes that system to an extreme, draining you before the run begins.

If you feel you're in over your head or not being pushed hard enough, you can scale challenges to meet newfound demands during the act of running itself. Say you've decided to run a half marathon with your friends. Their target time is 2 hours. You've never broken 2:10 before, but your training has gone well and you're hoping for a breakthrough. If a 2:00 pace feels difficult, you can always scale a goal back and shoot for running a PR. Conversely, if a 2:00 pace feels easy at halfway, you can consider pushing the pace even further. In either case, the key to feeling successful is to have an honest understanding of your present skill level against the backdrop of the challenge at hand.

The Road to Unambiguous Feedback

To best appreciate the role of feedback in a flow situation, consider Manzano's struggle entering the last lap of the 1,500 meters at the 2012 London Olympics. Until that point, Manzano felt good. The pace was moderate for a championship race, between 58 to 60 seconds per lap. The field was packed together, but no one was running on top of another. Manzano breathed hard, but so did everyone around him. With his focus tightly locked on the race, including elite competitors such as Makhloufi and Kenya's Asbel Kiprop, Manzano left no room to worry about his physical condition.

That changed when Makhloufi started his surge just before the bell sounded. The injection of pace was dramatic; it caught Manzano off guard. The 10 runners in front responded more quickly. In doing so, they made Manzano feel like he was a lesser athlete, that he was slow, that he was more fatigued. In the blink of an eye, Manzano went from supreme confidence in his abilities to depressed and wallowing in self-pity.

The story could have ended there with another American out of the medals, except Manzano got his thoughts under control. He realized the runners in front were running too fast, too soon. He was still running well. The fact that many of these athletes were making a tactical error gave him renewed hope. When the time came to kick to the finish, Manzano felt fresher than the rest of his competitors.

Nothing physically changed for Manzano during the emotional lull that snapped him out of flow. His pace remained static during the moments of equilibrium before the bell lap and the 100 meters (109 yd.) after it. What changed was the way he interpreted the internal and external feedback around him. As others pulled away, he felt inferior. His legs "felt so done." But as he rationalized his competitors' actions, he realized they were making an error. Suddenly his legs felt light and springy. Always renowned for his kick at the national level, Manzano suddenly found himself capable of running down almost the entire field of international competitors at the finish.

Feedback may not always have such do-or-die consequences, but to produce flow it needs to be totally aligned with your goals and expectations. It is called unambiguous feedback for the ways both internal and external processes interpret information in the same manner. This feedback needn't be all positive; if something isn't going well, you want your brain to alert you to it. The question is this: Can your body and mind get on the same page to solve the problem and keep you moving in a progressive manner?

The Perils of Ambiguous Feedback

A classic example of the opposite (ambiguous feedback) is getting lost running in the woods. For 10 miles (16 km) you could be having the time of your life, climbing mountains and jumping through streams. Your body feels strong, and mentally you're confident you'll finish the run with no obstacles. All of a sudden you realize the trail looks unfamiliar. Maybe you've missed the cutoff. Maybe you need to backtrack. Is there a phone nearby with service? What if you run out of water? As these questions and concerns swirl, all semblance of flow is lost. Nervous and afraid, your prefrontal cortex kicks in to process every option. Your pace slows as you begin to unconsciously conserve calories for the uncertain future. You may even come to a complete stop, ostensibly to help you make a decision. The very thought of trudging back up the mountain makes your legs quiver. One minute ago you felt fine. Now it's as if a 50-pound sandbag has been thrown on your shoulders. Nothing physical has changed; everything has to do with the mental interpretation of unfolding events.

While ambiguity can ruin even the greatest run, unambiguous positive feedback can take you to the highest level imaginable. Everything seems possible when your heart and lungs and legs feel strong and feedback from your coach, your watch, spectators, and environment is all positive. Paces you never thought you'd hit happen. Landmarks you never thought you'd reach on foot appear. Two-hour runs pass by in what seems like 20 minutes. And all because the mind and body are on the same page.

Feedback in All Its Forms

At any given moment while immersed in an activity you have numerous forms of feedback available. These can be lumped into two basic categories: internal and external feedback. Unlike intrinsic and extrinsic motivation, neither form of feedback is more valuable than the other. **Internal feedback** refers to anything coming from inside the body. People most commonly think of physical cues such as breathing rates and sensations of fatigue in the legs. Balance, proprioception, and heart rate are other forms of internal physical feedback. This feedback also encompasses mental processes. Your thoughts, attitudes, and strategies all fall into this category.

External feedback is theoretically even broader, because it contains all sensory data outside the person. This feedback includes data collected from GPS and heart rate watches, the mandates of a coach, crowd noise, weather and temperature, and competitors. External feedback can also include spatial information such as your place in a crowd, positioning on a track, and the landscape you're moving through (hilly vs. flat; smooth vs. technical terrain; and so on).

These two forms of feedback form the bedrock on which you can interpret how you are performing at any given moment. Much of this information is processed and handled automatically by implicit memories; think of a steady increase in heart rate or reacting to a competitor's surge instinctually. Other times, feedback needs to be carefully considered in the conscious mind. Questions such as *Is this pace sustainable?* or *Should I stick in the pack longer or go off on my own?* can't always be acted on immediately. Some ventures require a redoubling of effort and an acknowledgment of risk. It is the downside of chasing flow; the challenge and its demands may exceed your preparation. In those instances, you may have to heed the strongest feedback or risk your body doing it for you automatically.

One question you'll want to ask yourself during any challenging event is *Is the feedback I'm receiving relevant to the task at hand?* Because feedback can take so many forms, interference is common. Some runners hate to run in the wind or rain and find that it distracts their focus. A comical fan or rude competitor may make it hard to immerse yourself in a race. Even the most zoned-out trail run isn't going to produce flow if a misbehaving watch starts beeping every few seconds.

On the other hand, relevant feedback can make a world of difference. GPS watches are rapidly replacing chronographic watches for many runners, and for good reason. The instant availability of pace, distance covered, and distance remaining help runners better gauge their effort. Like a human speedometer, GPS watches help you quickly ascertain whether you have gone out too fast. While far from a perfect technology, they nonetheless provide a valuable clue in proper pacing.

More valuable than a watch is a coach or knowledgeable friend. While watches can externalize internal processes, coaches and other onlookers can

Flow and the Central Governor Model of Fatigue

Dr. Timothy Noakes is nothing if not thorough. The South African sport science researcher and physician has published four editions of *Lore of Running,* a 944-page tome on the science, history, and training philosophies of distance running. His work has influenced generations of coaches and athletes, making him one of the most influential people in the sport.

One of Noakes' (2002) more intriguing ideas is the central governor model (CGM). Put simply, the CGM holds that the body's ability to exert itself physically is limited by the brain. The brain's goal is to ensure that internal body homeostasis (normalcy) is maintained, thereby ensuring the heart is not damaged and body temperatures don't rise to dangerous levels. The brain is also looking out for itself, making sure it doesn't run too low on glycogen (blood sugar). The brain achieves these goals by limiting the recruitment of muscle fibers. This limit in turn causes the body to feel fatigue.

For Noakes, the CGM amounts to a change in pacing strategy. The brain is not telling us to stop, but rather to adapt by slowing down to a pace that doesn't put internal organs at risk. Essentially it puts a governor on our ability to produce force, capping our speed at a safe level. As Noakes puts it, "[A]ll that happens at fatigue, when we are no longer able to sustain 'the required force,' or running speed, is that we have simply adopted a new, albeit slower, pacing strategy" (Noakes 2002, p. 147). Because of differences in genetics, talent, and other variables, the governor will kick in at different paces and levels of exertion for different people.

Serious questions arose about both the existence of the central governor and whether athletes who are wholly invested in their goals could override it. These questions led to wondering whether athletes in a flow state ever bypassed this governor in the midst of accomplishing their greatest tasks, especially given what is known about downregulation in the prefrontal cortex.

Arne Dietrich, a professor at American University of Beirut whose work is featured prominently in these pages, doesn't think that's the case. While he agrees with Noakes in principle on the idea of central fatigue, he isn't sure the brain mechanisms match up. He also doubts passion, desire, or flow could override central fatigue, even when certain sections of the brain are shunting blood.

"I cannot think of a mechanism in which brain circuits in prefrontal regions—your 'will,' so to speak—can regulate this, at least not beyond a very limited range," he told *Running Flow* in a short e-mail interview. "I think flow in competition has to do with other variables, such as a working memory capacity (to exclude extraneous information) or attention span." In other words, if some part of your brain is looking out for the safety of our body, you're unlikely to push past your body's limitations, no matter how much you want it.

take in the entire race, helping you understand your place related to other key competitors or landmarks. Even just a few shouts of encouragement from a trusted person can lift your spirits and result in a needed shot of confidence.

Taking a mindful approach can also help you better use feedback. Top marathoners have talked about breaking the marathon into 26 1-mile races to keep their minds engaged and the distance manageable. This strategy makes good use of short-term goals—26 of them, to be precise—and increases the amount of feedback available. Every time a mile is on pace, the positive reinforcement and motivation to achieve bigger goals increases.

This mindful approach can also be extended to interpreting events without judgment. If Sam the Marathoner takes 7:45 to cover the 17th mile of his marathon instead of his target time of 7:15, he has several options. He can berate himself for slowing down. He can panic at the thought of trying to make back all that lost time. Or he can accept the 7:45 mile for what it is—a 7:45 mile. After that, how he responds—whether he tries to increase his pace to make up lost time or holds his effort steady under the assumption the slowness was caused by a hill or misplaced mile marker—is entirely up to him.

Putting It All Together

The beginning of this chapter examined how to set proper goals. Developing skills and finding suitable challenges came next, followed by the role of feedback.

These antecedents don't operate in a vacuum. If anything, they tend to work synergistically. Goals can lead to skill development and tougher challenges. Succeeding at a tougher challenge can lead to loftier goals. Unambiguous feedback can make challenges seem easier, leading to a higher perception of skill and the need for more challenging goals. Whatever the order, the antecedents set the table for flow to arrive. As you move on to chapters 6 and 7, you will look at using this synergy in all its various forms to make flow more likely in both noncompetitive and competitive situations.

Key Points

- You can more readily accomplish the first flow antecedent of setting clear goals if you use the SMART approach to goal setting; make goals **s**pecific, **m**easurable, **a**ttainable, **r**elevant, and **t**ime bound.

- When setting lofty or long-term goals, set smaller goals along the way. This way you can see your progress, which builds self-efficacy. Self-efficacy helps you feel more optimistic and persevere toward the long-term goals.

- Be realistic about the time you have to commit to achieving your goals.

- Skill building is a necessary part of achieving your goals. Skill building for running goals include physical skills (endurance, stamina, speed, strength, flexibility, efficiency) and mental skills (visualization, mindfulness).

- The second flow antecedent of challenge–skills balance is unique to each person. Some people require more challenge in order to experience flow, while others require a challenge that is relatively equal to their skill.

- Feedback, the third flow antecedent, must be clear and relevant to your goal.

- Feedback can be internal (heart rate, respiration, thoughts) or external (landmarks, race place, guidance from others, data from pace watch).

- Clear feedback helps you determine whether you are on target toward your goal. Feedback may be used to determine whether you need to adjust your performance or your goal.

- The central governor model (CGM; Noakes, 2002) suggests that the body's ability to exert itself is regulated (governed) by the brain. This regulation is a protective mechanism to prevent overexertion or physical damage to the brain or internal organs.

CHAPTER 6
Flow in Everyday Running

The highest point in Costa Rica is an inactive volcano known as Cerro Chirripó. Looming high above the ecotourists ziplining through the rainforest, Chirripó is one of the most prominent mountains in the world. At 12,583 feet (3.8 km), its peak rises almost from sea level. It is not surprising that most hikers take 2 to 3 days to complete the 24-mile (38.6-km) round-trip journey, with many spending the night at a base camp 3 miles (4.8 km) from the top in order to acclimate to the altitude. Thirty-three-year-old Betsy Dorsett decided to run it in a day.

Rising at midnight in late October, Dorsett put on a headlamp and hydration pack and walked out into the Costa Rican night. The journey would take most of the day, light and dark. The blackness made the lightning stark in the sky and the puddles and mud hard to see. One headlamp was already dead, so she pulled out a spare. She slipped and slid and splashed through the muck and mire. Dorsett wanted to turn back, to return to the safety and dryness of her hotel room. But each time she thought of turning back, this simple mantra returned: *I just have to keep moving for a day.*

After 6 hours of climbing, she approached base camp at almost a crawl. Altitude sickness struck hard, making her dizzy and lightheaded. Her head throbbed with the change in barometric pressure. The lack of specific conditioning didn't help; she had been training on the beach for the past several weeks and hadn't been to altitude in several months. Sitting down with a few potatoes and energy supplements helped, but the thought of pushing higher up the mountain on tough terrain seemed daunting.

So, Dorsett counted her steps. She counted and recounted each stride, letting the numbers slide the focus away from fatigue and back to the activity itself. Despite all the problems, she was still moving. In so doing she lost herself to inertia. Running, even up a brutal mountain 10,000 feet (3 km) above sea level, felt good. Nothing else mattered.

By now the sun was up. Birds chirped. Dorsett was above the tree line. The path was dry and the footing clear. Hikers from base camp appeared.

Courtesy of Betsy Dorsett.

Betsy Dorsett atop Chirripó.

She passed them at a canter, the thin air keeping her pace slow and steady. The trail's steepness left Dorsett scrambling at times, but that was okay; her other passion was rock climbing. At long last, she saw a large Costa Rican flag flapping at the summit. She had made it to the top. On a clear day, you could see the entire country in one long gaze.

"When I got to the summit, no one else was there," Dorsett wrote in her journal when she returned. "I wanted to cry and scream and jump up and down. But I didn't. I was only at the halfway point. I stayed there for a while, watching the clouds whip around me in the wind, catching glimpses of the valleys and mountains below as they parted and then came back together. I sat down and took it all in. I'd made it this far, but I had to keep moving forward."

The run down beckoned. She paced herself, mindful of the effects of plummeting 10,000 feet (3 km) over 12 miles (19 km). By the last three, every muscle and fiber in her body ached. A toenail had fallen off; another teetered on the verge. Haggard and red-eyed she descended into the village at the bottom of Chirripó. No one clapped. No one told her congratulations. The task was simply over.

"I don't know that I will ever have the words for the intensity of this experience," she wrote, "for how proud I was of myself for pushing through the pain, the sleepiness, the darkness, the altitude sickness. How far from fun that run was, but how incredibly happy I was after finishing it. Something amazing happens when you push the limits of what your mind and body can handle. It strips you bare. It leaves you utterly exposed and allows you to know yourself in a way you never could have otherwise."

Dorsett never trained as a competitive athlete; she works at the Bay Area Recreation and Outreach Program as a communications and development manager, and only began running and cycling after college. Her racing vitae includes a single organized marathon and a handful of shorter races. Her easy runs are often done at a pace of 11:00 to 12:00 per mile (1.6 km).

Despite this limited competitive background, Dorsett sets goals and actively chases large challenges. In addition to Chirripó, she recently finished the arduous 42-mile (67.5-km) Rim-to-Rim-to-Rim route from the North Rim to the South Rim of the Grand Canyon and back, a route that has over 21,000 feet (6.4 km) of elevation change. She also tacked on 30-milers (48 km) through Yosemite and the Desolation Wilderness of California. As her training has evolved, so have her ambitions.

"When I first started doing longer trail runs, I just wanted to see a lot of pretty things and have an adventure," she says. "It was a way to get outside. It was exciting and fun to go for a run in Desolation Wilderness and see landscapes that people would take all weekend to see, and it would just take me half a day. That was originally what made it compelling. And then it just changed into how far do I want to go, and how far can I go, how hard can I make it, and how much stuff can I see?"

Not all of Dorsett's quests necessitate that type of travel and commitment. In fact, many of her best flow experiences have happened on flat stretches of easy trails, places where she could, in her words, "sink into the run." In those instances the rhythm of running and the solace it produced allowed her to quiet her mind and enjoy the sensation of moving.

Other times, such as when tackling a massive challenge like Chirripó, the revelations seem much more profound.

"At some point that day, something shifted within me," Dorsett wrote. "All I had done for 13 hours was move forward, even when it was hard and I didn't want to and everything hurt. And that's what life is all about. We just have to keep moving forward, even when it's painful. Maybe especially then. That's the only thing we have to do. And sometimes, like on Chirripó, you end up right back where you started, but you are different when you get back there."

Runs that transcend the normal are part of what makes this sport so enjoyable. At times it can occur by happenstance, but you can cultivate flow in concrete ways in everyday, noncompetitive runs by adding in some key variables. This chapter examines the role of running partners, music, landscape, and the ability to find challenges that matter to you. It also looks at the risks of chasing flow, how flow can spark creativity, and how experiencing flow on these runs can inspire you to compete.

Finding Things That Matter

Ten years ago Dorsett left the Eastern Seaboard to try her hand at Northern California. Her reasons were simple and sound. The area provided the recreational and job opportunities that she needed to lead a life that felt exciting and fulfilling. In 3 hours she could be skiing in the High Sierras or running through a desert or climbing at Yosemite. These activities came to define her and gave her a series of skills to learn and goals to aspire toward.

"It makes me happy," Dorsett says, "even when I've been running 30 miles all through the night and the sun is rising and the light is hitting Cathedral Peak [in Yosemite National Park], and you're so tired. It just makes me feel small and insignificant but amazing at the same time."

You don't need to climb the highest peaks in Central American countries or traverse the largest canyon in the world to experience flow. In fact, many of Dorsett's favorite runs leading up to her Rim-to-Rim-to-Rim challenge came during the weekends leading up to the adventure, when she'd plan extravagantly beautiful runs in the Sierras to acclimate to the altitude and climbing that the Arizona desert would present.

"That was just an excuse to get me up there, running outside," she says. "I ran Mt. Whitney [the highest peak in the Continental United States at 14,448 feet/4,4000m] with a friend and did a bunch of things up in Desolation [Wilderness]. I did a climb on Cathedral in Yosemite National Park and then did a 30-mile run overnight. Rim-to-Rim-to-Rim was just a challenge that had a lot of challenges along the way which made it more fun."

Not all runners have mountains or oceans or deserts in our backyard (or even within easy driving range), but everyone can find runs and adventures that are personally meaningful. While the familiar flow equation of *goals + skills + challenge + feedback = flow opportunity* may sound rote, many everyday flow experiences come from feeling like you have mastery over a certain situation. It could come on a recovery day where your legs feel springy and light or a hilly run where you find you have the strength to push ahead.

For recreational runners who pursue the sport as a fitness hobby or competitive runners looking for a quiet recovery day, terms such as *goals* and *challenge* can seem unnecessarily intimidating. They connote rigorous planning, a type A personality, and competition. When all you're looking for is an easy hour escape in the woods, why should structure be involved?

In truth, the shortest short-term goals (such as running for an hour) are strong enough to engage you in the task when you are well practiced. Feedback indicating you feel strong and effortless can make running more enjoyable and automatic, freeing up mental energy. And, perhaps most important, performing a task that has personal significance makes you more likely to maintain attention for prolonged periods of time, even if the challenge is low.

The Art of Staying Focused

In August 2011, Dr. Christian Swann and three colleagues began trawling the internet for research on flow and athletics. Their goal was to analyze everything published on the topic. Their paper, "A Systematic Review of the Experience, Occurrence, and Controllability of Flow States in Elite Sport"

(Swann et al. 2012) lived up to its name. Certain themes emerged again and again as they sorted through the research. Of all of them, prolonged attention came up most commonly.

No number of goals, skills, challenges, or feedback can overcompensate for mentally checking out while running or performing any other meaningful task. Running can certainly be done on autopilot, especially on easy runs; in those instances your physical actions are controlled by the implicit memory, allowing your mind to wander wherever it wishes. However, when it wanders to the point that the act of running loses its meaning (running becomes just another automatic action like breathing, instead of something you're consciously excited about), you lose the opportunity for flow.

Therefore, experiencing flow requires you to concentrate for long periods of time. Sometimes an internal sense of well-being or big challenge is enough to keep your attention for the duration of a run. You feel so good or have so many obstacles to overcome that you have no psychic energy left to scatter your thoughts. Plenty of other times exist when staying in the present moment requires skill. Like all skills, attention and concentration can grow with practice.

In *Flow in Sports* (1999), Sue Jackson and Dr. Mike recommend a number of steps to increase your ability to stay focused. First and foremost is figuring out where to direct your attention. This task is specific to where you're running. For example, a trail runner will want to get comfortable watching her feet for rocks and roots for long periods of time, whereas a road runner may be better suited to take in a bigger view of traffic and landscape. All runners should work on identifying internal cues, such as breathing and heart rate. Jackson believes that practicing these skills in situations similar to what you'll face will help you best develop your concentration.

Learning to purposely direct your attention is another skill worth practicing. At the frenetic pace of modern life, people constantly shuffle between work, phones, future deadlines, and desires to be somewhere else. This lifestyle often feels scattershot, as if at any given moment people have no control of what they are thinking or working toward.

If you extrapolate that concept to running, you can see why practicing sustained attention is difficult. If you're running on a trail, do you need to be looking out for roots and rocks, listening to your breathing to keep it under control, or just enjoying the fresh air? When running on a busy street, do you want to hear the cars and noise around you, or do you want to keep up your internal monologue? There's no right or wrong answer as long as your safety is assured. However, learning to direct that focus to the action you're presently engaged in (in this case, running and the environment around you) is the best way to experience flow on recreational runs.

Just as running over time increases stamina and muscle strength, practicing some attention tasks can also improve your ability to stay focused, especially if this attention is a struggle for you. Meditation has been well supported as a great exercise for strengthening attention; as little as 20 minutes a day over a 5-day span shows lasting effects (Menezes & Bizarro 2015). Forcing yourself to block out external distractions and focus on things such as the number of words in a paragraph or on a page, counting backward from 100 to 0, and memorizing lists or poems are great ways to increase your attention. Repeat one or more of these strategies each day, and you will be surprised at how much more easily you can focus your attention within a short period of time.

Meditating on the Move

In its purest form, meditation is a practice of stillness and control of the mind. Running sits at the other end of the spectrum as a concerted effort to move the body forward. With mindfulness and sustained attention, which are two key attributes in flow experiences and two of the primary objectives in meditation, it begs this question: Can you meditate on the move?

Many Buddhist monks, who are some of the best purveyors of mindfulness meditation, believe the answer is yes. Deep in the forests of northeast Thailand, monks versed in the Forest tradition of meditation pace around their solitary huts for hours on end, trying to experience the same sense of emptiness the Buddha found before enlightenment (Cianciosi 2007). For runners, walking meditation serves these two main purposes: it sharpens the mind's focus for prolonged periods of time in a present-centered manner, and it does so while the body is in motion.

When meditating on the move, you should find a path clear of obstacles and that has fixed start and finish points. A suggested length is no more than 10 to 20 yards (9-18 m). Starting with good posture, your arms relaxed and your hands in front of your waist, begin walking. Keep your gaze on the ground a few steps ahead. Pay attention to each step. Note the sensation of your foot striking the ground and pushing back off. Try to keep all other thoughts at a distance; if you notice external thoughts creeping in, focus again on each step. When you reach the end of the path, evaluate your state of mind and return to where you started. In this way, you teach yourself to stay completely in the present moment with your full concentration on the task at hand (Cianciosi 2007). A good amount of time for beginners is 10 minutes, building up to as long as 30 minutes as you advance in the practice.

If you can master simple meditation while walking, you'll want to consider trying a similar approach while running. Sakyong Mipham, author of *Running with the Mind of Meditation* (2012), is quick to point out that meditation and running are separate entities. At the same time, the mental strength required in meditation is similar to the physical stamina required in running. A runner must put in years of training to achieve the bone, muscle, and tendon strength necessary to run fast, just as a master meditator must spend years developing the attentional powers needed to experience meditation and mindfulness in its highest form.

For Mipham, the biggest point of emphasis when meditating is the breath. "Paying attention to the breath as we exhale and inhale is extremely beneficial for the body and the mind," he says. "It helps to detoxify the mind from stress and negative thoughts and emotions, including regret. The breath is like the waves in the ocean that help circulate the water so that it does not become stagnant. . . . Generally our mental state becomes congested because we are thinking of the past or the future" (Mipham 2012, p. 24).

Staying in the present and focusing on small details is key to being able to meditate on the run. Creative thoughts often spark on runs, but just as often the mind ruminates on the past or dreams about the future. Shutting those thoughts off on occasion while running is beneficial. You can't entirely turn the mind off while running outdoors, though. Topography, passersby, and upcoming obstacles are all things your implicit memory will need to process and manage while you're running, even if you're doing your best to harness your mind.

To aid you in that quest, Mipham recommends "mildly [paying] attention to your feet and your breathing, rather than spacing out and thinking about other things. It's a matter of balancing mindfulness not too tightly, not too loosely. When you find that balance, all of a sudden the mind gets totally into the groove. We think of it as accidental, but something in the mind brought those conditions together" (Bond 2008).

That statement sounds a lot like flow. To get the most from it, start small. Pick a clear part of a path. Focus exclusively on your breathing and foot strike; pay attention to each inhalation, exhalation, foot landing, and toe-off. Later on, expand that awareness to ever longer stretches of a safe path. If you become advanced enough, you can master those skills on technical terrain for entire runs. Just make sure your mind never wanders so far into the quiet abyss that you put your safety at risk.

Environment and Flow

Simple as running may appear, it's never done in a vacuum. Open fields, city streets, mountainous trails, or your basement each serve as the environment that you will move through during the course of a run. Far from a static variable, the environment strongly influences how much you enjoy a run and how likely you are to experience flow.

Exploring and immersing yourself in your surroundings can provide motivation for a run, replacing the need for a challenge in order to experience flow. A steady run on a beautiful trail often elicits positive affect and invites flow for the runner who connects with nature. Dr. Mike has suggested in many previous writings that nature can be a huge contributor to the onset of flow; in fact, it may be a facilitator that encourages flow more readily than many other factors (Csikszentmihalyi 1990).

Researchers studying the restorative qualities of spending time in mountainous regions (Wöran & Arnberger 2012) found that flow can be more readily attained when you feel like your environment allows you to escape from your reality or distracts you by focusing on the interesting elements of nature. These same researchers note you are more likely to feel calm when you encounter pastures, mountain views, landmarks that clearly guide your way, and structured park-like settings. Other natural settings like unmarked dense forests or endless open plains are more likely to feel chaotic and stressful if they're unfamiliar, forcing you to divert your attention towards navigating the terrain.

A second working theory on nature's relationship to flow has started to gain traction in recent years. **Attention restoration theory (ART)** posits that you can concentrate better after being exposed to the natural world (Kaplan 1993). Whether at work, school, or parenting, much of the time people are forced to direct their attention toward a particular task. If this task fully engages them, a great deal of mental energy is required to keep them locked in. This requirement leads to a condition called **directed attention fatigue**. Researchers have found that after spending time in natural settings, people's minds are better able to cope with prolonged periods of directed attention, and performance on mental tasks increases (Kaplan 1993).

A light form of stimulation known as **soft fascination** may be at the root of this restorative effect. The natural environment offers many pleasant things for the mind to ponder, such as the shapes of clouds, the colors of leaves, or the trickling sounds of a creek. They effortlessly engage the brain in a totally different manner than urban landscapes, filled as they are with scores of people, machines, and man-made structures. Greater biodiversity in the natural landscape escalates this restorative effect. Even people with untrained eyes benefit from a varied setting of trees, plants, animals, and environmental features (Fuller et al. 2007). As your attentional capabilities restore, your ability to experience flow—either in the natural setting or later on in a more hectic race environment—increases as well.

This benefit is not only related to being outdoors. Study participants who spent time looking at nature scenes recorded similar benefits to those who explored outdoors (Wells & Evans 2003). These benefits contribute to more than attention span. Being able to look outside a hospital window greatly improved postsurgical recovery times in one study (Ulrich 1984), while exposure to nature increased psychological well-being and resiliency against life stressors in both adults and children in another (Wells & Evans 2003).

All that said, environments needn't be exotic in order to be conducive to flow. The sight of spring flowers or a manicured pond in a neighborhood provides the same flow potential as a park as long as the streets don't also provide any dangerous obstacles. Certain man-made objects, such as running toward a beautiful city skyline, also offer plenty to ponder. Bike paths that utilize underpasses and overpasses offer a great opportunity to lose yourself in a secure, traffic-free environment surrounded by a mix of natural and man-made beauty.

Just as important as the views around you are the views below you. Specifically, topography and footing can both make or break a flow experience.

Flow in the City
How Urban Running Environments Affect Flow

Stop and go. Green light, yellow light, red light. Pedestrians are clogging the sidewalks with dogs on leashes, deliveries are made on fixed-gear bikes, and horns are blaring at every intersection. To many the idea of navigating crowded city streets, to say nothing of running through them in a Zen-like manner, induces anxiety. However, some runners thrive on training in urban areas. So, can you experience flow one busy city streets? Surprisingly, the answer is yes—if your personality type matches the challenges of the environment around you (and the environment doesn't get too out of whack).

The biggest obstacle to experiencing flow in an urban environment is unpredictable traffic patterns on both the roads and sidewalks. Entering a flow state requires that you maintain a clear focus on your goals and internal and external feedback. That focus is likely to be shattered when a car alarm goes off or a hundred people in suits exit an office building directly in your path. Even if the sidewalks are clear, navigating vehicles in congested cities is exhausting. If you are already locked into flow, a sudden change in traffic will end with you either snapping out of flow for your own safety or a dangerous encounter with several tons of metal.

Runners who train extensively in urban areas usually find tricks to minimize the ebb and flow (no pun intended). That could take the form of running before or after rush hour traffic, sticking to minor thoroughfares with fewer stoplights, or spending more time in city parks or bike paths. Major cities such as New York, Boston, and Chicago have all utilized their proximity to large bodies of water to provide havens for urban runners.

Some runners seek out paths or drive out to run in quieter suburbs, and others seem to thrive on the controlled chaos of city running. Darting around double-parked cars or shooting into the road the second the crosswalk light illuminates, these runners make a challenge out of working against the dissonant aspects of city life to have successful runs. This attitude may stem from two personality traits in particular: **behavioral activation system** and **behavioral inhibition system**.

All humans are wired with these systems, but each activates them to varying degrees. Approach motivation (the tendency to find challenges pleasurable, even very difficult ones) is related to the behavioral activation system. Avoidance motivation, on the other hand, is correlated with the behavioral inhibition system. Runners who have highly sensitive inhibition systems are less likely to engage in the risky behavior of running through a busy city because of all the potential risks involved. People more attuned with the activation systems find the constant shifts in traffic and obstacles a pleasurable challenge. For these runners the city comes to life, and the constant shapeshifting means that no run ever feels quite the same as the last.

One runner's mountain, it appears, is another runner's Fifth Avenue.

A speedy runner looking for a fast time may become disheartened if a route proves to be hillier or more technical than expected. Similarly, a runner who finds runs in the wilderness recharging may feel estranged from a jog in a cluttered neighborhood. If you find yourself running in an environment that feels ugly or ill-fitting, work to find something beautiful about it. Even the least gentrified neighborhoods usually have some redeeming spark of beauty hidden in their midst. Whether it's an old bit of Gothic architecture or a tiny garden planted in a front yard is for you to find out.

One part of an environment that can shut flow down in a millisecond is a lack of security. Even in a deep flow experience, your brain continues to unconsciously monitor the world around you, tracking relevant, goal-related information and monitoring your safety. While Dietrich's theory of transient hypofrontality (Dietrich 2003; also mentioned in chapter 4) suggests that unnecessary portions of the prefrontal cortex and amygdala may shut down during a flow run, it does not mean your survival instinct also deactivates. The brain remains constantly vigilant in scanning your surroundings for potential dangers. This activity can inhibit or disrupt flow while running if your sympathetic nervous system is repeatedly activated in response to perceived dangers.

This uncertainty is one reason that runners seek out tracks and treadmills for runs. The static and safe environment these venues provide allow the mind to lock in fully on the task at hand, with no energy diverted toward managing traffic or footing. Even nature lovers may find the rhythmic effect of treadmill running hypnotic. If you can stop staring at the time/distance display and "sink into the run," to borrow Dorsett's phrase, treadmills and tracks can provide ideal flow opportunities.

What a Conversation Is Worth

When Allan Sillitoe penned *The Loneliness of the Long-Distance Runner* in 1959, he meant for it to convey the hardships and social class discord occurring in Great Britain after World War II. Long after the story has collected dust on most people's bookshelves, its title lives on as a powerful descriptor. Both recreational and competitive distance runners are imagined to be a breed of introverts putting in silent, solitary miles.

For many runners, nothing could be further from the truth. Group runs from running stores and microbreweries have become increasingly popular, with many drawing upwards of 100 runners at a time. These runners enjoy the social aspect of the sport and use it as a time to catch up with friends. The miles seem to fly by as the conversation takes hold. For a select few, this conversation can induce flow.

If you look forward to running with your fitness-minded friends, you probably also benefit from getting lost in conversation while you are racking up the miles. Not only does it afford a break from the monotony and pressures of everyday life, but talking also helps pass the time. At a higher level, conversation can induce flow for those well-versed in this forgotten art. Koudenburg, Postmes, & Gordijn (2013) found that a smooth conversation with minimal gaps between speakers provided feelings of contentment and **social validation,** that is, that their feelings were correct and justified. A fluent discussion requires less energy to be expended, allowing that energy to be better spent in other areas. A good conversation is like a dance, and the smooth give-and-take relationship between people in a deep conversation can produce flow. Conversations that are choppy or filled with awkward pauses have the opposite effect, leaving people anxious and distracted and concerned that their thoughts and opinions are somehow incorrect.

Aside from conversation, running with friends or in groups has other benefits. **Social facilitation,** a well-known theory from social psychology, suggests that when people do well-rehearsed tasks in the presence of others, they tend to perform better. Studies on social facilitation have looked specifically at runners (Strube, Miles, & Finch 1981) and found that, when compared to running alone, runners tend to run faster when in the presence of others. Striving to keep up with others may help you and your partners run faster than usual, thereby increasing the challenge. If you thrive on competitive situations, even as a recreational runner, this effect may be pronounced enough to help you succeed at a more difficult task. (It's worth noting that if you're not well-versed in a task, the opposite is true; no one likes to perform in front of an audience when they don't know what they're doing.)

If you're an introverted runner, this notion of running in a group while chatting and pushing the pace may sound like a nightmare. Running in a pack is likely to drain you unnecessarily, robbing you of energy you would rather spend on the run itself. For the introvert, running alone is best and more pleasurable. Introverts are more likely to gain energy in a solitary run by refueling their mind, tapping into the beauty around them, and enjoying the silence a run alone provides. Running alone can serve as a welcome reprieve from the hustle and bustle of life, providing a much-needed restorative effect for the mind and body.

When to Let the Beat Drop

Few topics divide runners more than music. We're not talking genres or artists, but whether you choose to pop some earbuds in and rock out while running. This is far from a niche debate. Websites today sell structured playlists that match a song's beats per minute (BPM) to your intended running speed and cadence. Tech companies reap millions of dollars from ergonomically designed headphones. Not to be outdone, scientists have also thrown their hats into the arena, examining the effects of music on aerobic exercise. Like most things in life, a mix of personality type, physiology, and environment play a role in whether music is beneficial in a given situation.

Music is a highly studied human creation with lots of positive outcomes. Costas I. Karageorghis and David-Lee Priest (2012) wrote this in the *International Review of Sport and Exercise Psychology:* "According to the available evidence, music captures attention, raises spirits, triggers a range of emotions, alters or regulates mood, evokes memories, increases work output, heightens arousal, induces states of higher functioning, reduces inhibitions and encourages rhythmic movement" (p. 45). Many of these findings coincide with good running.

In studies of music and aerobic exercise, music of all types is positively related to lower ratings of perceived exertion during moderate-intensity exercise (Potteiger, Schroeder, & Goff 2000). It seems that music acts as a passive distraction, pulling your attention away from feelings of pain and fatigue (if not literally deafening you to the sounds of your own breathing). Music that motivates you, whether for its rhythmic qualities or personal connotations, has been shown to delay fatigue and increase power output in people. This physiological response is entirely individualized; no two people respond the same way to the same song (Karageorghis & Priest 2012).

So, if music has all these inherently positive qualities, what's to stop you from starting every run with music? For one, music is isolating. Not only do you miss out on interacting with other people you may see on the path, you also miss out on all the sounds that surround you. If nature is a strong motivating force, not hearing the roar of a creek beside you may mitigate many of the advantages of being in the woods.

As one of your five senses, being able to hear also keeps you more alert and prepared in your environment. Runners often rely on their ears to know that a car is coming well before making visual contact with a vehicle. It is especially true for vehicles approaching from behind or around blind curves. People who run in parks or on sidewalks also lose the ability to sense the presence of others around them, increasing the risk of being startled or worse. Most every television crime show at some point depicts a headphones-wearing runner being attacked at night. Hollywood may be preying on people's fears, but no doubt you're less prepared to initiate a fight-or-flight response if you can't hear your attacker approaching.

Even if your safety is assured, music often robs you of one of your most important human abilities, creativity. With your mind focused on the lyrics and rhythm of a song, you lose the ability to get lost in thought. This loss is a shame, because both the mind wandering of a neutral run and the intense experience of flow can be valuable in problem solving.

Think about a time you struggled at work with a logistical problem or encountered writer's block while working on a paper. No matter how much mental energy you put into solving the problem, nothing seemed to help. Then, after walking away from the problem and engaging in something completely unrelated, you found you had your solution when you returned to the problem. It's easy to chalk this up as luck or an aha moment, but in reality your unconscious mind has been hard at work sorting through various options while you engaged in the unrelated task.

According to recent research (Sio & Ormerod 2009), the best incubation periods are filled with tasks that aren't too cognitively challenging and more extensive in length. Nonstrenuous running fits this definition perfectly. By filling your attention with running instead of music, you leave plenty of mental energy available for experiencing flow and coming up with creative solutions.

The Risk/Reward Ratio of Flow

Up until now, flow has often been portrayed as a positive outcome resulting from a high skill level, a strong challenge, clear goals, and unambiguous feedback. What about autotelic runners who experience flow on a regular basis and continually up the ante in their quest to overcome greater and more exotic challenges? For instance, think of Max King from chapter 4 and Dorsett in this chapter. Can being a "flow junkie" as a runner be positive? What are the negatives?

As long as it remains balanced with the rest of your life's priorities and doesn't put you at risk, pushing the envelope in pursuit of flow is generally a good thing. Seeking new challenges requires new and more refined skills, making you a better-rounded runner. A runner who once struggled to climb halfway up a mountain suddenly finds herself capable of summiting the highest peaks. A 30-minute run becomes an hour becomes 2 hours. Expanding your boundaries opens up the door to experiences and views never thought possible. As these boundaries grow, so, too, do people's perceptions of what is possible. With no limiting ceiling hanging over your head, the world brims with possibility.

Despite those positives, there are caveats. Like a euphoric drug, running and flow hunting can become addictive. And like all addictions, when you start pursuing running and flow to the detriment of other areas of your life, then you've tipped the scales too far and no longer have a healthy relationship with the sport. It's one thing to drive to the Sierra Nevadas on the weekend to run up amazing trails and see awe-inspiring views; it's quite another to quit your job and leave your family to live as a running hermit in the mountains.

Perhaps the biggest potential risk associated with hunting for flow is blowing up in pursuit of a big challenge. When Dorsett ran Rim-to-Rim-to-Rim, she did so on an injured ankle. Five miles from completing the route, her ankle gave out, forcing her to walk the remainder of the route out of the Grand Canyon. Hobbling home isn't exactly a pleasurable experience, but for Dorsett the risk of her ankle giving out was worth the experience of running all over the Grand Canyon.

Authors in Flow
Christine's Endless Long Run

Courtesy of Christine Weinkauff Duranso

It was a beautiful summer day in Northern Indiana as I laced up my running shoes. I hadn't been back to Indiana in 2 years, and I was looking forward to a flat run through a local forest preserve. As much as I love mountain runs in my adopted hometown in Southern California, I have to admit I was missing the ease of running for miles with nothing but the flat path in front of me. I was peaking in mileage as I prepared for the Nike Women's Marathon in San Francisco, so my plan was to find a nice pace and enjoy 20 miles' (32 km) worth of sights, sounds, and smells of the forest.

It was early in the morning on a weekday, so the asphalt trail was all mine, except for the sound of a babbling brook, the hum of bumblebees, and the occasional barking dog tracking me as I passed a fenced yard on the other side of the tree line. One mile turned to two. My breathing and heart rate synched comfortably. My thoughts wavered from the joy of seeing my son and his family to pace calculations to determine whether I was on target for my goal.

> *My son Brad is such a great father! The laughter that reverberates in his house is indicative of a life worth living, and I am so proud of him. Mile 3: Pace is good. My granddaughter Anna is so smart! And confident! She is going to be so successful in life. Mile 4: Speed up.*

*I love the way my daughter-in-law Lydia finds creative ways to spend
time with Anna and my grandson Lincoln. They are always coloring,
playing soccer, or making up stories. Mile 5: I wonder what my other
kids back in Southern California are doing. I miss them.
Mile 6: On target for goal pace.*

As I ticked off the miles, my legs worked effortlessly to keep the pace. As
I rounded curves and stopped for the occasional cross traffic, my mind and
body knew exactly what to do. The beat of my feet meeting the trail kept time
with my heart, and it all felt so good. I could feel my legs churning past miles
7, 8, 9, 10. Double digits and feeling great! More barking dogs. A soft breeze
greeting my face. A smile. I wiped the sweat from my face without losing step.
I felt like I could go forever. *I hope the Nike race feels this good!*

Because this was an unfamiliar trail for me, I mapped the route on my computer before I left Brad's house. I had a general idea of a trail marker that would
indicate the halfway point where I should turn around and head back home,
but I hadn't seen it yet. I wasn't worried. I felt so energized, there was no way
I'd passed it.

*Mile 12, 13, 14. My legs feel good. My pace is where I had hoped.
Wait! My pace? My pace! How long have I been out?*

A rush of mathematical calculations in my head suggested I was finishing
mile 15. I should have turned around 5 miles ago.

*Reverse course, keep running. Laugh. Wow, this is a great run
indeed!*

As I continued running, now on my way back toward home, I realized I'd
been experiencing flow for quite some time. I was thinking about things other
than running, but I was also constantly monitoring my pace. Too bad I hadn't
monitored my pace with enough detail to realize I had run beyond my turnaround, but I felt so good it hadn't occurred to me that I should be feeling the
need to turn around. My 20-mile run turned into a 30-mile run.

*Will I make it without hitting a wall? I hope so. I have never run 30
miles. I am going to be late getting back to the house. I hope no one
worries about me! Wow this feels great, though! I think it will be fine.
Mile 16. Yes, it will be fine. This will definitely require a rest day tomor-
row though. That's okay; more time with family. Mile 17, pace is good.
Mile 24, 25, 26; pace is a little slow, pick it up. Don't worry, Chris,
you've got this. Keep up the pace. My feet are a little tired but it isn't
bad. Keep going. Mile 27, 28, 29; one more mile! I am almost back
home! What happened to miles 18-24? Wow, I thought it was going
to be rough getting back when I tacked on an extra 10 miles, but the
time just flew by and I didn't realize it! Mile 30. Done.*

I kept my pace for most of the run, even though I added an extra 10 miles.
My legs were spent, my feet sore, but it was the best run I'd had in a very long
time. This was flow.

On a smaller scale people make these types of risk/reward decisions all the time. Do you stay on the flat route because your legs are tired or take the hillier path with the better views? Do you pick up the pace for 5 minutes or 10? Do you run for 1 hour or 90 minutes? Your physical and mental condition at any given moment may influence whether you take a riskier strategy with high rewards or play it safe with a more conservative choice.

What makes people choose the riskier option many times? Often it has to do with the pleasure-inducing outcome variables discussed in chapter 2, such as increased feelings of self-confidence, a loss of self-consciousness, and time transformation. Flow elevates your mood and buffers stress and is often accompanied by heightened awareness of your body moving through space (kinesthetic awareness), an absence of strain, and calmness. People have reported even more incredible sensations, such as a oneness with the world around you or having an out-of-body experience (Swann et al. 2012). These pleasurable experiences can lead to a sustained high after the activity ceases. For some, this high is worth the time, effort, and risk.

Building Toward Competition

Experiencing flow in everyday runs is an incredible, meaningful experience. As you have seen so far, it makes running more rewarding, helps you connect with nature, increases your motivation and mood, and is worth pursuing in its own right. Recreational runners who begin to experience flow more frequently may find a desire to compete in races, even if they've never competed in the past. Meanwhile, competitive runners may begin to wonder how flow experiences could enhance their performance.

In the next chapter, you will look at flow in competitive situations and see how the powers of a meaningful task and a high challenge often produce the best experiences of our lives.

Exercises

If you're looking to find flow in your everyday runs, try some of the following exercises.

Start your run with a reachable goal. Achieving even a small goal during a run can increase your confidence and increase the likelihood you'll positively engage with the activity. Before you start a run, come up with a goal that offers a small challenge. Adjust accordingly so that you feel a sense of mastery over the task. If you get bored, set the goal higher. If you are pushing so hard that you are anxious, then back off, slow down, and decrease the challenge. Ideally, you will raise your goals over time, producing a deeper, fuller flow experience as you meet harder challenges.

If you love running in natural settings, find places that don't require too much cognitive energy. Parks, nature trails, and well-marked mountain paths all increase the likelihood of experiencing flow because you can enjoy the scenery and sensations without worrying about getting lost. Running with a map or smartphone may sound like an inconvenience, but if you venture out into more remote areas it can put your mind at ease (and open it to flow) by allowing you to navigate.

If you're a socialite, find a group run in your area. The social elements of running are powerful and enjoyable for many athletes. Most communities now have group runs through running stores, running clubs, or local businesses. Many areas also offer less official running groups whose information can be found on websites and social media. Visit one of these runs, and see if it makes the miles pass by pleasantly.

Practice prolonged, focused attention. One good way to improve your attention span is to practice meditation (Lutz et al. 2009). If the idea of sitting still and focusing on nothing is overwhelming, consider starting with just a few minutes a day or joining a guided meditation group for added clarity and support. Another option is to practice visualization, as discussed in chapter 5. Both methods will help you maintain your focus for longer periods of time. Other possible exercises include counting the number of words in a paragraph without distraction. Over time, increase from a paragraph to a page; keep counting larger chunks of words each day or week to help practice the art of focused attention. Other training strategies include counting backward from 100 to 0 or memorizing lists or poems. As you are able to memorize one small list or one small poem, move on to larger lists or longer poems to train your mind to focus total attention on that one goal. Spending just 10 to 20 minutes per day on these tasks can result in measurable improvement in your ability to focus attention in everyday life and also in your running life.

See if music works for you. Some runners love it, some hate it, but the only way to see if music is a powerful motivating force in your running is to give it a try. If you worry about your safety with a pair of earbuds in, consider starting with music on a treadmill. You can also run with only one headphone in, allowing you to hear both music and the sounds of the world around you.

Key Points

- Experiencing flow requires concentration; running mindlessly (without purpose or goal) is not going to elicit flow.
- Staying focused is an important skill for flow. You can improve your focus using the exercises provided in this chapter.
- Running environment matters. Running is more likely to include flow if you practice it your preferred context (trail, track, treadmill).

- Nature seems to elicit flow more readily than other contexts.
- Social facilitation is the tendency to work hard (run faster) when you are with others.
- Running with music may distract from pain, discomfort, or exertion. Fast-tempoed music may help you improve your pace. However, music may also stifle creative thinking during a run and rob you of the pleasure of hearing the world around you. It can also be a safety hazard.

CHAPTER 7
Flow Racing

The city of Stockholm has something magical that extends far beyond the cobblestone streets of Old Town. Maybe it's the Gothic architecture or all the fit, healthy people riding around on their bikes or the national park within city limits. Whatever it is, former NCAA champion Katie (Follett) Mackey could sense an opportunity waiting when she came through the tunnel of the castle-like Olympic Stadium on a cool, July afternoon in 2015.

Built for the 1912 Games, the stadium now played host to soccer matches and concerts. Once a year that focus shifted to the world of professional track and field when the Stockholm Diamond League meet came to town. One of the premiere 1-day track meets in the world, Stockholm served up a host of Olympic and world champions in the many events contested that day.

Into this fray stepped Mackey, an elite U.S. distance runner trying to take her running to the next level. Just a few weeks earlier Mackey came up short of qualifying for the world championship team at 5,000 meters after stumbling with a lap and a half to go. Undeterred, Mackey continued her season, running good 1,500-meter races in Belgium and London. Winning a Diamond League race at 3,000 meters, though, would reclassify her entire season.

"I wanted to prove to myself and others that I belonged there, and I'd never raced with so much money ($10,000) on the line," Mackey says. "I felt pretty confident in my fitness. I knew that the 3K was a sweet spot for me and felt ready for anything. I didn't know all the girls in the race; I just knew that everyone was good and would be hard to beat."

From the time the gun sounded it was clear that this race would be a tactical one. Mackey stayed on the inside of the track, conserving energy while runners from Bahrain, Poland, Ethiopia, and the United Arab Emirates took turns maintaining the pace. The race followed this script until two laps to go, when two Ethiopian-born runners, Mimi Belete from Bahrain and Betlhem Desalegn of the United Arab Emirates, started pressing hard. They scorched the penultimate lap in 67 seconds. That was close to Mackey's pace for the 1,500 meters (an event half the distance she was covering now), but the strain of picking up speed never set in.

"There were several athletes that I knew would be racing for the win, and so I tried to just pay attention and make gradual moves as other girls died

Daniel Petty/The Denver Post via Getty Images

Katie Mackey, center, competing at the 2016 Olympic track and field trials in the 5,000 meters.

off to stay in the lead pack," Mackey recalls. "When we came around and heard the bell I was just off the leaders. With 300 meters to go I remember thinking, 'Damn, I feel pretty good!'"

As the pack splintered, Mackey kept contact with the two leaders. Coming into the final curve, she felt her momentum carry her out to lane 2. Now there was no going back, no time for fears or concerns. As she came into the home stretch, she slipped past Belete and Desalegn.

"It was a surreal and effortless feeling, like someone was behind me pushing me," Mackey says. "I just couldn't believe that I couldn't see the other girls in my peripheral vision anymore. Once I crossed the line my first thought was 'Did that really just happen? Am I dreaming?'"

As a television camera operator leaped onto the track and caught her every move, Mackey smiled and blew kisses to the folks back home. Meet organizers presented her with a single red rose, a small symbol of everything going right when it mattered most. As she caught her breath, the fact that she had won $10,000 and become just the fourth U.S. runner to win a Diamond League 3,000- or 5,000-meter race was far from her mind. In this moment, she simply felt pure joy.

"It was rewarding to see all the hard work and fitness pay off, to just keep believing, have faith, and work hard," she says. "I remember thinking after the race that faith is like a muscle, and the more you work it the stronger it becomes."

The importance of the meet, the right level of competition, the motivation to succeed after failure, and the faith in her fitness combined in synergy to put Mackey in a position to succeed. Her success in Stockholm wasn't a product of luck or chance; it was a well-planned physical and mental peak.

This chapter discusses how flow affects racing and vice versa. It describes the type of holistic training that can help you experience flow racing more frequently in everything from a 5K to an ultramarathon. The information in this chapter draws on research from sport psychology, mindfulness, motivational research, and exercise physiology. Synergizing all these disparate elements is the best way to make Mackey's experience tangible and possible for all runners who love to compete.

Cultivating Flow in Competition

Humans are naturally competitive creatures, and competition has the potential to bring out the best in people. While competition against the self is a strong motivator, competing against other people is an even stronger stimulus.

Social facilitation theory (defined and discussed in chapter 6) plays a large role in explaining this phenomenon. At its core, the theory states that people become physiologically aroused when asked to perform in front of or against others. In well-learned tasks that involve simple motor patterns, people tend to perform better. If people are asked to do a more challenging task that they are less comfortable with, they tend to perform worse. This tendency has been evidenced in studies involving runners (Worringham & Messick 1983), cyclists (Triplett 1898), and weightlifters (Rhea et al. 2003).

The process is more complex than simply running in front of others. Racing well takes months, if not years, of preparation. To build toward a race entails setting long-term, intermediate, and short-term goals that motivate you to develop your skills for long periods of time. Races also provide challenges that draw on your maximum capacities and require you to process feedback in order to make tactical adjustments. Processing this feedback requires sustained concentration, blocking out the usual irrelevant details that clutter your mind. Beneath all that lies motivation, the extra spark that got you training in the first place. The desire to run fast, test your limits, and surpass competitors offers an intangible drive that can override the effects (or, perhaps more accurately, the interpretation) of fatigue.

These benefits extend to all competitors. They're also the antecedents for flow. In those instances where flow presents itself, the opportunity to achieve even greater feats (such as Mackey's tremendous run in Stockholm) materializes. Even if your skill level surpasses the challenge at hand, important competitions provide enough motivation for you to achieve a flow state (Engeser & Rheinberg 2008). This effect can be especially true for runners in team sports such as cross country and track and field, where the team score often has greater value than individual success.

Although the antecedents are present, experiencing flow on the big day is not guaranteed. However, you can raise your chances. Understanding your desires, using cognitive strategies, establishing practices and routines, controlling the controllable, and building off past flow experiences make it more likely you'll feel your best when it matters most.

Effect of Motivation

Flow doesn't occur in a vacuum. It is the direct result of internal, external, and behavioral factors interacting together (Swann, Keegan, Piggot, & Crust 2012). One of the strongest internal factors is motivation. Motivation helps you set goals, increases your patience to allow for skill development, and gives you persistence to tackle difficult tasks. For this reason, some researchers have wondered whether motivation should be considered the tenth flow variable (Swann, Piggot, & Crust 2012). The stronger the motivation, the more likely you are to be resilient when setbacks occur.

For instance, Mackey was completely disheartened to miss out on the 2015 IAAF World Championships in track and field. In the lead pack at the U.S. championships for the entire race and possessing the fastest raw speed of the group, she believed her years of dedicated training were about to pay off with a top-3 finish and berth on the U.S. team. Instead she hit the track rail with her foot and stumbled, losing her momentum and precious seconds. Although she would make a late charge, the effects of the stumble disrupted her rhythm and allowed her competitors to pull away from her over the final quarter mile.

That loss stung, but Mackey persisted. She trained well before returning to Europe for a successful series of late season races. To make life better, Mackey's father, Kevin, flew out to Stockholm to watch her first Diamond League race. Standing on the line, Mackey felt physically and mentally prepared to race her best. Her motivations could be divided into these five categories, each of which offers unique motivational qualities:

1. Time-based motivation
2. Competitor-based motivation
3. Personal validation
4. Team-based motivation
5. External rewards

Leading into your next race, you might find yourself motivated by any combination of these categories. Motivation is a deeply personal drive, so it's not unusual if you find yourself more heavily motivated by one of these categories than another. For the purposes of flow, any motivation is better than none.

Time-Based Motivation

In any given race, only a select few runners will be gunning for the win. Because competition fluctuates by event, a more constant way of evaluating your performance is based on time. On a perfect day on a lightning-fast road course or track, you might seek a seasonal or lifetime best. If you have run a particular race multiple times, you might try to run faster on it than you have before. If you are early in your season and unsure of your fitness, you might make a guess based on workouts and try to achieve it.

Being motivated by time-related goals has its advantages. These goals are concrete and provide a lot of feedback. If your goal is to run 5,000 meters in 18:00, you know you need to be under 5:50 per mile (1.6 km). Seeing a mile split time of 5:45 would provide encouragement that you're performing admirably, while a time of 5:55 would indicate that you needed to pick up the pace or change your goal. The motivation to achieve these goals can grow as you get closer to succeeding. Interpreting this feedback helps make flow more achievable.

"My goal was to PR," says Mackey, who had to kick her last lap in 63 seconds to achieve it. "I felt pretty confident in my fitness."

Time-based motivation doesn't just push you through a race. Chasing a personal record (PR) can make putting in the work feel much easier, increasing your likelihood of being prepared to race your fastest and experience flow in competition.

Competitor-Based Motivation

Every race needs a champion. Whether it be the top woman, man, master, or grandmaster, everyone likes to recognize the swiftest and best-prepared runner in a race.

For Mackey, the chance to win a prestigious Diamond League race pushed her to give every last ounce as the race wore on. Even when a momentary gap opened up on the penultimate lap, she never stopped trying for the win. Instead, she began to interpret all the feedback around her to better understand when to make her last move.

"I was confident that if I was with the lead pack at the bell that I could run a competitive last 400 meters with anyone in the field because of where I was at with my fitness," Mackey says. "I don't know why I decided to swing wide on the curve; I think it was probably because of all the feedback I was getting in that moment, the stuff that becomes almost subconscious after years and years of racing—how labored the girls around me were breathing, if they were slowing slightly, if their form was starting to come undone. Those are all things that I am constantly assessing in races, especially ones where I'm not familiar with all the competitors."

However, the beauty of competition extends beyond the absolutes of winning and losing. Competing against others gives you motivation to see how you stack up against peers in your gender and age group. It lets you build friendly rivalries with people you compete against frequently. And, as seen earlier in this chapter, competing against others naturally draws out the best in people.

Personal Validation

Humans are competitive yet also fragile creatures. People crave assurance and acceptance. Even a world-class runner like Mackey, who could run a mile (1.6 km) in just over 4:20, still needs proof sometimes that she's worthy of being labeled a professional.

"I wanted to prove to myself and others that I belonged there," Mackey says of competing in her first Diamond League race. "I didn't know all the girls in the race; I just knew that everyone was good and would be hard to beat."

Validation extends beyond self-worth. Because races can bring out the best of your abilities, they provide an ideal opportunity to assess the absolute limits of your fitness. If you always run great workouts but come up short in races, proving to yourself that you can perform in the clutch is a strong motivator. If you recently had a subpar performance, erasing that memory with a good race can push you forward. As long as it's not overly ego driven, this motivation offers a pathway toward flow.

Team-Based Motivation

If you've never run on a team, attend a high school cross country meet (fall is cross country season). Watch the boys and girls in their matching uniforms, how they willfully push their bodies to the absolute maximum in an effort to help their teams place highly. Cross country has no time-outs, no chance to make a substitution, and no time to call for a redo. It's all or nothing, and it brings out skills and perseverance these kids never knew they had.

That love of team can be harder to find as you get older, but it's not impossible. USA Track and Field lists thousands of clubs on its website that are open to post-collegiate runners. Many of these clubs enter races that include team scores. Even if the clubs are just a social gathering for local runners, they offer a great way to meet athletes in your community and give you a section of runners to cheer for and compete alongside. Knowing your teammates will be watching your results with interest is another way that you can benefit your performance through social facilitation.

Although the world of professional track and field focuses almost entirely on the individual athlete, most elite runners today train in groups sponsored by apparel companies. Mackey runs with the elite Brooks Beasts in Seattle. Training with teammates and cheering them on in their own races helps her stay motivated to do her best, while competitions such as USATF Club Cross Country Nationals allow her to compete with the Beasts against other clubs from around the country.

Team Flow

The Contagion Effect

Is flow contagious? Coauthor Phil Latter first wondered this after watching his new team, the Brevard (NC) Blue Devils, respond from an abysmal start to win the 2015 North Carolina 2A Cross Country State Championship title in his first year at the helm.

The race couldn't have started any worse. Days of rain left the course pock-marked and muddy. When the Lady Blue Devils got off to a poor start (their presumed All-State runner, Eliza Witherspoon, was in 70th place at the half mile/0.8 km, with no one else faring much better), it looked as though they were stuck. Halfway into the 5,000-meter race, no runner was in the top 20. As she passed her coaches, tears ran down Eliza's face from the pain and frustration of things spiraling out of control. A long day looked to get much longer.

But then Phil and his assistant, Jackie Witherspoon (Eliza's mother), noticed something. Their number 4 and 5 runners were moving up—way, way up. In fact, if things kept progressing, they had a chance to be in the team title hunt if the others could turn things around. At the next vantage point, the coaches conveyed this information to the runners. They implored Eliza to find some reserve, to put the team before herself, and to believe she had the ability to turn the race around and make something magical happen.

What happened over the next mile (1.6 km) seemed scripted out of a movie. Eliza passed 15 girls and ended up All-State. Her teammate Ava finished just a few steps behind. Two freshmen ran the race of their lives to finish in the top 35. As each runner heard news of the team's success during the race, they found a way to increase their own pace. They engaged the race more with each stride. In the end, Brevard won the state title by a mere 2 points.

This scenario is the essence of group flow, a phenomenon whereby members of a team get in sync with each other and focus collectively on the same task in the same way. In this scenario teammates respond to each other instinctively and effortlessly.

Group flow seems to be the result of two things: performance feedback and environmental input, specifically from a coach or trusted advisor (Bakker et al. 2011). In the previously mentioned instance, seeing that they were moving forward through the field of racers and hearing their coaches say they had a chance to win a state title spurred the Brevard girls into a higher state of attention and performance. This provides more evidence for the importance of clear and unambiguous feedback. At no point did the coaches express doubt or disappointment in the early race outcomes. Instead, they provided clear strategies to remedy the situation and told the team how it was affecting their performance. The girls internalized that feedback and executed the race plan flawlessly. In the end, only 1:02 would separate the five scoring runners, by far the lowest margin of any contender that day. The contagious nature of flow had more than a little to do with it.

External Rewards

Sometimes doing well in a race carries with it a tangible prize. It could be a trophy, a medal, or sometimes even cash. Before her race in Stockholm, Mackey shared a meal with U.S. runner Brenda Martinez, a medalist at the 2013 World Championships in track and field. Martinez talked about how she had used her prize money to fund a camp for young girls. The thought of turning that money around for a greater benefit intrigued Mackey.

"I remember thinking, '$10,000 is a lot of money,'" Mackey says, "'and if I win I could start a girls' camp of my own in Seattle.'" With the vision of creating a workshop focusing on self-esteem, confidence, nutrition, and training in her adopted hometown of Seattle, Mackey fought all the way to the line.

In some instances, extrinsic motivation such as running for prizes, money, or even just the win can make experiencing flow more difficult. It is especially true for runners who have external demands from sponsors or who consider anything less than victory to be a failure. At the same time, those demands can help create a laser-like focus that makes engaging the task more likely. At the end of the day, according to leading sport psychologist Cindra Kamphoff, getting out there is what matters the most.

"We know that intrinsic motivation is really powerful," she says. "You love the joy, you love the satisfaction—that type of motivation is incredibly powerful. Extrinsic motivation is where you are doing it for some type of outcome. Either one of those, it's still motivation. As long as you're using it in a way that's beneficial to you, it's not controlling you and you're not making decisions based on competing against someone else, then it can be beneficial" (Kamphoff 2015).

Controlling the Controllable

With strong motivation driving your actions, the next step to achieving flow is to control variables that have been shown to increase the likelihood of flow and good performance. Much like motivation, these variables are individualized to a degree. However, in studies done on elite athletes, certain elements came up repeatedly (Jackson 1992; Jackson 1995; Sugiyama & Inomata 2005; Chavez 2008). They provide an excellent starting point for taking control of your actions related to finding flow.

Preparation

As discussed in chapter 5, being optimally prepared is one of the best ways to produce flow experiences. This preparation includes both the physical training leading up to your race and the psychological carryover of feeling strong and in control of your own destiny. Well-prepared athletes are more likely to have a realistic and positive outlook on their skill levels. They are also likely to have concrete and measurable goals, can take on bigger challenges, and are more adept at interpreting the feedback they are receiving from their own bodies and the environment around them.

You can still achieve flow in situations where you're less physically prepared as long as you adapt your goals and keep your ego from pushing you to an unrealistic pace. This task is harder than it sounds, because people often are loathe to let their competition run away from them early on. Doing so is prudent; an aggressive early pace, particularly when you're undertrained or coming off a tiring week, usually leads to blowing up. Nothing strikes a bigger blow to your self-confidence than feeling like you have sandbags on your back for the last half of a race (to say nothing of dropping out).

The best part about preparation is that it is under your control. Injuries and illnesses may lead to setbacks, but unless they're chronic they are usually obstacles that can be quickly hurdled. Skipping runs, staying up late every night, and eating fast food are all under your control. If running is a priority in your life and you want to experience flow in this sport, choose to follow a well-designed trained plan and put in the necessary miles.

Optimal Arousal

Getting a case of the butterflies is a common occurrence before races (and, to a lesser extent, before tough workouts). Nervousness results from caring about the outcome of an event and the uncertainty that surrounds it. While some runners seem preternaturally calm in those situations, all too often they let nervousness overwhelm their systems with a hearty shot of adrenaline before an event even begins.

Adrenaline is a fickle drug. The same fight-or-flight hormone that lets you perform heroic acts, such as lifting a car off an accident victim, also paralyzes you if too much floods your system at the wrong time. According to the Society for Endocrinology, adrenaline increases your heart rate and blood pressure, dilates your pupils, and increases blood flow to large muscle groups needed for sudden action (Society for Endocrinology 2015). For that reason, finding an optimal level of arousal is critical in performing your best (figure 7.1).

Nerves may seem uncontrollable, but plenty of methods have been shown to be effective in getting the benefits of adrenaline without the side effects of paralyzing nerves. Chief among these methods is mindfulness, which is

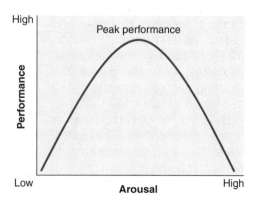

Figure 7.1 To achieve peak performance, arousal should be neither too high nor too low.

more closely examined later in this chapter. Nervousness stems from dwelling on future outcomes. Conversely, when you focus exclusively on the present, you can greatly reduce nervousness.

Another technique comes from cognitive behavioral therapy and is known as thought stopping and thought shifting. It involves stopping or shifting negative or nervousness-inducing thoughts as they pop up and willfully focusing on something else. If the thought of being crowded on the starting line gives you goose bumps, practice shifting your thoughts to something pleasant and relaxing. Although this technique works for many, one risk associated with it is that it may make you overly conscious of your fears and worries.

As you saw in chapter 6, music can also affect your mood and state of readiness. If you get in a good headspace through music, consider bringing headphones for your warm-up. Listening to familiar, motivating music before a big race may help you overcome nerves and get you physiologically primed.

Dick Beardsley

2:08 U.S. marathon runner, protagonist in famous "Duel in the Sun" 1982 Boston Marathon

Flow moment: 1981 Grandma's Marathon (and the workout 11 days before)

Dick Beardsley, an aspiring professional runner for New Balance, couldn't wait to call his coach late one spring evening in 1981. With coach Jock Semple based in Boston and he in rural Minnesota, the telephone would have to be the carrier of this news: Beardsley had just run the best workout of his life, a 23-miler filled with surges, floats, and a fast 4:45 closing mile. The amazing part was how effortless it had felt on a course filled with rolling hills. Had he tacked on another 3 miles, he would have run a 2:12 marathon—a world-class time. In Semple's opinion only one problem existed, and it was a rather large one. Beardsley's goal race, Grandma's Marathon in Duluth, was 11 days out.

Scott Mason Photography

"I'm telling you, if he could have put his hands through the phone and grabbed my neck he would have," Beardsley says today with a chuckle. "He started screaming at me. I think he thought I wasted it on that run."

Beardsley felt otherwise. The run had been encouraging, the action effortless. With a week and a half to rest, he felt he could recover. He also tried to stay true to his humble Midwestern roots. "I was confident in my effort," he says. "I had that inner confidence. Other people tried to put me on a pedestal, but I never did, certainly not to myself. I mean it's the marathon. One minute you can be feeling great, the next you're standing on the side of the road."

At Grandma's Marathon, Beardsley's confidence and training would be tested by Garry Bjorklund. The prodigiously talented Minnesota native had run 4:05 for the mile as a high schooler and gone on to represent the United States at the 1976 Olympics at 10,000 meters. The defending champion, it was considered by many to be Bjorklund's race to lose.

That was okay with Beardsley. He lived for competition and saw fast times as irrelevant. Bjorklund and Beardsley would run step for step with each other until mile 21. During those miles Beardsley would assess his position through internal feedback, such as how his legs and breathing felt. As the race wore down into the final miles, Beardsley would also analyze his competitors.

"Without absolutely staring at them, I'd take a glance at how their stride was, how their arm carriage was," he says. "I'd keep my ears open, too. If I heard someone's feet start slapping on the pavement, I'd think maybe they're getting fatigued, getting a little tired, and now's the time to maybe throw in a surge."

Beardsley's surge at Grandma's came at mile 21. When he went to check his split at mile 22, he saw for the first time that his wristwatch was dead. Without clocks at the mile marks and no pace vehicle barking out times, Beardsley ran hard off the hope of winning and his own pride. Crossing the line in 2:09:36, he was stunned; he had no idea he was running that fast. The whole race had felt so effortless, he had no idea he was running one of the fastest times in U.S. history.

"Even though I had a bit of a side stitch (the last few miles), it was one of those days where it just felt effortless," he says. "I look back and it would have been nice if they happened more, but in a way I'm glad they didn't because it made known I could run that kind of pace on days where I felt bad, like the first few miles in Boston in 1982 (where he ran 2:08). But boy those days where things were flowing . . . I don't know what caused it on that particular run or that particular day, but it was an incredible feeling to have."

Although Beardsley would become famous the next year for waging an epic battle with Alberto Salazar at the Boston Marathon in the aptly named "Duel in the Sun"—a race so captivating it would spawn a book and a documentary—Grandma's remains his favorite flow race. Perhaps it's because it captured that element he so often found in training runs but rarely in races.

"A lot of times it occurred on my weekly long runs, after I got out there," he says. "Honest to goodness, and there were plenty of times where I wish I could bottle this up, but there were times it felt so effortless. It felt like, if say I was doing a 24-miler at a fast pace, I could have kept going at that for another 24 miles. I always thought I should just try that sometime, just see how far I could keep going in that state."

Positive Mindset

Katie Mackey had a big decision to make in Stockholm. Being allowed to line up against some of the world's greatest runners could easily produce fear and anxiety. Many of those runners had personal bests that far exceeded hers. The risk of losing—and losing big—was a very real possibility. A poor showing not only risked personal embarrassment in a meet being broadcast around the globe, it also could keep her from being invited back to future Diamond League events.

Mackey turned this perspective on its head. She saw Stockholm as a tremendous opportunity. She would be running against the very best, and in doing so the very best would be drawn out of her. She visualized ways she could put herself in contention to race well. She focused on the challenges each moment presented to her. In the end, she came away with a victory.

Runners may not be able to control the weather, the competition, or how much sleep they got the night before the race, but they can control how they interpret events around them. Having a positive mindset that is rooted in a healthy view of reality offers you the best chance to experience flow. You are a self-fulfilling prophecy; believing you will do your best goes a long way in making that dream a reality.

Developing a Plan for Success

When you meet Mackey in person, the first thing that stands out is the strength of her personality. She is bubbly, witty, and gregarious; she wants to know you and everything that is special about you. In short, she is a well-adjusted person living out her dream as a professional runner. She has a strong support team and amiable teammates. For the last year, she has also seen a sport psychologist.

Mackey attaches no shame or stigma to working with a professional who prods deep into her mind. Mackey's psychologist has helped her develop skills that make running and the stresses around it easier to manage. What's more, she now has concrete tools she can use when the situation calls for them.

The situation inevitably will call for them. No matter how well you control the controllable, once race day arrives your emotions and concerns are likely to increase. Mackey and other elite athletes use the following strategies to help manage the difficult challenges that crop up before and during a race. All have been proven effective at helping manage the physical and emotional challenges that wait.

Following a Routine

Bryan Clay earned the title "World's Greatest Athlete" by winning the 2008 Beijing Olympic decathlon. The grueling 10-event, 2-day competition entails sprinting, hurdling, jumping, vaulting, throwing, and distance running. For all the abrupt starts and stops, Clay often found himself experiencing flow.

"I am always striving for it, learning to set the stage for it," he says. "Excellent athletes do. For me it was about the amount of repetition you do, [and] the process you put your body through.

"But it is also about the setup," he continues. "I always had a routine I would go through. Some call it superstition, but it triggers something in your mind and body to what is next. This is why you don't see young athletes experiencing flow as much as elite athletes, because you have to find your routine."

If serious athletes of all sports have one thing in common, it's what Clay points out. Each has a distinct routine that they follow to the letter before every important workout or race. Runners generally perform light running, drills, active stretches, and strides. A beginning runner might take 15 minutes to do their routine; an Olympic-caliber athlete may be out there three times as long. Some take it a step further, eating the same breakfast or wearing the same socks every time.

"The routines were crazy," Clay says. "Every detail was the same. The things I would tell myself in my head were the same. So my mind, body, and spirit know, 'Okay, here we go.' It's like Pavlov's dog. It's conditioning. Those routines teach your body something."

If you have your own warm-up routine, it likely started because a coach or fellow runner implored you to prepare your body physically before strenuous running. The difference between warming up and not warming up in a race can actually account for several percentage points in performance (Hajoglou et al. 2005), which is no small feat when you consider the difference between running 17:30 and 18:01 for 5,000 meters.

Over time you may have noticed that the routine presents a certain amount of comfort and consistency in an uncertain, stressful environment. You have no control over what your competitors are going to do in a race, but you absolutely can start jogging 45 minutes before the start of the event, do your familiar drills, put on your racing singlet, and change your shoes. These actions become a metaphorical talisman you carry into the race, readying you for whatever struggles you might encounter. They also allow you to relax, which is a key to good performance.

"Sticking to the same warm-up routine for big races and workouts helps me to turn my brain off and just go with the flow," Mackey says.

If your routine gets thrown out of whack because of travel, weather, or any other circumstance beyond your control, try not to fret. Anxiety kills flow and is counterproductive to performing well. Instead, focus on what you can control. Try to slip into the closest facsimile of your routine as possible given your circumstances. Even a shortened warm-up is better than no warm-up at all, and oftentimes the positive effects of race-time adrenaline can outweigh any time lost immediately before the race.

Positive Self-Talk

People are thinking creatures, and these thoughts have a voice. This internal narrator can tell you positive, uplifting things or drag you down into the mire. The Mayo Clinic defines self-talk as the "endless stream of unspoken thoughts that run through your head" (Mayo Clinic 2014). It is a voice that defines how you view the world.

Positive self-talk is just as it sounds; it is a way to tune the voice in your head toward positive outcomes. The more positive thoughts you have on a daily basis, the more likely you are to have an optimistic outlook on life. This positive disposition can help you better manage stressful solutions, such as preparing to race. If you are a mostly negative thinker, learning to engage in positive self-talk will take time and effort. After all, you're rewiring your brain to think in a new way, giving up old, engrained habits in the process.

One of the keys to positive self-talk is recognizing areas where you're frequently negative. If you show up to speed workouts thinking "I hate the track," you're less likely to have a successful run than if you arrive thinking "This isn't my forte, but I'll get faster by doing these workouts."

Negative self-talk isn't just doom and gloom, it's misappropriating or mis-interpreting events. When you **catastrophize**, one event not going according to plan ruins the entire day. When you **negatively filter** thoughts, you cancel out positive thoughts or praise and instead focus on criticism or mistakes. If you **polarize thoughts,** anything less than a perfect race or workout is seen as a failure (Mayo Clinic 2014). Understanding these errors in thinking (as cognitive behavioral therapy would term them) and working to replace them with more optimistic thought patterns can turn anxiety-inducing situations into moments of potential growth.

Staying Present and Being Solution Oriented

If you've read this book from cover to cover, you've noticed that mindfulness finds a way to slip into almost every chapter. That is because staying in the present moment (as opposed to ruminating on past mistakes or future out-comes) offers a wealth of benefits and helps you take control of your actions.

Being in the moment doesn't mean throwing caution to the wind. It means engaging it fully, giving it all the attention you can. When you treat the present moment as the only moment, you can devote more energy to solving problems as they occur. And in the throes of a challenging workout or competition, you can bet there will be speed bumps.

"Races hardly ever go according to plan, so being confident that I can run my best race that day in 20 different ways helps me remain calm when something isn't ideal," Mackey says. "Not getting emotional but just looking for a solu-tion helps me stay present and not miss anything or make a dumb mistake."

Mackey's "dumb mistake" wasn't necessarily hitting the curb and stum-bling during the 5,000 meters at the 2015 U.S. Championships; rather, it was making a rash, emotional decision to surge to the front of the pack as soon as she caught back up. Reeling in the leaders in a short period of time was no easy feat; Mackey could have used a moment of respite after the trip put her 10 meters behind the pack. Instead she sprinted past the leaders, only to be caught again 100 meters later. By the time the race winner was going to be decided, Mackey was struggling to finish in sixth place.

That mistake reaffirmed what her sport psychologist preached. Since then Mackey has tried to remove emotions from the equation. Part of mindfulness is taking in all that is around you in a nonjudgmental stance; you simply see things for what they are. When Mackey interpreted her stumble as a lost chance at making the U.S. team and a waste of all her years of effort, she responded emotionally. In retrospect, she may have done better if she had acknowledged the stumble, regrouped, and focused on calmly catching the lead pack, conserving as much energy as possible for a later kick.

Cheryl Treworgy/Prettysporty.com

Authors in Flow

Philip's Greatest Race

Stick with Purple! That was the mantra I recited over and over again on a 200-meter indoor track in Chapel Hill, North Carolina, in the winter of 2003. I was racing the 3,000 meters against a field loaded with collegiate talent from Atlantic Coast Conference (ACC) schools like the University of North Carolina (UNC) and North Carolina State. I ran at a smaller state school, UNC Asheville (UNCA); I doubt most of the competitors had even heard of me, especially since I only made the fast heat due to a late scratch. Now that I was competing with the best, I was going to make it worth my while. I was going to stick with Purple.

"Purple" was Jeff Fairman from High Point University. The talented Canadian had placed third at our conference cross country meet a few months earlier. I figured I'd be right in the mix with him for that spot, but some poor early race decisions combined with side stitches left me several minutes and 30 spots behind. It was the worst race of my life.

(continued)

Philip's Greatest Race *(continued)*

Now I had a chance to make amends. A winter of high mileage and long workouts had put me in the best shape of my life. Indoor track suited my temperament, offering lots of feedback every lap. The competition was solid, but it was not out of my reach. I had a goal time of 8:40 to 8:45 and wanted to represent UNCA to the best of my ability. And then there was Purple and all the validation running with him would bring.

From the gun, I felt good. The race was fast, much faster than I had ever run 3,000 meters before. For five laps I hung in there. I even contemplated taking the lead. But on the sixth lap I felt the pace in my legs. I looked around and saw runners who I knew would also slow down. I could settle in with them. But then my UNCA teammate, Carmin, stepped out into lane 6 and gave me the bit of feedback I needed: "Stick with them, man."

It seemed wise beyond all reason, so I did. Tucked in behind Purple and the lead pack, I passed the mile in 4:28—my high school PR. This time I still had almost another full mile waiting. That was okay, because the race seemed effortless. Rather, I was so excited to see how fast I could run that fatigue didn't distract me. I just looked at Purple's back, ran past the clock every 200 meters with a feeling of delighted shock, and clicked off the laps like it was an everyday run.

With three laps remaining I had this brilliant insight: if I didn't fall over, something amazing was going to happen. Clearly my prefrontal cortex was on low blood supply. No matter. By now the top two runners had surged away, but I was still with Purple and Devin Swann, a runner at NC State. Hearing the bell ring shot a last burst of adrenaline through my system. I swung wide and made a bid to move into third. Almost immediately, they surged away from me.

As soon as I crossed the line, I looked for my coach. "What did I run?" I asked. He held up the watch. *8:32.62.* What I said next isn't fit to print, but needless to say it was an outpouring of a thousand different emotions. In fact, I doubt many fans ever saw a happier fifth-place finisher before or after. But what could I say? I'd run a 24-second PR, set a school record, shattered my expectations, and run with Purple. For the first time ever I felt like a legitimate college runner. Not a star, mind you, but a solid athlete. My definition of what was possible changed. I tried telling all of this to Carmin. He just looked at me and smiled. "That's flow," he said.

It was the first time I'd heard that phrase (although I was familiar with "the zone" from basketball), but it created in me a deep-seated interest in how the body's physiological and psychological systems could work in such perfect harmony. I'm lucky that as a featured speaker at several running camps I get to relive my flow experience each year. It's been well over a decade, but if I'm completely honest with myself, that's one of the happiest moments of my life, right up there with my wedding day and the births of my two children. It took my running to a higher level; I set four school records and won a coveted conference championship later that year (defeating Purple for the first time in the process). I also found a way to combine my two passions, running and writing. That moment in Chapel Hill sprouted an interest that one day grew into this book.

Attributional Retraining

According to attribution theory, "people look for causes to explain outcomes and events in their environment, especially ones that are unexpected, important or negative" (Kallenbach & Zafft 2004, p. 1). All too often, people attribute outcomes based on a preconceived notion about the self. For example, imagine you score a 75 percent on a test. If the coursework was challenging, you might assume you're not intelligent enough to score much better than a C. **Attributional retraining** turns this idea on its head by helping you realize the test score may not have come from a lack of intelligence but rather a lack of preparation. With better study habits, your score is likely to improve.

Applied to running, you might assume you run a particular time because you're not fast enough or not talented enough. Like everyone else, you have a genetic ceiling on what you can achieve, but rare is the time where you're doing everything in your power to improve. Smarter training, better recovery, superior nutrition, and better equipment can all contribute to lowering your fastest times.

Attributional retraining can also help you see errors in how you approach a race. For example, say you enter a 5K race. Because several competitors in the race are faster over shorter distances, you assume they're faster than you over 5K as well. If they beat you in a sprint finish, you may think nothing could have been done. On the contrary, putting a surge into the middle of the race or starting your finishing kick from farther out may have allowed you to negate much of their speed and surpass those competitors.

If some of this sounds similar to the internal and external loci of control discussed earlier, it's because they are related. Attributional retraining helps you see how much control you really do exert over the many outcomes in your life, then takes it a step further by helping you recognize and use your strengths to their greatest advantage.

Each of the techniques in this section offers you a different way to regain control of your emotions and stay engaged with the task at hand. Staying focused for a long period of time is the hallmark of flow. As you move forward, it's time to look at the ways things grab your attention and how you can stay focused on races you care about for the full duration.

Sustaining Focus in Competition

If you could use only one word to describe the feeling of flow, "absorption" would be apt. Therefore, total immersion in what you're doing is the only way to court flow. That means you have to put all other distractions aside through either conscious or subconscious means. As elite sports researcher Edward Chavez (2008) notes, "In order to achieve the flow state, it is essential that the athlete eliminate any extraneous thoughts, thereby allowing him or her to be fully absorbed in the performance, thereby allowing the performance to feel effortless or automatic" (p.75).

Saying you'll give a race your full attention and doing it are two different things. All too often, especially when situations begin to sour, it can be easy to turn your attention away from the race and direct it toward fears, frustrations, and doubts. Other times you may accidentally disengage from a race or hard workout. In so doing, you're likely to slow down as your mind drifts and your body attempts to bring your labored breathing and high heart rate back under control.

Your attention span can be expanded. So can the ease with which you maintain attention. Mastering this skill can take your performance to a higher level and open the door for you to routinely experience flow.

Focusing on the Right Things

Every race environment is different. Track races may take you through a crowd 25 times during a race; rural road races and remote trail races may have no spectators at all. Each environment presents its own unique characteristics, each of which must be factored in when making a plan for an upcoming race. If you're in a large city marathon, should you focus on your place in the race, a friendly rival, or your watch? Should you monitor your heart rate or breathing rate on a hilly trail race? Should you listen for a coach's advice during a race or feed off the roar of the crowd?

Those answers are all individual, but they come out of the motivational framework described in this book. If time is a major motivator and you're running a race on a fast, flat course, it makes more sense to pace yourself as evenly as possible, regardless of what other competitors are doing. If you thrive on racing others and have a good internal ability to judge your effort, you may not even want to wear a watch. If being in a beautiful countryside or historical city inspires you more than the hubbub around you, focus on those mountains or ancient buildings. If the environment is just a conduit in which you race your rivals, then focus on those select competitors and save the sightseeing for after the awards ceremony.

This was the case for Mackey. After enjoying the beautiful architecture and environment of Sweden up until the starting gun, Mackey locked in fully on the people beside her on the track. "I felt laser focused," she says. "The race went by super quickly. If something wasn't going according to plan, I just kept thinking about how I could solve it and get back into position. I was trying to stay attached to the leaders no matter what and nothing else mattered at the time."

Your internal processes play a large role in what you focus on. Perhaps the biggest distractor of all is fatigue. It may seem like an absolute, but as you saw in chapter 5, all physiological sensations are controlled first and foremost by the brain. Your legs may feel dead tired, but that's because your brain is interpreting signals from your legs in that manner. If the race is particularly important and you're fully engaged in the moment, you very well may be able to override that fatigue and maintain your pace. Ultimately, if the exertion poses any risk of damage to your brain, you'll slow down. However, you can increase this threshold by occasionally challenging your perceived limits through workouts and other races.

Effortless Attention

A counterintuitive but no less intriguing view of attention and sustained attention is Dietrich's temporal hypofrontality theory (THT), which was introduced in chapter 4. To briefly recap, sustained movements such as running require a large amount of energy from your brain in order to coordinate. Dietrich gives the example of how a simple robot can beat humans at chess in eight and a half moves, but even with the lightning-fast microprocessors now available people still can't make a robot move with lifelike actions (Dietrich & Stoll 2010). Because it takes so much energy, the brain starts reallocating where available fuel goes. Parts of the brain that are less critical to sustaining movement are downregulated. When the prefrontal cortex is downregulated, you lose your ability to worry about the future or ruminate on the past. All energy is directed on the present task. When this occurs, action and awareness merge and you're more likely to experience flow.

Effortless attention also makes tasks enjoyable. This enjoyment applies to freely chosen tasks such as running and obligatory tasks such as studying. It is quite possible to find yourself in the middle of a marathon, running at close to your maximum capacity, and be content in the process. You're unlikely to feel true happiness—after all, the part of your brain that processes emotions is currently having its blood and calorie supply shunted—but running is now an almost effortless task, done on autopilot by the implicit memory as the world whirs around you.

The most interesting fact about effortless attention is that while it may be produced by downregulation of the brain, the effect creates *more* attention where it's needed most. The more things can be handled by the implicit memory, the more they seem automatic, the more room there is for you to focus on responding in the moment to any little cues that call your attention. If you were responsible for moving every limb while thinking about the past and worrying about the future, you'd be unable to detect a subtle shift in pace or a competitor stalking away from the field. But with these processes automated, your whole being can be engaged in racing.

You can court effortless attention in two ways. One is to practice meditation or mindfulness. Staying focused on the present helps limit negative internal noise. If you can take each mile, minute, or stride for what it's worth, focusing on the task to the exclusion of all else, then your engagement will be complete and flow will be more likely. The other approach is indirect. In this case you simply do a task to the best of your ability and trust that in time the attention will become effortless. When it comes to cultivating sustained attention, it seems both the chicken and the egg arrived at the same time.

Regaining a Lost Flow State

Getting into a flow state is highly desirable when competing. But what about when you get knocked out of it? Both 1,500-meter specialist Leo Manzano and Katie Mackey have experienced flow on some of the biggest stages imaginable. Both have also had those flow experiences come screeching to an abrupt halt when an unexpected blip occurred. For Manzano, it was a sudden injection of pace with 400 meters to go that left him questioning his self-worth and chances at finishing well. For Mackey, it was stumbling at the 2015 U.S. Championships. Manzano regrouped and won a silver medal; Mackey responded emotionally and faded to sixth.

Being in the middle of a flow experience and suddenly losing it jars your mind and body. It's as if everything you thought you knew evaporated. In a race you could get tripped, turn the wrong direction, realize you went out way too hard, or be overcome by heat or dehydration. A coach or teammate could yell something, your watch could give you incongruous feedback, or a pebble could get in your shoe. Whatever the case may be, losing flow can cost you more than just a few moments of enjoyment; it can cause you to lose the levelheadedness that brought you the flow experience in the first place. But can flow ever be fully regained in a race after it has been lost?

Chavez (2008) explored this idea and found in his study that 81 percent of college athletes believed flow could be restored. Positive thinking was seen as the best way to achieve this turnaround. It involved having both a positive outlook on the situation and using positive self-talk to help the mind reengage the task at hand. Other prominent themes for restoring flow included **task orientation** (the ability to focus on the task you're performing), relaxing, and clearing the mind.

Taken together, these traits show why being solution-oriented can help restore order and help you regain flow. If everything suddenly blows up on you, it behooves you to work through possible solutions to the problem and then reengage the race as quickly as possible. Ruminating on what went wrong or catastrophizing the incident is a surefire way to keep flow at a distance.

When flow occurs in a competitive environment, it provides a large dose of encouragement and motivation. Nothing makes you want to train hard and compete like experiencing a peak moment. In extreme cases, it can provide a highlight of your life.

What about those times flow doesn't occur when you need it most? Chapter 8 faces this question head on, looking at why flow is so fleeting and helping you learn how to recover from those times when everything crumbles around you.

Exercises

The following exercises can help you find flow on race day:

Use a training log or computer software to assess your fitness before setting a final goal. Setting a goal is paramount to having a flow experience during a race. However, an unrealistic goal will send loads of negative feedback to you early in a race, leaving you disappointed and distracted. To remedy this, assess your training log honestly. If you've been doing workouts like 5 × mile at a 10K pace in 6:00, don't go out at 5:40 in your race. The effort will be too high, the pace will start to slow quickly, and you'll lose motivation as you begin to struggle. If you're running an off distance (e.g., 15K) or a new event, use an online race calculator like the one at McMillanRacing.com to help assess your fitness over a range of distances.

Practice mindfulness during workouts. No environment better simulates a race than a hard workout. Whether it's a sustained tempo run, short intervals, or a long run, workouts push the body to new levels while challenging the mind, which makes them a wonderful place to experiment. The next time you hit the track or roads for a tough workout, practice the key tenets of mindfulness. If you're running mile repeats, monitor your pace and effort with each stride, taking in the landscape and what's around you in a nonjudgmental way. Steer your mind away from thoughts of how many intervals you have left. If you feel the exertion creeping up, focus on that for a moment, acknowledge that the effort is increasing, and then refocus on the act of running. Fatigue that was once overwhelming may seem more manageable now.

Talk to yourself nicely. The only person you're guaranteed to be around all day and night is you. That can lead to some harsh words and poor feelings. Make a note of negative thoughts you form in your mind but don't say out loud. Then try and turn them into positive thoughts. If monitoring your thoughts all day is wearisome, try it at critical moments, such as when you're running or in a meeting at work. The better you can get at steering negative thought patterns to positive ones, the happier and more satisfied you are likely to be.

Establish a consistent warm-up routine. From regional runners to Olympians, nearly all elite runners have a routine they follow to the letter leading up to a race or challenging workout. For some it begins with a ritual, such as eating pancakes for breakfast or wearing a pair of lucky socks. Others only begin their process when the event is imminent. In either case, figure out what warms your muscles up while putting your mind at ease. Most runners do some combination of light jogging, dynamic stretching, form drills, and strides. Others may build in a pit stop, a music playlist, or a uniform and shoe change before heading to the starting line. As you grow accustomed to your routine, notice how it settles your nerves and keeps you occupied during the tense moments before the gun goes off.

(continued)

Exercises *(continued)*

Practice problem solving. No one likes to be caught unaware. It could be a change in pace, a sudden storm, or a surprise competitor you weren't counting on. Problems only impair you when you are not prepared. Before your next race, work through various scenarios that could play out, and think about how you'll react. What if you go out too fast? Too slow? What if the course is hillier than you read online? What if your rival stalks behind you for the first three quarters of the race? What if she takes off on you from the gun? Practice that problem solving by tinkering with workouts, such as running a negative split (finishing faster than you started), or performing fartlek workouts during which you surge and recover at random. People all have wonderful imaginations. Put yours to use before race day.

Key Points

- Motivation is a strong internal factor that contributes to flow.
- Many runners experience five types of motivation: time-based, competitor-based, personal validation, team-based, and external rewards.
- Control the controllable factors. Preparation, a realistic assessment of your skill level, and an ability to adeptly respond to feedback are controllable variables that can improve the likelihood of experiencing flow.
- Using techniques to manage your nerves, such as meditation or positive self-talk, can help you find your optimal level of arousal.
- A positive mindset can improve your chances for flow.
- Develop a plan for success. Follow a routine, use positive self-talk, stay focused on the present, be solution oriented, and practice attributional re-training if necessary.
- Arne Deitrich's theory of transient hypofrontality proposes a downregulation of the prefrontal cortex during prolonged physical exertion. This downregu-lation results in an interesting paradox called *effortless attention*. While you remain focused and vigilant on your performance feedback and the ever-changing context of your running experience, your ability to stay focused feels effortless. This effortless attention helps you perform at your best.
- Flow can be restored after a sudden interruption. Thinking positively and maintaining a task orientation will make it more likely.

CHAPTER 8
Flow's Limitations

Todd Williams knew the 1996 Atlanta Olympic Games were going to be his crowning achievement. For the last year, the 26-year-old had lived, breathed, eaten, and slept nothing but the 10,000 meters. The Games would be close to his adopted home of Knoxville, Tennessee. He would be America's best hope for a medal in the long distance events. If a backup plan existed, some lower level of achievement that could be deemed a success, Williams hadn't thought of it yet.

To achieve this goal, Williams mapped his life out to the minute. He trained 13 times per week, plus weight room sessions. He did 500 crunches and 500 pushups a day, every day of the week. He counted calories with the same level of precision he counted miles. Running was the be-all, end-all. It was his life, his passion, his obsession.

Four years earlier, Williams qualified for the Barcelona Olympic Games as a mostly unheralded graduate from the University of Tennessee. Those Barcelona Games were owned by the Dream Team, a legendary American basketball squad made up of NBA stars such as Michael Jordan, Larry Bird, and Magic Johnson. Their outsized talent and personalities captivated the world. Williams was there for the gold medal game, just as he was for the gold medal tennis match featuring all-time great Pete Sampras. Soaking in the experience and inspired by the brilliance he was witnessing, Williams surprised the pundits by making Olympic finals in the 10,000 meters and placing 10th. "It felt like my own gold medal," Williams says.

That perspective evaporated in 1995. Williams ran his greatest race ever that year, a North American record of 42:22 for the 15K at Jacksonville's Gate River Run. It built upon a stellar 1:00:11 half marathon from 1993. That mark was then the second fastest ever by a U.S. athlete. On the track he was just as deadly, running 27:31 for 10,000 meters and 8:14 for 2 miles (3.2 km). With those performances came greater expectations.

"It was different before the Internet and social media, but everything in the running world, like *Track and Field News,* was saying, 'Medal, medal, medal,'" Williams says. "It was like everyone was saying, 'Todd's going to win a gold medal. And if Todd doesn't win a gold medal, it's a failure.'"

To meet those external pressures, Williams pressed. He fractured his sacrum from the volume and intensity of work. Williams estimates that of the 70,000 miles (112,654 km) he ran in his career, 50,000 (80,467) were under the pace of 6:00 per mile (1.6 km). The fracture in his lower back curtailed that mileage in the fall of 1995, but instead of stepping back, Williams cross-trained with a manic intensity. Two-hour sessions on an arm bike were surrounded by pool running sessions. He maintained his fitness and won the U.S. Olympic trials 10,000 meters in the searing Atlanta heat. But the stress of carrying a nation's expectations on his back was quickly wearing him down.

"I still loved it, because you have to love it to get out and run," Williams says, "but compared to what it was in high school, all through college, no, it wasn't the same. All the expectations on an elite-level runner are if you don't win, you're a failure. If you take that all the way up to the Olympic level . . ." Williams pauses for a second, then laughs at the absurdity of it in retrospect. "It's like, 'C'mon, I'm at the Olympic Games!'"

Wally McNamee/CORBIS/Corbis via Getty Images

Todd Williams' experience in the Atlanta Olympics shows that flow cannot be summoned on command.

That perspective was long overdue at the time. When Williams took the line in the semifinal round of the Olympic 10,000 meters, he was physically and emotionally spent. The opening lap felt like an all-out sprint. Williams did everything he could to hang on, but after 14 laps he fell off the lead pack of eight who would qualify for the finals. Dejected, he stepped off the track and recorded a DNF (Did Not Finish) in the biggest race of his life.

"I remember coming out of the stadium and smashing my hand, punching the brick wall under Atlanta Stadium, crying," Williams says. "It was a tough thing. I got on the van back to the Olympic Village, and Coach Brown, my coach at the time, told me it's going to be a tough time and then you're going to come back just like you've always come back."

Williams thought he'd done everything in his power to prepare himself for the race of his life. He knew about flow, "the zone," a place that made his

American record 15K feel like a walk in the park. Clear goals? He had those, too, and the talent to make them seem realistic. His training had gone well, as had his tune-up races. Sure, he'd had that sacral injury, but coming back so strongly in the Olympic trials made it a moot point in his mind. And then there was his passion. On this count, there could be no denying he had the right makeup, right?

However, Williams didn't have a flow experience in the Olympic Games. In fact, he had the worst race of his life. This is the inherent risk that all runners face, that they might come up wanting when they want it most. As you've already seen throughout this book, flow is a phenomenon for which you can set the stage, but it does not appear on demand. This lack of control makes flow both breathtaking and frustrating.

In the absence of flow, however, opportunity exists. Learning and growing from adversity is important in your growth as a runner and a person. Difficult times throw your passions and character into sharp relief, offering you new perspective and an opportunity to reevaluate your goals, skills, and motivation. This chapter looks at various scenarios that may have kept flow from occurring. It also looks at flow's limitations and how they can direct you in your physical and mental training. Finally, it examines how disappointing results offer the opportunity for growth. New challenges and goals always await, no matter how highly invested you've been in a particular run, race, or even sport.

No-Flow Scenarios

It has happened to every runner. It's a big race, a beautiful spring morning, or a 3-hour trail run with a great friend. The conditions are perfect. The legs feel light and springy. You anticipate that you'll have a magical run, one where you disappear into the moment and let the act of running take you to a mentally sacred place.

Then something happens. Your legs feel like sandbags, or your mind can't shut off thinking about all the work waiting for you in the office. You stare at your watch every half mile, willing the GPS to move the mileage up just a bit. This was supposed to be your shining moment, a time when you locked in and loved every footfall. But now it's blown up. It's miserable. It's anti-flow.

Even the greatest runners cannot summon flow on command; neither can the greatest sport psychologists. Sometimes flow doesn't show simply because flow doesn't show; other times, your actions and thoughts hold you back from experiencing it. The following four examples examine ways that people conspire against themselves in terms of flow.

Scenario 1: Running is my life. I've given it everything I have. I sometimes experience flow during great workouts or low-key races, but when it matters most I end up having my toughest races. Now that I've done poorly, I feel worthless. I put everything into this race, and I came up short. I'm a failure.

Many variables work together in flow experiences. One of the most important is passion. In the case of Todd Williams, it was clear he loved running. The 120-mile (193-km) weeks, the long workouts in the high humidity of Tennessee, the wonderful surge of endorphins after a successful long run or great race—Williams fed on all of it.

That passion morphed as the stakes rose from great high school runner to elite professional. The pressure intensified. His goals shifted from seeing what his potential was to meeting the expectations of others. As that happened, Williams became ever more meticulous, to the point that the sport ruled his life.

"I mean I was obsessed," Williams says. "Every single minute my mind was on how I could run the fastest I could run. When I was in my [heavy training] zone, I always tell people you really need to be a little borderline obsessed and a little nuts to be the best you can possibly be. I know some might disagree with that, but every day I had my plan. I got up and knew it was time to do my pushups and crunches, time for my morning run. I watched every calorie I ate 50 weeks out of the year, I had 13 [running] sessions each week, I lifted weights. Yeah, it was an obsession."

The dedication to put in the miles year after year comes from a fire burning deep inside you. Hopefully it is borne from loving the act of running, immersing yourself in a task with lots of feedback, and challenging yourself to reach your fullest potential. Other motivators, such as external rewards and fulfilling others' expectations, can push you just as strongly. If flow never came in your biggest race—if, in fact, you wanted this race more than anything but felt mentally drained by the start and physically wiped out well before the finish—one possible explanation may reside in whether you're fueled by harmonious passion or obsessive passion.

On the surface both types of passion share a lot in common. Broadly defined, passion is engaging an activity you like or love, that has value, and which you devote a significant amount of time and energy into pursuing (Mageau et al. 2009). These are not frivolous things that you enjoy, but ones you emotionally invest in. Why you're putting all your energy into the task can go a long way in determining whether or not you experience flow.

Harmonious passion results from an autonomous engagement with the activity, which is to say that you're doing it because you want to. Much like the autotelic concepts discussed earlier, harmonious passion stems from an inherent love of the activity. In the case of running, you're in control of your training and are doing it because you love it. Even if you have a coach or follow a training plan, you're using that guidance because you believe it will help you achieve your personal goals.

Recent research indicates harmonious passion stems from people coming to an activity on their own terms and freely engaging in it. As a result, the activity becomes a key part of their identity, fully integrated with their life at large (Mageau, Vallerand, Charest, et al. 2009). The drive to be the best and to maximize one's potential can be just as high for someone who is obsessively passionate, but because harmoniously passionate people are open and self-directed, they're able to experience outcomes (both good and bad) with less judgment attached.

On the flipside, **obsessive passion** is borne from a controlled environment where people don't think they're acting under their own direction. In the case of an obsessively passionate runner, he or she may become wrapped up in the sport because of demands from parents, coaches, fans, or sponsors (as in Williams' case). The athlete may also feel socially pressured by teammates or friends to enter the sport. The athlete's self-esteem ends up completely tied into the outcome of certain workouts and races. This scenario occurs frequently in U.S. athletics, where so-called helicopter parents push their kids into sports with the idea that it will lead to college scholarships down the road. These kids may not have initially enjoyed playing football, soccer, basketball, or running, but with their parents cajoling them on, they put an incredible amount of time and effort into maximizing their potential.

Williams felt this type of pressure at the highest level of the sport. He believed his shoe sponsor had done a lot to elevate his profile; as a result, he literally broke his back trying to justify their investment. Even once he healed from that fracture, he entered the Atlanta Games with the mindset that anything less than gold was a failure. This standard wasn't one he set for himself; rather, he internalized it from outside sources.

When you become obsessively passionate about an activity like running, you tend to view outcomes as black and white. Your personal, academic, or professional life may begin to spiral downward as all your energy is directed toward meeting external objectives. With no balance in your life, an activity like running becomes singular in importance. If a race goes well, you're ecstatic; if it goes poorly, you're despondent. Because the outcome becomes more important than the activity, flow experiences are nearly impossible to come by. Even more deleterious are the effects this mentality can bring once you're back home. Cutting courses short, using performance enhancing drugs, and eating disorders become justified means to an end, although the end usually isn't as predicted.

If an important run goes up in flames, it's worth examining the roots of your passion in the sport. What is driving you? Are you training because you love running and pushing your personal boundaries, or are you running because you feel you have to, as if you'll let others down if you come up short of perfection? Has your passion morphed in one direction or another over the years? Taking a serious look at these questions is the only way to determine whether you control your running or running controls you. That answer can go a long way in helping you understand your openness to flow experiences and, in turn, to a healthy, balanced life.

Scenario 2: *My target race just happened, and it was a disaster. I had confidence in my abilities and was sure the race was going to go well. I* *just knew I was going to have a flow moment. But then my competitors ran away from me from the start. I felt so slow, like I was running through molasses. Needless to say, I didn't have a flow experience. I couldn't stay focused after I got dropped by my main competitors. I must have done something wrong.*

Flow's fleetingness makes it tough to summon on command. In fact, actively wishing for a flow experience makes it unlikely you'll experience it. You can't focus on racing hard if all your energy is diverted toward finding flow. It must be an outgrowth of immersion in an activity; flow doesn't work in reverse.

That said, if you were fully engaged in the task at hand and had a healthy approach to the sport, the next place to look is back to the beginning—the antecedents. Setting goals, developing skills, finding challenges, and interpreting feedback are all familiar concepts. Often people misinterpret one variable or another. Other times an extraneous variable gets thrown into the mix, too, instantly scrambling the best-laid plans. Goal-oriented runners may have a hard time altering their plans when things don't go according to script, pressing on in what is likely to be a futile effort.

Being honest with yourself is a good place to start. Even if his buildup had gone perfectly and his mental outlook had been more conducive to flow, Todd Williams' goal of winning an Olympic gold medal was probably a little bit beyond his skill level. In 1995, his finest racing season, Williams only ran the 17th fastest time in the world ("only" is used with all due deference). He had proven himself a capable racer in Olympic-style races, placing 7th and 9th, respectively, at the 1993 and 1995 track and field world championships. Even in his 7th place race, however, Williams was more than 45 seconds off the gold medal—a substantial amount at the world-class level.

To make an honest assessment of your skill level, look back at how your running has gone over the past few months. Hindsight usually offers greater clarity. "My high school coach always said look at all the effort you put into that training log [before a race]," Williams says, "and when you start to get nervous about failure, you won't be nervous about failure anymore because that log is filled with hard work."

Williams' quote rings true when the accumulated work matches your expectations. Other times you may overestimate your fitness given the data you have in hand. Just because you can hold 6:00 pace for a workout of 3 x mile (1.6 km), it doesn't necessarily mean you can hold that same pace for a 5K race. Other factors such as rest, weather, and total training volume all play a role in what you're able to achieve on race day. At the same time, if you run at a pace of 6:00 per mile during workouts but assume flow will pull you to a 5:40 pace on race day, you're courting disaster by misinterpreting the power of flow. If you feel you judged your fitness correctly, analyze your competitors. If they ran away from you, you need to assess whether they're simply at a different place in terms of training and talent or if you just had an off day.

Off days happen to all runners, from beginners up to elites. Life has a funny way of intruding on your best plans. Take sleep, for instance. Family, work responsibilities, or social engagements can overrule your desire to get a good night's sleep and hinder your ability to run at your best. The restorative theory of sleep suggests that sleep deprivation reduces your body's ability to recover from a heavy training load and causes cognitive fog, making it difficult to run efficiently. It can also impair the body's ability to flush out neurotoxins. The result is a diminished capacity to function both physiologically and psychologically on a run of any duration or intensity (Gallagher 2013).

Neuroscientists and sleep researchers have found that sleep is an essential part of a healthy immune system, too. Sleep helps you stay focused and clear, consolidates memories, reenergizes your bodily organs, repairs damage to bones and muscle tissue, and creates better lines of communication between synapses in your brain (Frank 2009). Absent of sufficient sleep, you'll be unlikely to perform at your best, much less experience flow. If you have the chance, change your expectations for that day's run lest you come home deflated.

Busy schedules can also impact your nutritional needs and intake. Often busy schedules lead to shortcut eating; fast food or highly processed foods take the place of wholesome meals. This response is not without consequence. Researchers found that one bad nutrition day (defined as excess consumption of highly processed foods or a meal high in unhealthy fats and sugars) results in increased tissue inflammation, cognitive fog, and hyperglycemia (O'Keefe, Gheewala, & O'Keefe 2008). None of these factors are conducive to good running. Skimping out on hydration or drinking lots of sugary beverages instead of water will have similar effects.

If none of these factors add up, see if other antecedents may play a role. Perhaps you got into a race that had more challenging terrain than you prepared for. Maybe no one was running at your pace during the race and you felt lost without competitors. Feedback could be thrown off by misplaced mile markers or a rude spectator; your goals may have been unrealistic given the environment (including other competitors). Taking the time to thoroughly evaluate the antecedents and your lifestyle factors is the only way to find out whether your no-flow experience stemmed from something within your control.

Laughing Away Failure

When Todd Williams exited the Olympic Stadium track in 1996, he was about as dejected as a person could be. Furious and embarrassed, Williams stormed off. It could have marked the end of his competitive career. Instead, Williams came back the next year to win U.S. titles on the track and on the roads and made a successful debut in the marathon with a time of 2:11.

If you are unlucky enough to bomb your goal race after months of concerted effort, you might want to laugh. So says research by doctors Joachim

Stoeber and Dirk Janssen (2011) in the United Kingdom. In a study of 149 students, they found those who used humor, **positive reframing,** and acceptance positively coped with disappointment. Those who vented to friends and family, disengaged, self-blamed, or denied personal responsibility for the outcome fared significantly worse.

Humor offers an interesting approach to dealing with failure. For decades, research has shown that humor relieves stress. Recent research suggests that humor can help everyone, including doctors who deal with terminally ill patients and elderly adults who learn to cope more effectively (Williams 2011). Even self-deprecating humor counts. As long as you're not the butt of your own joke too often, it can help speed the healing process.

While laughing at a bad race won't make all the disappointment go away, a good laugh and a smile can definitely help.

Scenario 3: *I like routine, which is why I carefully plan a monthly schedule of long runs, tempo runs, fartleks, and other conditioning activities. This structure helps me stay on task for my performance goals. Seeing my times come down has been great; it gets me motivated. But I still rarely experience flow, if ever. Why can I make a plan and see it through my training but not flow?*

People who are highly structured and like routine have, by definition, a **type A personality.** People with type A personalities are punctual, highly competitive, and more likely to value performance orientations than mastery orientations; in other words, they care more about being good at an activity than feeling like they are masters of their craft. The more people with type A personalities read about flow, the more likely they are to set out on their runs with the intention of experiencing this phenomenon.

The downside to that approach is that it will almost always backfire. It feels counterintuitive to a person who has always thrived under a heavy dose of planning and structure. Being meticulous can be advantageous in many life arenas, but when it comes to courting flow, it's quite the opposite. It has to be an outgrowth of the activity you're passionate about, not the passion itself.

Fortunately, meticulousness does have some perks, the chief one being that people with type A personalities are likely to put in the time and effort necessary to achieve a high level of fitness, which can make flow more likely. Studying various training ideologies or finding a coach or book that can help put those methods into a coherent plan is a must when one is looking to get into great shape. This thinking plays into the hands of a highly rational and thorough type A personality.

However, you need to make the important distinction between meticulousness and neurotic tendencies. People who are neurotic overreact to criticism and negative feedback. They are anxious, indecisive, and sometimes struggle with social interaction. These traits hinder flow. Meticulousness is an eye for detail and wanting everything to be orderly. As long as those tendencies don't control your life, they won't impinge flow.

While you can alter personality traits to a small degree, when it comes to experiencing flow as a person with a type A personality, it makes more sense to play up to your strengths. When you are planning your monthly schedule, focus on performance goals so that your routine in and of itself encourages improvement. As you set specific goals and head out to meet them with each carefully planned run, you can focus on your goals and the running itself. This way of goal setting increases your likelihood of experiencing flow.

Even if you don't regularly experience flow, you can take great satisfaction in measurable progress. Improvement is satisfying; recognizing the progress you make as you set out on each run can motivate you when the joy of running itself isn't quite enough. As you focus your attention on your achievements in running longer and faster, you are likely to find a sense of peace and satisfaction. With the expectation of feeling flow diluted, you might find yourself pleasantly surprised when it does arrive.

Scenario 4: *Now that I have read about flow, I keep trying to make it happen. Every time I lace up my running shoes, I get excited . . . and every time I come home empty-handed. I try to focus all my energy on finding flow when I'm running, but it's just not working out.*

One of the greatest challenges in experiencing flow is its fleeting nature. The more you yearn to experience it, the more difficult it is to obtain. Paradoxically, the more you try to avoid the thought of flow, the more likely it is to burst into your conscious awareness. Persistent desires are difficult to set aside even when you're working hard at your craft, but with practice you can learn to focus your attention more diligently. Practices such as meditation and mindfulness strengthen this ability to direct your attention to what matters in the present moment. If you want to experience flow, keeping your mind on running when you're running is the first step.

All of that advice is easier said than done. Flow is a peaceful yet exhilarating experience. People want to experience it because it feels so good. It is also paradoxical. Most of what is enjoyable about flow is within the person, yet it is heavily influenced by external surroundings. Sometimes you seem to have mastery over your thoughts and your environment; other times they wreak havoc on you. Setting the stage for flow requires you to control the controllable. More than just the antecedents, it means decluttering the mind of anxiety, worry, and thoughts of flow itself.

The limited capacity of the brain to process information at any given moment, especially when the motor cortex is highly active in running, demands this decision: Are you going to focus on the external stimuli in the moment, or are you going to focus inward? These decisions are split-second decisions, often made at an unconscious level, that determine how you experience a given moment. If you can enter a run or race with a positive, accepting attitude and let go of the idea of controlling flow, your mind is more likely to enjoy the run, giving you the best chance to experience flow.

Flow's Realities

Pretend for a moment that Todd Williams felt great during the preliminary round of the 10,000 meters. He finished in the top eight and advanced to the final, run under the lights and shown to an audience of almost a billion people on prime-time television. Even more than that, pretend that Williams had a flow experience during that race. His legs felt light, his focus stayed tight, and every lap seemed to fly by more quickly than the last. He remained aware of the great competitors around him, legendary runners such as Haile Gebrselassie and Paul Tergat, but they didn't frighten him. He was too engaged in the race for thoughts like fear to enter (never mind that the prefrontal cortex was being shunted in an effort to deliver more blood to working muscles, limiting room for those thoughts). He experienced fatigue, but his mind interpreted this fatigue as a sign of a great effort and a fast pace, not as that of muscles wearing out.

Given this flow experience, Williams wins a gold medal, right?

Probably not.

Flow can do many things. It can heighten the enjoyment you experience during a run. It can enhance your performance by filtering out distractions, improving focus, and strengthening the mind–body connection, thus merging action and awareness. Flow can bring you back, over and over, to the trail, the track, and the treadmill. It can make a 3-hour run feel like 30 minutes. It can reignite your love for the blood, sweat, and tears it takes to be the best version of yourself. Once you've experienced flow, the pull of experiencing it again can pry you out of bed before the sun ever rises. It can do all of this and more. However, flow also can*not* do a lot of things.

Flow cannot magically inject speed, fitness, or skill into your running life; those characteristics take a hard work. Flow cannot propel you to the front of the pack; that advantage takes work *and* patience. Flow cannot improve your pacing strategy or your form; those techniques require you to study the sport and yourself. Flow is not a shortcut; it's an outgrowth and reward stemming from a long-term commitment to do something right.

Sometimes people see the miraculous and assume flow did it. Casual sports fans still talk about Michael Jordan's 1997 "flu game," where he overcame a 103-degree fever, dizziness, chills, and nausea to lead the Chicago Bulls to a last-minute victory in the NBA Finals. Jordan was confined to his hotel room for 2 days and only arrived at the arena an hour before game time. Even then, he hid in a dark room off the locker room, physically drained and frightened of failing on the world's biggest stage due to illness. Then he played the game of his life.

Jordan overcame his physical malaise through an incredible competitive drive and locking into the moment completely. Every time the whistle stopped play, Jordan slumped. Sweat cascaded off his body. His eyes were red and glazed over. He sometimes had trouble staying upright. But every time play resumed, Jordan reengaged. He had no room for doubts or self-loathing. All that mattered was the 48 minutes on the court. He scored 37 points that night.

Jordan's performance was heroic and unexpected, but it was not impossible. Jordan was already the best player in the game, if not of all time. While it's true that most players wouldn't have been able to play through those conditions, most players also didn't have that skill set (both physical and mental) to begin with. Jordan used flow to summon his greatest effort when it mattered most. He also had the most talent and had put in the most work to begin with.

Williams' work ethic was no less impressive. He was a meticulous runner who pushed himself further in the sport than anyone one would have guessed. Even then, his genetic ceiling was simply a little lower than the world's best runners, making the gold medal he dreamed of an unrealistic dream from the start.

"The setup for failure in your mind is a powerful thing," Williams says. "I look at the psychology of elite athletes, and there are plenty of people who might look back and think, 'Ahh, I didn't live up to what I could have done.' I say baloney. I look back, and I ran 70,000 miles, and the majority of those were sub 6-minute pace. A lot of hard, hard efforts to run my fastest. I'm pretty sure I did everything I could."

Flow may help you experience a wonderful race in a unique way, but its absence won't stop you from achieving your potential. Flow is a performance enhancer in that it encourages you and changes your perception of effort and fatigue. Plenty of other great races simply hurt. On those days it will be years of hard work, combined with passion and a cast-iron drive to succeed, that will lead to the best outcomes.

"I can probably count on one hand how many times I felt in the zone during a race," Williams says. "The rest of them just hurt so badly."

Accepting Flow for What It Is

If flow is such a mystery, such a riddle, such a paradox, why do we keep coming back to it? Philosophers since the times of Confucius and Socrates have pondered the meanings of pleasure, engagement, and the value of experience; they advised people to *chop wood, carry water*. Psychologists have said that the greatest moments in life are unexpected and come from engaging in tasks without expecting anything in return.

People press on with these riddles and chase after the intangible ghost of flow because it makes life feel somehow more complete. Living in the moment makes you care about the actual moment, not the moments from before or the moments yet to come. With regret and apprehension gone (at least for the moment), your body and mind are fully in sync. You can get lost in a book, a conversation, a hike, or a run. And when it's over, you can look back and say, "Wow, that's what I call living."

You will never be able to take a pill for flow or follow a 12-step program that can guarantee its arrival. However, the lack of a guarantee may be what makes flow beautiful. If you are willing to work hard, set goals, sustain your focus, and engage in challenging tasks, you might in return be gifted a transformative experience that will help you create a better version of yourself.

Flow can never be the goal; it can only be the outcome. For a runner, that comes from engaging the sport on a near-daily basis, making it a critical part of your life, and treating it with respect and dignity. Set out with the goal of being the best runner you can be, and you'll have a good chance of encountering flow along the way. That experience will be beautiful and motivating. And, if you take the time to really understand what made it happen, it opens up the opportunity to experience a more fulfilling, engaging life outside of sport.

Exercises

The following exercises can help you work through moments when flow seems hard to come by.

Keep a race journal. More detailed than a training log, a race journal allows you to examine in great detail a particular race. In a training log you record mileage, time, pace, and maybe a few notes about the course or partners you ran with. In a race journal, you'll want to dig down to the nitty gritty. Record how you felt beforehand, how the race progressed, and how you rate it on a scale of 1 to 10. Then make two columns, listing what things you could control and what things you couldn't. Be honest with yourself; this journal is for you and you alone. By taking the time to see what factors came into play, you stand the best chance to correct mistakes and set yourself up for flow.

Go naked. Everybody needs some naked time. Keep the clothes on, though; "naked" means about running without a watch. It might skew your training log for a moment, and it can feel like you're running too fast or too slow, but every now and then the watch may need to stay behind. Running without a watch (or at least with the auto lap beep turned off) allows you to run free of judgment. If you can't see your pace, you can't have a good run or a bad run; it's simply a run. By throwing away the judgment of the Almighty Watch, you free yourself to listen to internal cues for effort and external cues for enjoyment. Stop to read that interesting nature sign. Pick it up because it feels good. No, it won't get you any personal records, but it might restore some sanity to your run.

Smile. Of all the pieces of research we've stumbled across while writing this book, this fact made us the happiest: Smiling can reduce stress, release endorphins and serotonin, lower blood pressure, reduce anxiety, and even make you more attractive to members of the opposite sex. The best part is that in studies, it happened whether the subject was feeling happy or sad when asked to smile (Kraft and Pressman, 2012). These effects hold true as long as you give a legitimate Duchenne smile (where your cheeks, eyes, and mouth all engage). You'll already be smiling after the good races; now consider smiling after the bad ones, too. You may not experience flow, but you'll cope that much faster.

Key Points

- Even the greatest runners (or anyone for that matter) cannot summon flow on command.

- Running with a harmonious passion is more likely to bring flow than running with obsessive passion.

- If you want to experience flow, you must perform an honest assessment of your skill level. Finding the appropriate challenge–skills balance is not possible otherwise.

- Bad feedback (misplaced mile marker, broken pace watch) can throw off your performance and inhibit flow.

- Laughter and positive reframing can go a long way in helping you deal with challenges and disappointments.

- You are more likely to experience flow and to enjoy your running life if you practice a mastery orientation instead of a performance orientation.

- Flow helps you find your peak performance, but it will not push you to perform better than you are physically capable. Flow is not magic.

- Flow is elusive. The more you think about it, the less likely you are to experience it. It cannot be the goal of your run, but it can be a wonderful, surprising outcome.

CHAPTER 9
Flow Beyond Running

Tim Catalano was teaching his high school psychology class in Cherry Creek, Colorado, when his world altered. Up until that point the class focused on memories and perception and the neuroscience that accompanied it. To Catalano this topic presented this existential question: Are humans simply their brains, or are they somehow something bigger than a series of electrochemical reactions inside of the cranium? "I came to the conclusion of well, no, not really," he says. "If you look at who you are, you're pretty much a collection of your experiences in concert with your genetic makeup."

To build on this conclusion, he performed a simple experiment. He asked his class how many days they could remember in the last year. Without specific cueing, most students could only remember the details of 20 to 25 days (with cueing, that number jumped to 100 to 120). The events that triggered memories tended to be extreme and random: births, deaths, relationships starting and ending, memorable nights with friends.

"If that's the case, and you've taken a trip around the sun, and you can only remember 20 days without being cued, that means the rest of those days you didn't live," Catalano says. "So I always tell people the goal of your life is to create as many memories, as many 'pieces of wow,' that stick out. That's living. When you get comfortable, and you're in your routine doing the same thing over and over again and nothing really changes from one day to the next, the things you remember often happen by accident. My question is 'How can we purposely put ourselves in situations where we're creating memories?'"

Standing in front of his class, Catalano realized he wasn't living his own truth. A former elite runner at the University of Colorado, he had done a lot for the cross country program. With a master's degree in psychology, he felt comfortable bringing the subject alive to his students. At the same time, he could see his career path etched in predictable stone—20 years of teaching and coaching followed by retirement and a long walk into the sunset.

"So I moved to Honduras," Catalano says. "I thought I was going to be living on a dirt floor in a little shack in this poor Central American country. It ended up being a whole lot better than that, but I was ready for that because I knew I could take that for 2 years."

Courtesy of Tim Catalano.

Tim Catalano's (shown here in Vietnam) life goal has been to create as many memories as possible.

Or longer, as it turned out. The thrill of living in foreign lands, learning new languages, and challenging himself in ways he had never been challenged became addictive and pleasurable for Catalano. First he taught in Dubai. Then he managed activities for elite guests, including neighboring princes and kings at the Atlantis Hotel. When he returned to the United States, he wagered on himself by taking a year off from work and self-publishing a book with his former college teammate and Olympian Adam Goucher. *Running the Edge* (2011) challenged readers to examine their lives and their running to overcome any obstacle. Today, his platform has more than 150,000 followers on Facebook and has spawned a series of virtual events that connect runners from across the globe.

Catalano wasn't finished. Although he was over 40 and hadn't trained seriously in years, writing the book and talking to thousands of runners at lectures and conferences made him realize there was plenty left to explore in the sport that had helped him find flow in the first place. He entered a 100-mile (160.1-km) race in Ohio and began training in earnest. His longest training run ended up being 30 miles (48 km).

"I didn't know how it would go, but I figured it would be interesting," he says in his understated fashion. "If the average person remembers 20 days a year, I have 20 stories in a 24-hour period from that race. So if you just want to live and create as many memories as possible in 24 hours, go run 100 miles." In typical memory-creating form, Catalano also carried a ring in his shorts the entire 100 miles. At the end, woozy with dehydration and fatigue, he got down on a knee, looked up at his girlfriend, and proposed. Not surprisingly, they ended up eloping in Thailand at the feet of Buddhist monks before returning to the States to celebrate with friends and family.

Courtesy of Tim Catalano.

Tim Catalano competes in the TransRockies Run stage race.

"A lot of people do tell me that I have more stories than the average human," Catalano says, "but I think that's intentional."

Catalano skis in the Rockies during the winter and hikes in the high country during the summer, but he is not an adrenaline junkie. He has done 120-mile (192-km) stage races through the highest peaks in Colorado and once trained alongside two future Olympians, but he is not obsessed with the sport. He writes, lectures, travels, and has created an enormous social media following, but it doesn't feed his ego.

If there were a poster boy for living a life of engagement, it's Catalano. He seeks out challenges for the pleasure of developing skills and overcoming challenges. His life feels fulfilling, because he is always working to better himself by creating new and exciting goals. When the task has been mastered, he doesn't wait around for glory. Instead he seeks out the next adventure looming on the horizon. And when all is said and done, he's not afraid to smile and savor the wonderful memories he has created.

The majority of this book has looked at how you can experience flow in running and how it can help you become a better, happier runner. Being a faster, fulfilled athlete is one thing; being a more engaged, happier person in multiple areas of your life is another. This final chapter examines how the skills garnered by experiencing flow in sport can be transferred to experiencing flow in life. It covers the many places you can experience flow—work, relationships, a short walk around the block—and how the autotelic personality ties it all together. To get there, first look at what leads to a happy, full life in the first place.

The Full Life

What does it mean to flourish, to thrive, to be satisfied with life? Researchers in positive psychology have been studying these questions for nearly 20 years. Up until then, most of psychology was based on understanding and treating mental illness. Great strides were made in understanding the deepest troubles of the human mind (and how that mind developed in the first place), but little emphasis was placed on figuring out what led to happy, satisfying lives. In 2000, Dr. Mike partnered with Dr. Martin Seligman to focus attention on a new field of inquiry that would examine the traits of healthy people (Seligman & Csikszentmihalyi 2000). Since then, psychologists have learned a lot about the elements of a flourishing life. Chief among those are purpose, engagement, and pleasure.

Purpose

Finding purpose in life is a common pursuit for all people; it is one that humans have grappled with since evolving into rational beings. For millennia philosophers and theologians have dedicated their lives to seeking meaning. Today this process is mainstreamed through self-help books, therapists, and life coaches, so that everyone may find a personal validation to their own existence.

This pursuit is not trivial. When people find that purpose for themselves, life has meaning, they feel goal directed, they experience greater hope and optimism about the future, and they are generally happier and satisfied with their lives (Feldman & Snyder 2005; Lavasani & Mohammadi 2013; Snyder et al. 1991). However, purpose can shift as circumstances change, so being flexible in their sense of purpose is important to people's well-being (Hanssen et al. 2014).

The potential for this type of shift is abundant in adulthood. Some of these shifts may be the natural course of aging, such as the physical or cognitive limitations of an aging body, or the ever-evolving role of parenthood. As the parent of young children, your sense of purpose may focus on being the best mother or father you can be for them. Maybe it is about making the best snack for the preschool party or providing a home environment filled with love and encouragement. As your children grow, their needs change as does your role in meeting their needs. When your children leave home for college or careers, your meaning in their lives changes again, resulting in a necessary shift in focus for your overall life purpose, too. Clinging to that previous role in their lives will result in some emotional and relational challenges for you. It is best to acknowledge the change in family dynamics and adjust your focus toward new goals, new aspirations, new hobbies, and a new direction for your identity and sense of meaning.

Changing family dynamics are not the only reason you may need to alter your sense of purpose, and other reasons may be less in your control. For instance, a changing economy, job loss, or reaching the pinnacle of your career may present a barrier to future goals. Or, like Catalano, you may change your personal mission after a period of self-reflection and self-assessment. If you are not happy with the current state of your life, maybe you need to reconsider your current trajectory. That could mean a shift in perspective, values, career path, or purpose. It may also mean finding focus in areas that have previously been lacking in clarity or commitment.

Authors in Flow

Dr. Mike's Flow Moment

I have had the good fortune of having been able to experience flow from so many things I have done that the hard part is to narrow it down to a manageable list. So, I will focus instead on the first time I remember getting really immersed in an activity, which was when I learned to play chess. I had recently celebrated my 9th birthday when World War II suddenly took a nasty turn. Everywhere my family moved, either bombs fell from the sky with monotonous regularity or they came horizontally from the artillery of various armies or partisan groups. Most of the days I spent hiding under furniture or running down into the basement "bomb shelter," which nobody really trusted anyway to be a safe place if we were hit.

Mihaly Csikszentmihalyi. Photographer: Peter Gardiner.

(continued)

Dr. Mike's Flow Moment *(continued)*

As weeks, then months, passed in the chaos of a collapsing society, it became increasingly confusing; the meaningless, unpredictable way of living started to get at me. Fortunately, my older brother Karcsi, who by the end of the year was killed by the advancing Soviet troops, taught me how to play chess in the summer of 1944.

I soon found out that when playing a good game (namely, one where my opponent was neither much better, or else even worse at chess than I was), the sound of exploding artillery shells were no longer audible, and the red burst of explosions no longer visible. All my attention was taken by the moves on the board, and if I became distracted by the war, I was likely to lose a bishop or a pawn needlessly. Not only that, but I would start getting really scared by the stupid, random, ugly reality outside the windows.

Since then, my most memorable flow activities came from rock climbing, from painting, from singing in a choir of Italian mountaineers, from hiking with my family, from trying to interpret the result of research studies . . . In fact, from almost every aspect of life. But those first chess games taught me an invaluable lesson: It is within our power to create a safe and orderly place to live even when all around hatred and ignorance reign.

Engagement

When we have clarity and commitment to our sense of purpose in life, we are much more likely to feel engaged. Engagement has been shown in a variety of studies to be an important element in the life well lived. Engagement is being present in the moment. It is taking an active role in your life and being absorbed in your activities. It is about showing up and plugging in. It may also be about taking risks; nothing keeps you in the present moment like the chance something could go wrong.

This description sounds a lot like a formula for experiencing flow, and not surprisingly flow's biggest contribution to a full life stems from enhancing engagement. Peterson, Park, and Seligman (2005) found that experiencing flow and being present and engaged in your relationships, work life, and hobbies are key elements in enjoying a satisfying existence. According to this research, the full life is one that balances a sense of purpose, active engagement, and the pursuit of pleasurable experiences.

Flow requires persistent focus and engagement, just as engagement leads to flow. On the job, being engaged means you go beyond the minimum requirements for your position, seeking opportunities to improve your skills, to lead, and to step outside of your comfort zone. Flow workers find meaning in their jobs by putting their whole attention into their work and not dreaming about what they'll do when the workday is done. A pastry chef is more likely to experience flow if she is focused totally on creating a cake, with all its nuances of flavor and frosting designs, instead of wondering how much she can sell it for. Even jobs that offer little room for creativity, such as factory work, can produce flow when you find a rhythm to the work and get lost in the moment (Csikszentmihalyi 1990).

Much like being at work, engaging with your family requires more than simply showing up. You need to invest energy. Instead of watching television in the evening, engage your family members in a discussion about their days, participate in a group activity, or cook a meal together. Go for hikes on the weekends instead of staying home on your smart phones. Share your passions. The ways you choose to engage with your family contributes to the third area Seligman and his colleagues (Peterson, Park, & Seligman 2005) spoke of in their research on the full life, namely, pleasure.

Pleasure

Although not as strongly correlated with life satisfaction as purpose or engagement, pleasure is still a large component of the life well lived (Peterson, Park & Seligman 2005). For the sake of simplicity, pleasure can be divided into two categories: hedonic and eudaimonic. **Hedonic** pleasures cover a wide span of short-lived, instantly gratifying moments. Basic drives such as food, drink, and sex all provide microbursts of pleasure. Spending money and consuming goods lasts a little longer, perhaps a few days, but eventually the shine wears off and you're back to your happiness baseline. At its heart, hedonic pleasure seeks to maximize pleasure while minimizing pain (Boniwell & Jane 2013).

Being idle is also a pleasure, and it may be genetically wired in people. Research (Hsee, Yang, & Wang 2010) has shown that when given the option between expending energy or sitting around, people tend to opt for lazing, even though those same study participants reported being happier when active. This evidence explains in part why watching television often sounds good at the time but ends up leaving you restless and anxious (Argyle 2001; Csikszentmihalyi & Hunter 2003; Dempsey et al. 2014).

Whether you enjoy family runs, chess, or prefer solitary activities such as reading or playing music, making time for these pleasurable moments matters. If you spend money on memorable experiences instead of consumable goods, you will find a more deeply felt sense of pleasure called **eudaimonia.** Similar to contentment, the word *eudaimonia* literally means "conducive to happiness." This type of pleasure has a long-lasting impact on your sense of satisfaction with life. When seeking pleasure that will contribute to your well-being, you should look for this type of experience. Eudaimonic experiences are not self-indulgent or cheap thrills. They come from a place of self-realization and self-determination. They may involve self-sacrifice and have less raw pleasure than hedonic pursuits, but they carry greater meaning.

Imagine you're given a choice between climbing a 14,000-foot (4.2-km) peak in Colorado on your own or spending a weekend staycation camping with your family. The thrill of the Rockies, and the raw edge of strapping on crampons and ropes and climbing through ice fields, won't be happening in the backyard. However, spending time with your children, and helping them experience the joys of sitting around a campfire and falling asleep to the rush of a nearby creek, provides a different kind of pleasure; it fulfills you in a different way. These experiences do not have to be extravagant to be powerful. Going for a walk with a friend, taking a beautiful bike ride with someone you care for, or meditating in a peaceful garden all provide eudaimonic opportunities.

Another important element of the eudaimonic approach is that of prosocial behaviors. These altruistic behaviors consist of doing good for others without any tangible benefit gained in return. This idea runs counter to many cultural messages in which people are told to pamper themselves and do some "retail therapy" after a bad day. People are led to believe this behavior will improve their mood, but for most people it produces only temporary happiness. It is indicative of hedonic happiness, which ultimately ends in a quick return to their original state of mind. Many people report feelings of guilt for self-indulgence rather than improved mood (Nelson, Layous, Cole, & Lyubomirsky 2016).

The better fix, it turns out, is to help someone else. Recent research (Nelson, Layous, Cole, & Lyubomirsky 2016) found surprisingly significant differences in state of mind in a study where participants were instructed to either (1) track their daily activities, (2) engage in self-focused acts of kindness, (3) engage in prosocial acts toward specific others, or (4) engage in prosocial acts toward humanity or the world. People in the last two groups experienced significant, long-lasting improvements in reported positive emotions and overall psychological well-being.

The pursuit of pleasure can't be constant. Life's responsibilities sneak up and strangle opportunities for both hedonic and eudaimonic pleasures. It isn't problematic for your overall sense of well-being as long as it doesn't become the new normal. Leisure activity is so important for stress reduction and overall well-being, it should not be ignored. For instance, Alexander and colleagues (1993) found that meditation practitioners experience less work tension and overall anxiety in life. Whatever your pleasurable leisure time activities may be, inking them into your calendar in even the busiest of times can help you manage the stress of catastrophic events (divorce, job loss, financial strain) as well as daily hassles such as commuting or family responsibilities (Caltabiano 1994; Iwasaki, Coyle, & Shank 2010).

As research in full life suggests, it is important to find a sense of purpose, ways to engage, and healthy sources of pleasure. As difficult as it may be to find time for leisure activities, finding balance can also be challenging. Everyone has cycles in life when one of these areas stole most of their waking moments. Purpose-driven activities such as completing school, cultivating a career, and beginning a family require lots of time, which is inevitably borrowed from leisure activities. Other times hobbies and passions take front and center, leaving purpose in the background.

No matter how balanced you may feel, these fluctuations are a part of adult life. Short bouts of time when your career takes precedence over leisure can propel you toward more meaningful job opportunities, but routinely prioritizing purpose over engagement and pleasure results in burnout, dissatisfaction, dissolution, and loneliness. Similarly, focusing on pleasurable activities at the cost of purpose or engagement may leave you feeling dissatisfied, lonely, or lacking direction. Disheartening as it may be at times, keep striving for balance even when under stress. As you acknowledge the importance of purpose, engagement, and pleasure throughout your life, and as you work toward a balance between them, your potential to experience the full life grows. And, thanks to running and flow, you already have a leg up.

The Marathon Monks of Mount Hiei

Some people run for fitness, some run for sport, and some run for enjoyment. On the sacred Mount Hiei in northern Japan, a group of monks run for enlightenment.

Known as the "marathon monks" of Mount Hiei, they practice a form of religion known as Tendai Buddhism. This Japanese version of the worldwide faith is replete with rituals, rites, and traditions, all of which seek to bring the believer closer to enlightenment. Meditation is considered an essential part of becoming enlightened, but in the Tendai faith it rarely happens in a static manner. Instead, seated meditation is augmented by moving meditation, half-moving meditation, and freestyle meditation, where every moment of one's life is seen as a religious gift (Stevens 2013).

Above all of these rituals and rites is a practice known as *kaihogyo,* a roughly 30-kilometer (18.6-mile) walk-run route performed by all Tendai priests and nuns at least once. Those who wish to become abbots in the faith must perform this journey for 100 consecutive days. It is no ordinary 3 1/2-month nature hike. Carrying only a paper lantern and straw raincoat when they depart the massive Enryaku-ji temple complex, the monks begin their journey

AP Photo/Shizuo Kambayashi

Genshin Fujinami is one of the "marathon monks" of Mount Hiei, Japan.

(continued)

The Marathon Monks of Mount Hiei *(continued)*

every morning at 1:30 a.m. The course is a weaving network of dirt trails on Mount Hiei, replete with rocks, roots, thousands of stairs, and occasionally venomous animals. Despite these obstacles, the monks wear only straw sandals. These sandals become flimsy and fall apart in the rainstorms, which are common in the temperate rainforest region. The monks must use their stock wisely, for they are allocated only 80 pairs over a 100-day period (Stevens 2013).

On the trail, the monks are expected to recite a mantra while moving and stop at 255 designated worship stations along the way. These stations include manmade temples, shrines, tombs, and graves, in addition to sacred natural features such as mountain peaks, stones, trees, and waterfalls. At each stop the monks recite a special prayer. Sometimes the prayer takes a few seconds; other times, it can be a minute or longer. Once the monks return to the temple, they eat a small vegetarian meal, attend services, and are expected to head to bed as early as possible. Not surprisingly, many experience serious physical issues early in their endeavor, including Achilles tendinitis, diarrhea, hemorrhoids, fevers, infections, and frostbite; after day 30, however, their bodies generally adapt well (Stevens 2013).

A select few monks may petition their Tendai elders for a 1,000-day version: the *sennichi kaihogyo*. This journey takes 7 years; years 4, 5, and 7 involve two 100-day sessions each. In the sixth year, the route extends to 60 kilometers (36 miles); in the seventh year, the first 100 days are 84 kilometers (52 miles) in length. Daunting as it seems, the greatest challenge has already taken place.

The *doiri* is an extreme ritual after the fifth year, where the monk will not eat, drink, or sleep for 182 hours. Other than a 2 a.m. trip to a well to retrieve water for a Buddhist deity, the monk sits in lotus position and recites an eight-word mantra upwards of 100,000 times. When saliva dries up after day 5, the monks often begin to taste blood (they are allowed to wash their mouths to keep from permanently damaging their cheeks). At all times, the monk going through *doiri* has two assistants sitting next to him to keep his head erect and prevent accidental sleep. This deprivation is generally considered the hardest part of the ordeal (Stevens 2013).

If this sounds incredibly harsh, those who come out the other side of *doiri* think it is worth it. After facing death—and many physiologists have noted the monks should be dead from these conditions—these devotees often develop extreme sensitivity to sound and smell. John Stevens, the author of *The Marathon Monks,* describes how they can hear ash falling or detect a meal being cooked miles away. Their reintroduction in the world has a "feeling of transparency," he says. "Nothing is retained; everything—good, bad, neutral—has come out of them, and existence is reveled in crystal clarity" (Stevens 2013).

These existential bits are critical, for the monks are severely tested in the final year. Completing the 84-kilometer circuit each day on little more than rice balls, tofu, and a few hours of sleep each night has led to these monks being called the greatest athletes in the world (Hayden 2002).

During the last set of 100 days, the route changes dramatically. Instead of working their way through the lush greenness of Mount Hiei, the monks run a route through the ancient Japanese capital of Kyoto. There they constantly give blessings to laypeople who follow their paths, each hoping this nearly enlightened monk can pass on some measure of good fortune or beneficence (Stevens 2013).

Since 1885, fewer than 50 monks have completed the *sennichi kaihogyo*. The 30-kilometer loop is filled with unmarked graves of monks who took their own lives upon failure. Despite the ardent difficulty and esoteric nature of the quest, people can learn a lot from these high-endurance athletes, such as the following:

- **Find a greater purpose for your run. . . .** It doesn't have to be religious or part of some elaborate ritual. Just as the Tendai monks believe these runs bring them closer to experiencing enlightenment, you, too, can find ways for your runs to have a higher purpose. Whether it's taking your fitness to a higher level, relieving stress, helping you meet your health goals, practicing your faith, or finding an hour of solace for yourself, believing the run is part of something greater than yourself can keep you motivated.

- **. . . But also stay in the moment.** Despite the many stops and starts during their journey for sacred sites, the monks stay immersed in the moment. Staying present is a critical tenet of Tendai Buddhism. Every time a monk reaches one of the 255 sacred sites, he devotes his full attention toward it; while running or hiking, monks recite a mantra and stay grounded in their task. Stay in the moment, and you'll have a better chance of experiencing whatever that moment has to offer.

- **Never underestimate your abilities.** Before setting off on their first 100-day journey, the monks focus on utilitarian tasks such as chopping wood and carrying water. They also master their breathing. Beyond that basic strength and lung work, the monks get most of their endurance training by helping others on their 100-day journeys (Stevens 2013). None are professional athletes, and few have an athletic background entering the journey. It is through willpower and belief that they push through sleep deprivation, muscular fatigue, and a low-calorie diet to achieve their dreams. "If mind and body are unified, there is nothing that cannot be accomplished," writes Stevens. "Strive to attain the ultimate, and the universe will someday be yours" (Stevens 2013, p. VIII). That's something everyone can take heed of.

- **Make running a part of your life.** A monk in the midst of a 100-day ritual never has to ask himself what he's going to do that morning. That consistency enables him to grow as an athlete and person. When you identify yourself as a runner—not someone who runs—you won't find yourself questioning your motives every day. Run because it's who you are.

Transferring Flow from Running to Life

Few running meccas in the United States can match Boulder, Colorado. Situated at the base of the Rockies along the stunning Flatirons Range, Boulder has drawn elite runners, cyclists, and triathletes to its vicinity for the past 50 years. The challenging mountain trails and rolling dirt roads of the city's reservoir offer endless variety for those putting in the miles. When backed by the camaraderie and esprit de corps that's forged by having so many dedicated athletes pushing their limits, Boulder has proven to be one of the best places in the world to run.

In the late 1990s, Catalano knew these roads and trails very well. He harbored dreams of making the Olympic trials in the 3,000-meter steeplechase. The event, which includes hurdling 35 barriers, 7 of which sit in front of a 12-foot-long (3.6-m) water pit, demands a unique blend of speed, strength, and athleticism. A recent college graduate, Catalano continued running high mileage in the foothills surrounding Boulder under the tutelage of his now legendary college coach, Mark Wetmore. Wetmore would go on to lead the University of Colorado to a handful of national titles, but at the time he was only beginning to be recognized for his brilliance.

Catalano's brilliance, meanwhile, was flaming out. A tibial stress fracture and resulting case of plantar fasciitis limited his training. Catalano pushed forward, always believing he was just one lucky break from making it to the trials. After a particularly bad 14-mile (22.5-km) run on a loop affectionately dubbed "Certain Death," he saw Wetmore waiting for him. The two made small talk about injuries and the run for a moment before Wetmore issued a simple edict: quit.

"You've gone as far in running as you can go," Wetmore told him. "Now go be great at something else."

At the time the verdict stung. Catalano had dedicated the last decade of his life toward being a successful runner; now he was being told by the biggest influence in his life to drop the sport altogether.

Over time, Catalano came to realize Wetmore's point. He was a good runner who trained hard, but he simply didn't have the talent to make a living in a low-ceilinged sport. Instead, it was time to take that focus, dedication, sense of purpose, and passion and apply it elsewhere. Thanks to running, Catalano owned the traits necessary to successfully make the transition into his life's next great adventure.

The Value of Flow's Antecedents

Some people get stuck in a rut or wander aimlessly through life, never happy with their pursuits and seemingly lost on what to do. They may work menial jobs or spend a lot of time in passive, unengaging activities such as watching television, reading soft news articles, surfing the Internet, or abusing painkillers. Heavy computer users often describe going down the rabbit hole, where a series of clicks leads to website after website after website. Entire days may get eaten up without a single memorable or enlightening moment occurring.

In a culture of instant gratification and entertainment overload, it can be easy to have your attention constantly pulled in one direction after another, with none of it amounting to anything memorable. Luckily, if you're a runner who has experienced flow, you have a trump card in your pocket when it comes to experiencing a full life; that is, you have the antecedents of flow, namely, setting goals and developing skills over a long period of time.

The **transfer of learning theory** states we are capable of taking skills and knowledge learned in one area and applying it to another. Sometimes these transfers are simple. These **low-road transfers** are evident when you type on a computer at the library instead of at home. Although several keys may be in different spots and the size and spacing of the keys may vary slightly, you are able to type just as efficiently in either location. **High-road transfers,** on the other hand, require a high degree of thought to apply in different scenarios (Perkins & Salomon 1988). For these transfers, you'll need to spend some time pondering the parallels between two disparate ideas that have some commonalities. If you're a war veteran well versed in military tactics, you may coach an American football game differently given this knowledge. The ability to protect key assets and exploit weaknesses in a defense are common to both sports, giving you a widened perspective on engaging the opponent.

When it comes to experiencing flow in areas outside of running, you're likely to experience a mix of low-road and high-road transference. In aerobic sports such as swimming, mountain biking, hiking, and skiing, the similarities of moving through the environment under your own power, the rapid pumping of your heart, and the cadence of your breathing bring a degree of familiarity to the sports. Not only are you indirectly prepared for these sports because of a high level of running fitness, but experiencing flow is more likely because of low-road transference. The same mentality and approach that allowed you to engage in running and experience flow in that setting is likely to pay off here.

Aerobic exercise is only a fraction of the whole of your life. To take flow and engagement outside of your exercise habits requires a high-road approach. Think of Catalano. After his epiphany teaching high school psychology, he had to figure out a way to make his new dream come true. Moving abroad, learning a new language and culture, and taking care of all the odds and ends that are associated with leaving the United States is no easy feat. It required time, patience, a willingness to stumble, and the passion and dedication to push through adversity. This laundry list of obstacles may have flummoxed many others, but after a decade of serious running, Catalano had developed strong endurance. Training taught him the value of hard work and deferred gratification. He also knew from mile repeats and 20-mile (32-km) runs that he could endure anything. Thanks to that, he found a passion for teaching in other countries, one that enriched his life and the lives of the students he taught.

What activities you choose to pursue is largely a personal matter and can develop over time. A person may be passionate about video games in their teens, rock climbing in their twenties, and work in their thirties. So long as you have challenges and measures of progress, almost any activity you can imagine can lead to engagement, passion, and flow. People who find a way to transfer this approach to the largest number of areas in their lives end up reporting the most fulfillment (Seligman 2002). The way you define a challenge can change over time, too. In your youth, you may have paddled class V rapids on fast-flowing rivers for the ultimate thrill. As you settle in and have a family, the challenge may be getting your kids out on the water and teaching them the techniques and nuances of piloting a boat. The sheer rush of plummeting over a 20-foot (6-m) fall may be gone, but the joy and sense of satisfaction of watching your offspring engage in your passion more than makes up for it.

If a key to happiness exists in this approach, it was what Dr. Mike has rec-ommended in many talks, books, and lectures: *Have as many flow moments as you can.* Even when they're not of the earth-shattering, hallelujah variety, these moments of engagement keep you in the here and now. They give you a chance to develop skills, make goals, and feel success. Those moments add up. They are, in fact, the very stuff of life.

The Autotelic Personality and Well-Being

When you step back and take a broader view of the moments that make life worth living, it seems appropriate to revisit the autotelic personality. Buried underneath the academic-sounding word is a viable framework for the life well lived. Consider it a roadmap to the full life. Whether your journey is about making significant life changes like Catalano's or subtly shifting your trajectory toward greater meaning, learning to live the autotelic life is a big step toward optimal living.

A person with an autotelic personality, by definition, creates a full life—one with purpose, engagement, and pleasure. With an autotelic personality, you are naturally motivated to choose engaging experiences and relationships, meaningful opportunities and goals, and pleasurable activities that fit both of those categories. Your life is peppered with interesting and challenging goals, people you love, and flow-inducing activities. You are generally a positive and curious person. Like Catalano, you say go, not no. You live to say yes to new experiences and appreciate the value in having few regrets as a result.

It doesn't mean you drive by this roadmap blindly, saying yes to every whim and request. As an autotelic person, you understand the value in slow-ing down and unplugging sometimes. Life can be so busy, you need to learn to say no to some things so you that can unplug (literally and figuratively), relax, meditate, go for a walk, enjoy nature, and savor life.

Learning to savor the past, present, and future by engaging all of your senses in a moment of stillness is strongly correlated with well-being (Bryant & Veroff 2007), and something an autotelic appreciates when enjoying some well-deserved solitude.

Have you ever spent time reliving a great memory? A vacation? The birth of a child? Your first race? When you relive that moment with all of your senses, you relive the same joy and happiness you felt in the original experience. Savoring is not exclusive to past experiences, though. You can savor the present moment by lingering on the positive feelings you are experiencing in real time. Future plans can be savored, too, through anticipation. Engaging your senses in what you think may happen in that future event gives you a preview to the positive feelings you are likely to feel when that moment arrives. Unlike fretting and rumination, it is a healthy form of engagement. Savoring in all its forms contributes to the full life.

Perhaps this approach is best encapsulated by the work of a German psychologist and philosopher named Erich Fromm (1900-1980). Fromm wrote about the optimal personality and the value of a *being orientation* versus a *having orientation* (Fromm 1976). To have, Fromm says, is to focus on the acquisition of material things and power. In this theory, people with a *having* orientation get what they want through exploitation, hoarding, marketing themselves, or patiently waiting for events to change. These people usually dissociate these traits from themselves, believing they are a necessary means to get what they need.

Forging a life worth living, according to Fromm, is to *be*—to live, to love, to engage the world around you. It involves risking vulnerability so that you may truly feel what love offers. It means being passionate about something enough to risk failure in order to achieve. To be, Fromm says, is to will one thing into your life, to find your passion, and to pursue it with energy and persistence. It involves being fully awake, present, engaged, and aware of your surroundings. A person with this orientation concentrates on the present moment and will meditate in order to make being more possible (Fromm 1976). Fromm's idea of being serves as a nice complement to flow, to the autotelic personality, and to the full life. To *be* is to live like an autotelic. To *be* is to experience flow. To *be* is to live and flourish.

As this book comes to a close, its aim is to enable you to experience a full life. Combining our passions for running and flow created the impetus for this book, but it's just the tip of the iceberg. As you experience flow more in your daily life, perhaps you will be inspired to engage just as fully with your work, relationships, and hobbies. Find your passions. Live your truth. Run. Flow. Flourish!

Key Points

- In 2000, Dr. Mike and Dr. Martin Seligman introduced the field of positive psychology, the study of the life worth living (flourishing).
- The life worth living is a full life, with a sense of purpose, engagement, and meaningful leisure activities.
- Finding a sense of purpose is an important element in the full life, and purpose can change over time.

- Engagement is about being present in the moment, taking an active role in your life, and being absorbed in your activities. It is about showing up and plugging into your life.

- Flow's biggest contribution to a full life stems from enhancing engagement.

- You can experience flow in running, other hobbies, relationships, and work.

- While occasional hedonic experiences are a normal part of life, the full life is filled with more eudaimonic experiences. Hedonic experiences are typically about the acquisition of material things, power, status, or indulgent pleasures. Eudaimonic experiences are meaningful, purpose-filled experiences that often include significant others and can focus on helping others instead of yourself.

- When people feel down, prosocial behaviors improve mood more than self-indulgent behaviors. Most people report short-lived pleasure mixed with feelings of guilt over self-indulgence.

- Flow is not just for running. You can transfer what you know about flow in running to other areas of your life. The full life is highlighted with moments of flow in all areas of life.

- A person with an autotelic personality frequently experiences flow, seeks purpose, enjoys challenge, appreciates meaningful experiences with others, pursues engagement in many areas of life, and typically finds life to be very full.

- Savoring contributes to flourishing. You can savor past experiences by reliving the moments in your mind. You can also savor the present by fully engaging in it and appreciating it. You can savor future experiences by anticipating them.

- Erich Fromm (1976) spoke of the good life as one that encapsulates the *being* orientation instead of the *having* orientation. The *having* orientation is about the acquisition of power, wealth, and status. The *being* orientation is about love, engagement in the world around you, and being passionate about life.

GLOSSARY

achievement flow—The motivation to return to an activity over and over again for the intrinsic value provided by improvements that come from practice.

action orientation—A tendency to take action to resolve a problem instead of mulling over options before taking action.

antecedents—Elements of the flow experience that are required before flow can happen. The antecedents for flow include clear goals, challenge–skill balance, and unambiguous feedback.

approach-motivated person—Someone whose behavior is motivated by a desire to pursue challenge, personal growth, and improved skill or ability, despite the risk of potential failure. Risk and failure are seen as opportunities to improve.

attention restoration theory (ART)—A theory stating that exposure to nature restores a person's ability to sustain concentration in directed behaviors, such as doing a project at work. Greater biodiversity in the natural environment escalates the restorative effect.

attributional retraining—Retraining yourself to attribute the source of your outcomes and events more accurately. For example, attributional errors take place when you do not acknowledge your own efforts that have contributed to your successes.

autotelic experience—From the Greek word *autotelēs,* meaning "self goal." An experience done for its own sake, such as going for a run just because you enjoy running.

autotelic personality— Behavioral and attitudinal traits leading a person to consistently seek out challenges and flow experiences. A person with an autotelic personality seeks autotelic experiences and finds satisfaction in them. This person tends to be open to new experiences, has a strong sense of curiosity and desire to engage in the things that are the source of curiosity, to improve skills, and seek challenge.

avoidance motivated—Behavior motivated by a desire to avoid failure rather than to achieve success. With this approach, a person is driven to avoid the discomfort of failure by lowering goals or standards, avoiding challenging experiences, and reducing risk. Challenge results in anxiety.

behavioral activation system—A model of appetitive motivation that explains a person's tendency to pursue and achieve goals. This system is activated when it receives cues for reward.

behavioral inhibition system—A neuropsychological system that explains a person's tendency to avoid unpleasant experiences or risk failure or discomfort. This system is activated when a person receives environmental cues for boring, negative, or uncomfortable events that may result in anxiety, punishment, or frustration.

catastrophizing—A tendency to exaggerate the potential for negative events to take place, or to exaggerate negative outcomes that may happen or have already happened.

challenge–skills balance—A rather equal balance between current skill level and current challenge. The optimal balance for flow is typically equal, or with a challenge just slightly beyond the current skill level.

conscientiousness—Personality trait indicating a tendency for self-discipline, reliability, ambition, organization, and initiative.

directed attention fatigue—Neurological phenomenon that occurs when the brain struggles to filter out unwanted stimuli while focusing on a specific task for long periods at a time.

downregulation—Deactivation or reduced activation. Used frequently to describe brain activity.

effortless attention—The result of significant practice and repetition, which is visible in the reflexive responses of an expert in any field, including sport.

endocannabinoids—Compounds that act as a natural version of THC, the chemical in marijuana that makes a person high. They are produced in the brain and are thought to be a main source of runner's high.

endorphins—Morphine-like opioids produced by various parts of the central nervous system. Some research that endorphins are implicated in runner's high.

eudaimonia—A philosophical term often used by Plato that refers to a life that focuses on meaningful experiences and a purpose-driven life instead of the pursuit or attainment of material goods, wealth and power. Eudaimonic pleasure is a broader, longer-term approach to happiness that focuses on meaning, purpose, and self-realization.

event-specific enjoyment—The pleasure experienced while participating in a specific activity, which is different than global.

explicit memory—A part of long-term memory that relies on active conscious recollection or attention. This requires focused attention, thus reducing the amount of mental energy remaining to attend to other information. Some tasks begin in the explicit memory but transfer, over time with practice, to the implicit memory system.

external feedback—Sensory data outside the person. This includes information such as noise, coaching, weather and temperature, positioning in a field of competitors or on a track or trail, landscape, time, pace, GPS coordinates, or other feedback from a smart watch or timer.

external locus of control—A state in which you believe that you have very little control over your circumstances, thus ascribing outcomes to the hands of others, fate, or destiny.

flow—An optimal experience during which the mind and body work harmoniously while honed in on a task. The nine components of flow, often called antecedents and process outcomes, include clear goals, challenge–skill balance, unambiguous feedback, focused attention, merging of action and awareness, sense of control, loss of self-consciousness, distorting of time, and intrinsic motivation.

flow personality—Personality that is predisposed to frequent flow experiences and includes these characteristics: goal oriented, intrinsically motivated, mastery oriented, realistic perception of ability, high self-esteem, internal locus of control, conscientious, engaged in meaningful, goal-oriented activities.

focused attention—A state in which you concentrate on one thing while also blocking out other sources of stimuli.

global happiness—An overall sense of happiness, optimism about the future, and feeling of contentment with life.

group flow—Flow experiences shared in a group, such as a relay team or cross country squad working together towards a common goal.

harmonious passion—A passion for, or intense commitment to, an activity that stems from an inherent love for the activity, is a key element of an individual's identity, and integrates into one's life and values or priorities.

hedonic pleasure—From the Greek word *hedonic*, which means "sweet." This type of pleasure is typically immediate, yet short lived, and focuses on the attainment of pleasure and the avoidance of pain or discomfort.

high self-esteem—Combination of attitudes and beliefs about your competency that suggest you feel worthy and capable of succeeding. This results from experiences of success that support this attitude and belief.

high-road transfers—Transfer of knowledge when the areas being transferred to/from are very different, such as using skills learned playing American football to organize and lead a team project in the workplace.

implicit memory—A part of long-term memory that relies on past experiences to remember things without thinking, such as routines or tasks that have been repeated so many times they become reflexive. These tasks are quick and efficient and free the mind to concentrate on other information.

in the zone—A description for flow often used by athletes. *Being in the zone* describes the mental state involving total concentration on your experience with no distraction.

inflated self-esteem—A combination of attitudes and beliefs about your competency that suggest you feel worthy and capable of succeeding. It results from a misjudgment of skill, typically because there are no experiences of success that support the attitude and belief.

internal feedback—Information from inside the body. This includes information such as heart rate, breathing, sensations of pain or fatigue, balance, proprioception, muscle tension or contraction, to name a few. Internal information also includes mental processes such as thoughts, attitudes, beliefs, and strategies.

internal locus of control—A belief that you have a high degree of control over the events of your life.

inverted-U theory of performance and anxiety—Also known as the Yerkes-Dodson law, this theory suggests that humans generally improve performance as the pressure to succeed heightens, but only to a certain point. As the pressure to succeed continues to mount, increased anxiety or worry results in diminished performance.

low self-esteem—Combination of attitudes and beliefs about your competency that suggest you are not worthy or capable of success, even if there are experiences of success to support ability. This results in a misjudgment of skill that is lower than actual potential, and feelings of shame.

low-road transfers—Transfer of knowledge when the areas being transferred to/from are very similar, such as when keyboarding skills transfer from one QWERTY keyboard to another.

mastery orientation—A mindset that focuses on mastering new skills and the process of the skill to be mastered rather than on the outcome. In running, it would be the difference between focusing on form and technique in order to improve running time versus focusing on finishing place as a measure of success.

mindfulness—A state of active attention on the present moment without evaluating or judging your thoughts or feelings.

negatively filtering—Canceling out positive thoughts or praise and focusing on criticism or mistakes.

neuroticism—Personality trait characterized by emotional instability, anxiety, and passivity.

obsessive passion—A passion for, or intense commitment to, an activity that stems from a controlled environment where a person doesn't feel they are acting under their own direction, or where they become overly focused on the activity or goal while ignoring other elements of their identity, life, or value system.

peak experience—An experience accompanied by a euphoric mental state or heightened sensory experiences. Many people who experience this describe it similarly to flow, in that they both include loss of self-consciousness, feelings of effortlessness, complete immersion in the present moment, and distorted sense of time. Unlike flow, however, peak experiences also result in a burst of energy and are triggered by external events.

performance orientation—A mindset that focuses on performance outcomes instead of the process of mastering new skills. The win, for instance, is more important than the skills needed to achieve the win. It values demonstration of superiority over others (beating others in a race) more than on improvements in skill or technique.

polarizing thoughts—Thoughts that are extreme, such as when anything less than perfect is seen as a failure

positive reframing—A way of rethinking or rewording events, ideas, concepts, or emotions in a more positive way.

positive-striving perfectionism—Behavioral and mental tendency to set high standards for yourself, to set specific benchmarks to measure progress toward or achievement of those standards, and to exhibit the drive necessary to persevere.

prefrontal cortex—An area of the cerebral cortex that covers the frontal lobe of the brain, located in the forehead area, that is responsible for rational thought. It is responsible for tasks such as complex cognitive decision making and an awareness time and time passage. It is implicated in the release of endorphins during endurance running.

process outcomes—The components of flow that may unfold after the antecedents are present. The process outcomes include focused attention, merging of action and awareness, distorting of time, and intrinsic motivation (autotelic).

runner's high—The "high" experienced after a run. This includes a flood of positive thoughts, feelings of euphoria, increased pain tolerance, intensely clear thought, all of which can remain for hours after the run is over.

self-actualization—A phrase first introduced by psychologist Abraham Maslow signifying one's desire to pursue personal growth and fulfillment of potential. According to Maslow, this state is possible when a person's basic needs (physiological, safety, love, self-esteem) are met.

self-critical perfectionism—Behavioral and mental tendency to set high standards, then have critical self-evaluations of personal performance, focusing on mistakes and negativity when performance does not meet high expectations.

self-efficacy—Your belief about your ability to succeed in a specific situation or task.

social facilitation—Also known as the audience effect, this theory suggests that people tend to perform differently when in the presence of others. For runners, the research suggests that we tend to run faster when in the presence of others than when we run alone.

social validation—Confirmation from others that your feelings or thoughts are valid or justified.

soft fascination—Objects in the natural world that attract a person's attention but require no cognitive effort to enjoy.

state orientation—A tendency to consider options and to study potential outcomes before taking action to resolve a problem.

stimulus theory of human motivation—Theory that stimulation or challenge is a necessary need for humans; without it they become bored, agitated, or even disoriented.

task orientation—The ability to focus on the task you are performing. Also called focused attention.

transfer of learning theory—A psychological theory that suggests people are capable of taking skills and knowledge learned in one area and applying it to another area.

transient hypofrontality theory (THT)—A theory developed by Arne Dietrich (professor of psychology at the American University of Beirut (AUB) in Lebanon). This theory suggests that extended physical exertion, like that experienced during running, requires investments of neural energy to the motor cortex, which results in less energy available for other areas of the brain, such as the prefrontal cortex. The downregulation (deactivation) of the prefrontal cortex explains some of the flow outcomes, such as loss of self-consciousness and distortion of time.

type A personality—Type A and B personality theory describes contrasting behavioral tendencies. Type A indicates a more competitive, outgoing, organized, ambitious and impatient behavioral repertoire; type B indicates a more relaxed personality.

REFERENCES

Chapter 1

Allan, P. 2014. Four "confusing" Zen quotes and what you can learn from them. *LifeHacker.* lifehacker.com/four-confusing-zen-quotes-and-what-you-can-learn-from-1676177538

Conley, C. 2007. *Peak: How great companies get their mojo from Maslow.* San Francisco: Wiley.

Csikszentmihalyi, M. 2003. The evolving nature of work. *NAMTA Journal, 28*(2), 87-107.

Csikszentmihalyi, M. 1990. *Flow: The psychology of optimal experience.* New York: HarperCollins.

Csikszentmihalyi, M. 1975. Play and intrinsic rewards. *Journal of Humanistic Psychology, 15*(3), 41.

Csikszentmihalyi, M. 1988. The flow experience and its significance for human psychology. In M. Csikszentmihalyi, I.S. Csikszentmihalyi (Eds.), *Optimal experience: Psychological studies of flow in consciousness* (pp. 15-35). New York: Cambridge University Press.

Dietrich, A. 2004. Neurocognitive mechanisms underlying the experience of flow. *Consciousness And Cognition: An International Journal, 13*(4), 746-761. doi:10.1016/j.concog.2004.07.002

Dietrich, A., & Audiffren, M. 2011. The reticular-activating hypofrontality (RAH) model of acute exercise. *Neuroscience and Biobehavioral Reviews, 35*(6), 1305-1325. doi:10.1016/j.neubiorev.2011.02.001

Dunn, E.W., Gilbert, D.T., & Wilson, T.D. 2011. If money doesn't make you happy, then you probably aren't spending it right. *Journal of Consumer Psychology, 21*(2), 115-125. doi:10.1016/j.jcps.2011.02.002

Fetters, K. 2014. How to achieve a runner's high. *Runner's World Online.* www.runnersworld.com/running-tips/how-to-achieve-a-runners-high

Gleiser, M. 2016. How runners get high. *13.7 Cosmos and Culture.* www.npr.org/sections/13.7/2016/04/20/474863739/how-runners-get-high

Gunaratana, B. 2002. Buddhist concept of happiness. *Bhavana Society.* www.bhavanasociety.org/resource/buddhist_concept_of_happiness

Jackson, S.A. & Csikszentmihalyi, M. 1999. *Flow in sports: The keys to optimal experiences and performances.* Champaign, IL: Human Kinetics.

Maslow, A.H. 1954. *Motivation and personality.* New York: Harper.

Maslow, A.H. 1962. Cognition of being in the peak-experiences. In A.H. Maslow *Toward a psychology of being* (pp. 67-96). Princeton, NJ: D. Van Nostrand. doi:10.1037/10793-006

Von Tevenar, G. 2007. *Nietzsche and ethics.* Bern: Peter Lang AG.

Chapter 2

Baer, R. 2003. Mindfulness training as a clinical intervention: a conceptual and empirical review. *Clinical Psychology,* 10(2), 125-143.

Cooley, C. 1902. *Human nature and the social order.* New York: Scribner's Sons.

Csikszentmihalyi, M. 1997. *Finding flow: The psychology of engagement with everyday life.* New York: Basic Books.

Csikszentmihalyi, M., Rathunde, K.R., Whalen, S., & Wong, M. 1993. *Talented teen-agers: The roots of success and failure.* New York: Cambridge University Press.

Dietrich, A. & Sparling, P.B. 2004. Endurance exercise selectively impairs prefron-tal-dependent cognition. *Brain and Cognition,* 55(3), 516-524. doi:10.1016/j.bandc.2004.03.002

Dietrich, A. & Stoll, O. 2010. Effortless attention, hypofrontality, and perfectionism. In B. Bruya, (Ed.), *Effortless attention: A new perspective in the cognitive science of attention and action* (pp. 159-178). Cambridge, MA: MIT Press.

Dweck, C.S. 1986. Motivational processes affecting learning. *American Psychologist,* 41(10), 1040-1048. doi:10.1037/0003-066X.41.10.1040

Emmons, R.A. 1992. Abstract versus concrete goals: Personal striving level, physical illness, and psychological well-being. *Journal of Personality and Social Psychology,* 62(2), 292-300. doi:10.1037/0022-3514.62.2.292

Jackson, S.A. 1996. Toward a conceptual understanding of the flow experience in elite athletes. *Research Quarterly for Exercise & Sport,* 67(1), 76.

Jackson, S.A. & Csikszentmihalyi, M. 1999. *Flow in sports: The keys to optimal experiences and performances.* Champaign, IL: Human Kinetics.

National Institutes of Health. 2016. Mindfulness meditation reduces pain, bypasses opioid receptors. NCCIH Research Blog: https://nccih.nih.gov/research/blog/mindfulness-meditation-pain

Smith, E.R. & Mackie, D.M. 2007. *Social psychology.* 3rd ed. Hove: Psychology Press.

Stavrou, N.A., Jackson, S.A., Zervas, Y., & Karteroliotis, K. 2007. Flow experience and athletes' performance with reference to the orthogonal model of flow. *The Sport Psychologist,* 21(4), 438-457.

Sugiyama, T. & Inomata, K. 2005. Qualitative examination of flow experience among top Japanese athletes. *Perceptual & Motor Skills,* 100(3), 969-982.

Tang, Y., Ma, Y., Wang, J., Fan, Y., Feng, S., Lu, Q., ... & Posner, M.I. 2007. Short-term meditation training improves attention and self-regulation. *Proceedings of the National Academy of Sciences of the United States of America,* 104(43), 17152-17156. doi:10.1073/pnas.0707678104

Ullen, F., de Manzano, O., Almeida, R., Magnusson, P.K.E., Pedersen, N.L., Nakamura, J., Csikszentmihalyi, M., & Madison, G. 2011. Proneness for psychological flow in everyday life: Associations with personality and intelligence. *Personality and Individual Differences,* 52, 167-172.

Yerkes, R.M. & Dodson, J.D. (1908). The relation of strength of stimulus to rapidity of habit-formation. *Comparative Neurology and Psychology,* 18, 459-482.

Chapter 3

Csikszentmihalyi, M., Rathunde, K.R., Whalen, S., & Wong, M. 1993. *Talented teenagers: The roots of success and failure.* New York: Cambridge University Press.

Csikszentmihalyi, M. (1997). *Finding flow: The psychology of engagement with everyday life.* New York, NY, US: Basic Books.

Dietrich, A. & Sparling, P.B. 2004. Endurance exercise selectively impairs prefrontal-dependent cognition. *Brain and Cognition, 55*(3), 516-524. doi:10.1016/j.bandc.2004.03.002

Dietrich, A. & Stoll, O. 2010. Effortless attention, hypofrontality, and perfectionism. In B. Bruya, (Ed.), *Effortless attention: A new perspective in the cognitive science of attention and action* (pp. 159-178). Cambridge, MA: MIT Press.

Dweck, C. S. (1986). Motivational processes affecting learning. *American Psychologist, 41*(10), 1040-1048. doi:10.1037/0003-066X.41.10.1040

Elliot, A.J., Gable, S.L., & Mapes, R.R. 2006. Approach and avoidance motivation in the social domain. *Personality and Social Psychology Bulletin, 32,* 378 –391.

Goldberg, L.R. 1990. An "Alternative description of personality": The big-five factor structure. *Journal of Personality and Social Psychology, 59*(6), 1216-1229.

Hanson, R. 2013. *Hardwiring happiness: The new brain science of contentment, calm, and confidence.* New York, NY: Crown Publishing.

Hudson, N. W., & Fraley, R. C. (2015, March 30). Volitional Personality Trait Change: Can People Choose to Change Their Personality Traits? *Journal of Personality and Social Psychology.* Advance online publication. http://dx.doi.org/10.1037/pspp0000021

Jackson, S. A., & Roberts, G. C. (1992). Positive performance states of athletes: Toward a conceptual understanding of peak performance. *The Sport Psychologist, 6*(2), 156-171.

McCrae, R.R. & Costa, P.T.J. 1990. *Personality in adulthood.* New York: Guilford.

Smith, E.R. & Mackie, D.M. 2007. *Social psychology.* 3rd ed. Hove: Psychology Press.

Strachman, A. & Gable, S.L. 2006. What you want (and do not want) affects what you see (and do not see): Avoidance social goals and social events. *Personality and Social Psychology Bulletin, 32,* 1446-1458.

Ullén, F., de Manzano, O., Almeida, R., Magnusson, P.K.E., Pedersen, N.L., Nakamura, J., Csikszentmihalyi, M., & Madison, G. 2011. Proneness for psychological flow in everyday life: Associations with personality and intelligence. *Personality and Individual Differences, 52,* 167-172.

Chapter 4

Baumann, N. 2012. Autotelic personality. In S. Engeser, S. Engeser eds., *Advances in flow research* (pp. 165-186). New York, NY, US: Springer Science + Business Media. doi:10.1007/978-1-4614-2359-1_9

Baumann, N. & Scheffer, D. 2011. Seeking flow in the achievement domain: The achievement flow motive behind flow experience. *Motivation and Emotion, 35*(3), 267-284. doi:10.1007/s11031-010-9195-4

Boecker, H., Sprenger, T., Spilker, M.E.,Henriksen, G., Koppenhoefer, M., Wagner, K. J., Valet, M., Berthele, A., & Tolle, T. R. (2008). The Runner's High: Opioidergic Mechanisms in the Human Brain. *Cereb. Cortex, 18*(11), 2523-2531. doi: 10.1093/cercor/bhn013

Csikszentmihalyi, M. 1982. Toward a psychology of optimal experience. In L. Wheeler (Ed.), Review of personality and social psychology (Vol. 2, pp. 13–36). Beverly Hills: Sage.

Csikszentmihalyi, M. & LeFevre, J. 1989. Optimal experience in work and leisure. *Journal of Personality and Social Psychology, 56*(5), 815-822.

de Manzano, Ö., Theorell, T., Harmat, L., & Ullén, F. (2010). The psychophysiology of flow during piano playing. *Emotion, 10*(3), 301-311.

Dietrich, A. 2004. Neurocognitive mechanisms underlying the experience of flow. *Consciousness and Cognition: An International Journal, 13*(4), 746-761. doi:10.1016/j.concog.2004.07.002

Dietrich, A. & Sparling, P.B. 2004. Endurance exercise selectively impairs prefrontal-dependent cognition. *Brain And Cognition, 55*(3), 516-524. doi:10.1016/j.bandc.2004.03.002

Dietrich, A. & Stoll, O. 2010. Effortless attention, hypofrontality, and perfectionism. In B. Bruya, B. Bruya (Eds.) , *Effortless attention: A new perspective in the cognitive science of attention and action* (pp. 159-178). Cambridge, MA: MIT Press.

Dietrich, A. & Audiffren, M. 2011. The reticular-activating hypofrontality (RAH) model of acute exercise. *Neuroscience & Biobehavioral Reviews, 35*, 1305-1325.

Engeser, S. & Schiepe-Tiska, A. 2012. Historical lines and an overview of current research on flow. In S. Engeser, S. Engeser (Eds.), *Advances in flow research* (pp. 1-22). New York: Springer Science + Business Media. doi:10.1007/978-1-4614-2359-1_1

Garfield, C.A. & Bennett, H.Z. 1984. Peak performance: Mental training techniques of the world's greatest athletes. Los Angeles: Tarcher.

Hamilton, J.P., Farmer, M., Fogelman, P., & Gotlib, I.H. 2015. Depressive rumination, the default-mode network, and the dark matter of clinical neuroscience. *Biological Psychiatry, 78*(4), 224-230.

Hoff, B. (1982). Tao of Pooh. New York: Penguin Group.

Jackson, S.A., Ford, S., Kimiecik, J.C. & Marsh, H.W. 1998. Psychological correlates of flow in sport. *Journal of Sport & Exercise Psychology, 20* (4), 358-378.

Jackson, S.A. & Csikszentmihalyi, M. 1999. *Flow in sports.* United Kingdom: Human Kinetics.

Jackson, S.A. & Roberts, G. C. 1992. Positive performance states of athletes: Toward a conceptual understanding of peak performance. *The Sport Psychologist, 6*(2), 156-171.

Jackson, S.A. & Marsh, H.W. 1996. Development and validation of a scale to measure optimal experience: The Flow State Scale. *Journal of Sport & Exercise Psychology*, 1817-35.

Keller, J. & Bless, H. 2008. Flow and regulatory compatibility: An experimental approach to the flow model of intrinsic motivation. *Personality and Social Psychology Bulletin, 34,* 196-209. doi:10.1177/0146167207310026

Landhäußer, A. & Keller, J. 2012. Flow and its affective, cognitive, and performance-related consequences. In S. Engeser (Ed.), *Advances in flow research* (pp. 65-85). New York, NY, US: Springer Science + Business Media. doi:10.1007/978-1-4614-2359-1_4

Loehr, J.E. 1984, March. How to overcome stress and play at your peak all the time. *Tennis*, pp. 66-76.

Masters, R.S.W. 2000. Theoretical aspects of implicit learning in sport. *International Journal of Sport Psychology, 31*I, 530–541.

Masters, R.S.W., Polman, R.C.J., & Hammond, N.V. 1993. "Reinvestment": A dimension of personality implicated in skill breakdown under pressure. *Personality and Individual Differences, 14*, 655–666.

Maxwell, J.P., Masters, R.S.W., & Eves, F.F. 2000. From novice to know-how: A longitudinal study of implicit motor learning. *Journal of Sports Sciences, 18*, 111–120.

Moneta, G.B. 2004. The Flow Experience Across Cultures. *Journal of Happiness Studies, 5*(2), 115-121. doi:10.1023/B:JOHS.0000035913.65762.b5

Pfitzinger, P. & Latter, P. 2015. *Faster road racing: 5K to half marathon.* Champaign, IL: Human Kinetics.

Ravizza, K. 1973. A study of the peak experience in sport. Unpublished doctoral dissertation, University of Southern California.

Ravizza, K. 1984. Qualities of the peak experience in sport. In J.M. Silva & R.S. Weinberg (Eds.), Psychological foundations of sport (pp. 452-462). Champaign, IL: Human Kinetics.

Rheinberg, F., Vollmeyer, R., & Engeser, S. 2003. Die Erfassung des Flow-Erlebens [The assessment of flow experience]. In J. Stiensmeier-Pelster & F. Rheinberg (Eds.), Diagnostik von Motivation und Selbstkonzept (pp. 261-279). Göttingen: Hogrefe.

Schuler, J. & Brunner, S. 2009. The rewarding effect of flow experience on performance in a marathon race. *Psychology of Sport and Exercise, 10*(1), 168-174. doi:10.1016/j.psychsport.2008.07.001

Takizawa, R., Nishimura, Y., Yamasue, H., & Kasai, K. 2014. Anxiety and performance: The disparate roles of prefrontal subregions under maintained psychological stress. *Cerebral Cortex, 24*(7), 1858-1866.

TED. 2011. Arne Dietrich TEDx Talk in Beirut. http://tedxtalks.ted.com/video/TEDxBeirut-Arne-Dietrich-Surfin

United States Tennis Association. (2016). Sports Psychology: Mental skills for achieving optimum performance. Retrieved from: https://www.usta.com/Improve-Your-Game/Sport-Science/117746_Sports_Psychology_Mental_Skills_for_Achieving_Optimum_Performance/

Wenz, B. & Henschen, K. 2012. Sports psychology. From *IAAF Medical Manual.* Edited by C. Brown. www.iaaf.org/about-iaaf/documents/medical

Chapter 5

Aherne, C., Moran, A.P., & Lonsdale, C. 2011. The effect of mindfulness training on athletes' flow: An initial investigation. *The Sport Psychologist, 25*(2), 177-189.

Brown, K.D. and Ryan, R.M. (2003). The benefits of being present: mindfulness and its role in psychological well-being. *Journal of Personality and Social Psychology,*

*84(4), 822-848.*Clarey, C. 2014. Their Minds Have Seen The Glory. *New York Times,* February 23, 2014, pp. 1-8.

Daniels, J. 2004. *Daniels' running formula, second edition.* Champaign, IL: Human Kinetics.

Davis, D.M. & Hayes, J.A. 2011. What are the benefits of mindfulness? A practice review of psychotherapy-related research. *Psychotherapy, 48*(2), 198-208. doi:10.1037/a0022062

Dietrich, A. (2016). Personal correspondence. 5 Jan 2016.

Epstein, D. (2013). The sports gene. New York: Current.

Garfield, C.A. & Bennett, H.Z. 1984. Peak performance: Mental training techniques of the world's greatest athletes. Los Angeles: Tarcher.

Johnson, S. (1840). The works of Samuel Johnson, LL.D. Volume II. New York: Alexander V. Blake Publishers.

Jung, A.P. 2003. The impact of resistance training on distance running performance. *Sports Medicine, 33*(7), 539-552.

Keller, J. & Landhäußer, A. 2012. The flow model revisited. In S. Engeser (Ed.), *Advances in flow-research* (pp. 51-64). New York: Springer.

LeVan, A.J. 2009. Seeing is believing: The power of visualization. *Psychology Today Online.* https://www.psychologytoday.com/blog/flourish/200912/seeing-is-believing-the-power-visualization

Locke, E.A. & Latham, G.P. 2002. Building a practically useful theory of goal setting and task motivation: A 35-year odyssey. *American Psychologist, 57*(9), 705-717.

Locke, E.A. & Latham, G.P. 2006. New directions in goal-setting theory. *Current Directions in Psychological Science, 15*(5), 265-268.

Noakes, T. 2002. *Lore of running.* 4th ed.. Champaign, IL: Human Kinetics.

Paavolainen, L., Häkkinen, K., Hämäläinen, I., Nummela, A., & Rusko, H. 1999. Explosive-strength training improves 5-km running time by improving running power. *Journal of Applied Physiology, 86*(5), 1527-1533.

Pfitzinger, P. & Latter, P. 2015. *Faster road racing: 5K to half marathon.* Champaign, IL: Human Kinetics.

Statistic Brain. (2015). New years resolution statistics. Source: http://www.statistic-brain.com/new-years-resolution-statistics/

Thompson, R.W., Kaufman, K.A., De Petrillo, L.A., Glass, C.R. and D.B. Arnkoff. (2011). One year follow-up of mindful sport performance enhancement (MSPE) with archers, golfers, and runners. *Journal of Clinical Sport Psychology, 5(2),* 99-116.

Wiese, B.S. & Freund, A.M. 2005. Goal progress makes one happy, or does it? Longitudinal findings from the work domain. *Journal of Occupational & Organizational Psychology, 78*(2). 287-304. doi:10.1348/096317905X26714

Chapter 6

Bond, P. (2008, April). Running with the mind of meditation. *Trail Runner Magazine.* Retrieved from: http://trailrunnermag.com/people/1648-running-with-the-mind-of-meditation

Cianciosi, J. 2007. Mindful nature walking one step at a time. *Yoga Journal Online.* http://www.yogajournal.com/article/practice-section/mindful-nature-walking-one-step-at-a-time/

Csikszentmihalyi, M. 1990. *Flow: The psychology of optimal experience.* New York: Harper Collins.

Dietrich, A. 2003. Functional neuroanatomy of altered states of consciousness: The transient hypofrontality hypothesis. *Consciousness and Cognition: An International Journal, 12*(2), 231-256. doi:10.1016/S1053-8100(02)00046-6

Fuller, R.A., et al. (2007). Psychological benefits of greenspace increase with biodiversity. *Biology Letters, 3*(4). 390-394.

Kaplan, R. 1993. The role of nature in the context of the workplace. *Landscape and Urban Planning, 26*(1), 193-201.

Karageorghis, C.I. & Priest, D. 2012. Music in the exercise domain: A review and synthesis (Part I). *International Review of Sport and Exercise Psychology, 5*(1), 44-66. doi:10.1080/1750984X.2011.631026

Koudenburg, N., Postmes, T., & Gordijn, E.H. 2013. Conversational Flow Promotes Solidarity. *Plos ONE, 8*(11), 1-6. doi:10.1371/journal.pone.0078363

Lutz, A., Slagter, H.A., Rawlings, N.B., Francis, A.D., Greischar, L.L., & Davidson, R.J. 2009. Mental training enhances attentional stability: Neural and behavioral evidence. *The Journal of Neuroscience, 29*(42), 13418-13427. doi:10.1523/JNEUROSCI.1614-09.2009

Menezes, C.B., & Bizarro, L. 2015. Effects of a brief meditation training on negative affect, trait anxiety and concentrated attention. *Paidéia, 25*(62), 393-401. doi:10.1590/1982-43272562201513

Mipham, S. 2012. *Running with the mind of meditation.* New York: Harmony Books.

Potteiger, J.A., Schroeder, J.M., & Goff, K.L. 2000. Influence of music on ratings of perceived exertion during 20 minutes of moderate intensity exercise. *Perceptual and Motor Skills, 91*(3, Pt 1), 848-854. doi:10.2466/PMS.91.7.848-854

Sio, U.N. & Ormerod, T.C. 2009. Does incubation enhance problem solving? A meta-analytic review. *Psychological Bulletin, 135*(1), 94-120. doi:10.1037/a0014212

Strube, M.J., Miles, M.E., & Finch, W.H. 1981. The social facilitation of a simple task: Field tests of alternative explanations. *Personality and Social Psychology Bulletin, 7*(4), 701-707. doi:10.1177/0146167281074030

Swann, C., Keegan, R.J., Piggott, D., Crust, L. (2012). A system review of the experience, occurrence, and controllability of flow states in elite sports. *Psychology of Sports and Exercise, 13*(6). 807-819.

Swann, C., Keegan, R., Piggott, D., Crust, L., & Smith, M.F. 2012. Exploring flow occurrence in elite golf. *Athletic Insight: The Online Journal of Sport Psychology, 4*(2), 171-186.

Ulrich, R.S. 1984. View through a window may influence recovery from surgery. *Science, 224*(4647): 420-421.

Wells, N. & Evans, G. 2003. Nearby nature: a buffer of life stress among rural children. *Environment and Behavior, 35*(3), 311–330.

Wöran, B., & Arnberger, A. 2012. Exploring relationships between recreation specialization, restorative environments and mountain hikers' flow experience. *Leisure Sciences*, *34*(2), 95-114. doi:10.1080/01490400.2012.6525

Chapter 7

Bakker, A. B., Oerlemans, W., Demerouti, E., Slot, B. B., & Ali, D. K. (2011). Flow and performance: A study among talented Dutch soccer players. *Psychology of Sport and Exercise*, *12*(4), 442-450. doi:10.1016/j.psychsport.2011.02.003

Chavez, E.J. 2008. Flow in sport: A study of college athletes. *Imagination, Cognition, and Personality*, *28*(1), 69-91.

Dietrich, A., & Stoll, O. (2010). Effortless attention, hypofrontality, and perfectionism. In B. Bruya, B. Bruya (Eds.) , *Effortless attention: A new perspective in the cognitive science of attention and action* (pp. 159-178). Cambridge, MA, US: MIT Press.

Engeser, S. & Rheinberg, F. 2008. Flow, performance and moderators of challenge-skill balance. *Motivation and Emotion*, *32*, 158-172.

Hajoglou, A., Foster, C., de Koning, J.J., Lucia, A., Kernozek, T.W., & Porcari, J.P. 2005. Effect of warm-up on cycle time trial performance. *Medicine & Science in Sports & Exercise*, *37*(9), 1608-1614. doi:10.1249/01.mss.0000177589.02381.0a

Jackson, S.A. 1992. Athletes in flow: A qualitative investigation of flow states in elite figure skaters. *Journal of Applied Sport Psychology*, *4*(2), 161-180. doi:10.1080/10413209208406459

Jackson, S.A. 1995. Factors influencing the occurrence of flow state in elite athletes. *Journal of Applied Sport Psychology*, *7*(2), 138-166. doi:10.1080/10413209508406962

Kallenbach, S. & Zafft, C. 2004. Attributional retraining: rethinking academic failure to promote success. *National College Transition Network: Research to Practice*, 1, 1-3.

Kamphoff, C. 2015. Personal conversation. 26 August 2015.

Mayo Clinic. 2014. Positive thinking: Stop negative self-talk to reduce stress. Healthy Lifestyle: Stress Management. www.mayoclinic.org/healthy-lifestyle/stress-management/in-depth/positive-thinking/art-20043950

Rhea M.R., Alvar, B.A., Burkett, L.N., & Ball, S.D. 2003. A meta-analysis to determine the dose response for strength development. *Med Sci Sports Exerc*, *35*(3): 456-64.

Society for Endocrinology. 2015. You and your hormones: adrenaline. www.yourhormones.info/Hormones/Adrenaline.aspx

Sugiyama, T. & Inomata, K. 2006. Qualitative examination of flow experience among top Japanese athletes. *Perception and Motor Skills*, 100 (3), 969-982.

Swann, C., Keegan, R., Piggott, D., Crust, L., & Smith, M.F. 2012. Exploring flow occurrence in elite golf. *Athletic Insight: The Online Journal of Sport Psychology*, *4*(2), 171-186.

Triplett, N. 1898. The dynamogenic factors in pacemaking and competition. *American Journal of Psychology*, *9*(4), 507-533.

Worringham, C.J. & Messick, D.M. 1983. Social facilitation of running: An unobtrusive study. *The Journal of Social Psychology*, *121*(1), 23-29. doi:10.1080/0022 4545.1983.9924462

Chapter 8

Frank, M.G. 2009. *Current advances in sleep biology.* New York: Nova Science.

Gallagher, J. 2013. Sleep 'cleans' the brain of toxins. *BBC News.* www.bbc.com/news/health-24567412

Kraft, T.L., & Pressman, S.D. 2012. Grin and bear it: The influence of manipulated facial expression on the stress response. *Psychological Science, 23*(11), 1372-1378. doi:10.1177/0956797612445312

Mageau, G.A., Vallerand, R.J., Charest, J., Salvy, S.J., Lacaille, N., Bouffard, T., & Koestner, R. 2009. On the development of harmonious and obsessive passion: The role of autonomy support, activity specialization, and identification with the activity. *Journal of Personality, 77*(3), 601-646.

O'Keefe, J.H., Gheewala, N.M., & O'Keefe, J.O. 2008. Dietary strategies for improving post-prandial glucose, lipids, inflammation, and cardiovascular health. *Journal of the American College of Cardiology, 51*(3), 249-255. doi:10.1016/j.jacc.2007.10.016

Stoeber, J. & Janssen, D.P. 2011. Perfectionism and coping with daily failures: Positive reframing helps achieve satisfaction at the end of the day. *Anxiety, Stress & Coping: An International Journal, 24*(5), 477-497. doi:10.1080/10615806.2011.562977

Williams, R. 2011. How to deal best with failure and stress. *Psychology Today Online: Wired for Success.* www.psychologytoday.com/blog/wired-success/201107/how-deal-best-failure-and-stress

Chapter 9

Alexander, C.N., Swanson, G.C., Rainforth, M.V., Carlisle, T.W., Todd, C.C., & Oates, R.M. 1993. Effects of the transcendental meditation program on stress reduction, health, and employee development: A prospective study in two occupational settings.

Anxiety, Stress & Coping, 6, 245-262.

Argyle, M. 2001. *The psychology of happiness.* 2nd ed. East Sussex, England: Routledge.

Boniwell, I. & Henry, J. 2013. Developing Conceptions of Well-Being: Advancing Subjective, Hedonic and Eudaimonic Theories. In C.L. Cooper, I.T. Robertson (Eds.), *Management and Happiness* (pp. 3-18). Elgar Research Collection. International Library of Critical Writings on Business and Management, vol. 21. Cheltenham, U.K. and Northampton, Mass.: Elgar.

Bryant, F.B. & Veroff, J. 2007. *Savoring: A new model of positive experience.* Mahwah, NJ: Lawrence Erlbaum Associates.

Caltabiano, M.L. 1994. Measuring the similarity among leisure activities based on a perceived stress-reduction benefit. *Leisure Studies, 13,* 17-31.

Csikszentmihalyi, M. 1990. *Flow: The psychology of optimal experience.* New York: Harper Collins.

Csikszentmihalyi, M. & Hunter, J. 2003. Happiness in everyday life: The uses of experience sampling. *Journal of Happiness Studies, 4,* 185-199.

Dempsey, P.C., Howard, B.J., Lynch, B.M., Owen, N., & Dunstan, D.W. 2014. Associations of television viewing time with adults' well-being and vitality. *Preventive Medicine: An International Journal Devoted to Practice and Theory, 69,* 69-74.

Feldman, D.B. & Snyder, C.R. 2005. Hope and the meaningful life: Theoretical and empirical associations between goal-directed thinking and life meaning. *Journal of Social and Clinical Psychology, 24*(3), 401-421.

Fromm, E. 1976. To have or to be? New York: Harper & Row.

Hanssen, M.M., Vancleef, L.G., Vlaeyen, J.S., Hayes, A.F., Schouten, E.W., & Peters, M.L. 2014. Optimism, motivational coping and well-being: Evidence supporting the importance of flexible goal adjustment. *Journal of Happiness Studies, 6*(6), 1525-1537. doi:10.1007/s10902-014-9572-x

Goucher, A. and Catalano, T. (2011). *Running the Edge.* Self-published.

Hayden, C. 2002. *Marathon Monks of Mount Hiei.* Watertown, MA: Documentary Educational Resources.

Hsee, C.K., Yang, A.X., & Wang, L. 2010. Idleness aversion and the need for justifiable busyness. *Psychological Science, 21*(7), 926-930. doi:10.1177/0956797610374738

Iwasaki, Y., Coyle, C., & Shank, J. 2010. Leisure as a context for active living, recovery, health and life quality for persons with mental illness in a global context. *Health Promotion International, 25,* 483-494.

Lavasani, M.G., Ejei, J., & Mohammadi, F. 2013. The relationship between meaning of life and optimism with subjective well-being. *Journal of Psychology, 17*(1), 3-17.

Nelson, S.K., Layous, K., Cole, S.W., & Lyubomirsky, S. 2016. Do unto others or treat yourself? The effects of prosocial and self-focused behavior on psychological flourishing. *Emotion,* April 21, 2016. [Advance online publication.] http://dx.doi.org/10.1037/emo0000178

Perkins, D. N., & Salomon, G. (1988). Teaching transfer. *Educational Leadership,* 22-32.

Peterson, C., Park, N., & Seligman, M.E.P. 2005. Orientations to happiness and life satisfaction: The full life versus the empty life. *The Journal of Happiness Studies, 6,* 25-41.

Seligman, M.P. 2002. *Authentic happiness: Using the new positive psychology to realize your potential for lasting fulfillment.* New York: Free Press.

Seligman, M.E.P. & Csikszentmihalyi, M. 2000. Positive psychology: An introduction. *American Psychologist, 55*(1), 5-14.

Snyder, C.R., Irving, L.M., & Anderson, J.R. 1991. Hope and health. In C.R. Snyder, D.R. Forsyth (Eds.), *Handbook of social and clinical psychology: The health perspective* (pp. 285-305). Elmsford, NY: Pergamon Press.

Stevens, J. 2013. *The marathon monks of Mount Hiei.* Brattelboro, VT: Echo Point Books & Media.

INDEX

Note: The italicized *f* and *t* following page numbers refer to figures and tables, respectively.

ABOUT THE AUTHORS

Mihaly Csikszentmihalyi is a bestselling author, world-renowned researcher, and one of the fathers of positive psychology. His seminal work, *Flow: The Psychology of Optimal Experience* (1990), was a *New York Times* best seller and introduced the concept of flow to mainstream audiences. Once the head of the psychology department at the University of Chicago, Csikszentmihalyi founded the Quality of Life Research Center at Claremont Graduate University. His work has influenced figures such as Bill Clinton and former British Prime Minister Tony Blair.

Now a professor at Claremont Graduate University in southern California, Csikszentmihalyi has written more than 120 journal articles and book chapters and has authored a dozen books related to positive psychology. He continues to research flow and motivation as the founder and codirector of the nonprofit Quality of Life Research Center. He lives in Claremont, California.

Philip Latter is the coauthor of *Faster Road Racing* (Human Kinetics, 2015) with two-time Olympian Pete Pfitzinger. A former senior writer for *Running Times* and current contributor to *Runner's World* and runnersworld.com, Latter has profiled more than a dozen Olympians and written extensively on training methodology, exercise science, and sport psychology. He regularly lectures on flow at summer running camps and has used many of the techniques described in this book with the high school, college, and post collegiate athletes he coaches.

A runner for almost two decades, Latter earned five all-conference honors at the University of North Carolina at Asheville and holds personal bests of 14:47 for 5K, 31:24 for 10K, and 1:12:11 for the half marathon. A former NCAA Division I head cross country coach at Radford University, Latter coaches runners at Brevard High School in the Blue Ridge Mountains of western North Carolina. He lives just outside of Brevard with his wife and two daughters.

Christine Weinkauff Duranso is a professor of psychology at both Woodbury University in Burbank, California, and California State University at San Bernardino. As a PhD student at Claremont Graduate University, Weinkauff Duranso studied under the mentorship of Mihaly Csikszentmihalyi and focused her research on the role of flow and exercise and how they contribute to thriving. Her dissertation considered how exercise, flow, and nature strengthen resilience and enhance well-being for college students.

Weinkauff Duranso has completed races ranging from 5K to marathon distance and has ventured into the triathlon world. She enjoys speaking to various groups about the role of flow and exercise in well-being and how flow can provide the motivation to persist in new exercise endeavors. A mother of four, she lives in Claremont, California, with her three youngest children.